Children growing up with religion: Ten narratives explored

Edited by
Lucy Birtwistle & Lindsay Smith

First published 2012 by
Lucy Birtwistle & Lindsay Smith

Design Services by
Philip Jones
www.philipjonesdesign.com

Published and Printed by
York Publishing Services Ltd.
64 Hallfield Road,
Layerthorpe,
York YO31 7ZQ
www.yps-publishing.co.uk

ISBN – 978-0-9572580-0-6

To our families:
Colin
Simon & Amy Louise
Amy
Tim
Nigel
Jack
Lucy

To our contributors:
Peter Gubi
Catherine Hand
John McCourt
John Rowan
Jane Simmonds
Sharon Stinson
Anni Townend
Wendy Weston

Acknowledgements
Kim Etherington, who inspired this research
Alistair Ross
William West
Alan Dunnett
Jill Burns
Christine Kennett
Carole Ashton
Peter Cook
Staff & Students at University of York St. John
Jack Smith
Philip Jones
Tim Birtwistle
David Mercer
Cathi Poole
Also thanks to all the friends and family members, mentors and supervisors of those involved who provided support and acceptance giving confidence to the writers to tell their stories.

Preface

This is a book about the effect that mainstream religion can have on the lives of those who had a childhood in which it played a significant part. The co-editors Lucy Birtwistle and Lindsay Smith qualified as counsellors in the same year and have worked together on various professional, supervisory and training projects since then, forging a strong and lasting friendship at the same time.

The interest in this subject grew from their individual experiences of religion as children, Lucy in rural Lincolnshire with her vicar father and Lindsay in suburban Wimbledon with her Catholic Apostolic mother. They wanted to know more about the experiences of others and whether any commonalities could be extracted that might inform and enlighten. They found eight others who generously shared their own stories. They discovered, from these, that there were important themes that could usefully inform professional practice in this area.

Laying out your experiences in a public arena is not something undertaken lightly. The narratives included here were written with courage and commitment, and as a gift to you the readers. The nature of writing means there has been quite a delay between the writing and the publication of this book so it is hoped you will be aware that changes and developments will have occurred since these contributors offered their stories, and as their personal development journeys have continued.

These narratives aim to offer you insight into experiences you might have had of religion when you were a child and, in addition, help you understand the possible significance of religious influences on others with whom you may be living or working.

Contents

1
INTRODUCTION

Religion is one element among many influences in childhood. We have attempted in this book to abstract it from its various noisy neighbours including social class, economic status, physical health, geographical location, education and race in order to see what part it plays in psychological development.

The definition of God that we use throughout is one that generally applies to monotheistic religious adherence, i.e. a belief in a creator and supreme ruler of the universe. The definition of religion can be described as a belief in and worship of that God in a system of faith. We refer to 'contributors' to describe those who have written autobiographically for this book. Their narratives describe their experience of religion in childhood and how it has affected them as adults.

Each person's experience of growing up is unique and idiosyncratic. The threads of influence on a child are tightly woven. It would be an impossible task to completely separate religion from other influences and trace exactly how it impacts on a child growing up. However, because of our own experiences of religion, we have felt it important enough to examine and to allow this aspect of socialisation to be heard above the hubbub. In order to get at this information we invited eight contributors to identify for themselves, and in their own words, where religion fits into their lives.

Rather than a book driven by a particular perspective this book presents a set of volunteered narratives from which some qualitative data emerges examining the influence of religion on children from an insider's perspective, and with the hindsight of adulthood. The two co-editors have worked hard to maintain a balance of perspective in analysing the narratives, but acknowledge that this has not always been straightforward. So as to make our perspectives and possible prejudices as transparent as possible we have included our own stories. The reader can then judge our analysis, commentaries and conclusions using that information.

When we conceived of this research, we did not set out to sell any religious or spiritual message nor to attack any religious faith or organisation. We are satisfied that our attempts to avoid these pitfalls have been successful. We hope that this book will make a contribution to raising each reader's awareness of the nature of religious influence in childhood, its connection to other events and experiences and the way in which this contributes to adult thought, feelings and behaviour.

The lived experience of personal narratives as a qualitative research method is now well established. (McLeod 2001, Etherington 2009) and it is from this tradition that we drew our research methods, the details of which we set out in Chapter 2.

We did not look for contributors who felt themselves scarred by childhood experiences of religion, or who needed to recover from them in order to move on. Nor did we set out to find people who had only positive things to say about their experience. What we found in the narratives were descriptions of the experiences of people who had struggled to examine the religious ideas and practices that they experienced as children in religious households. Some found that those influences had constrained their adult lives and some were led to doubt their own worth. Others seemed to have found their religious experience a springboard for exploration. All our contributors identified a serious engagement with the ideas, beliefs and experiences of the faith in which they were raised. The outcomes of their individual journeys are best expressed in their own words in Chapter 3. In this chapter the narratives must be considered as a snapshot of the perspective of our contributors at a given moment in their lives. Since writing their accounts, and submitting them for publication, their perspectives may have changed and their understandings altered. Many of our contributors reported that the act of writing generated a new journey of discovery which will have continued far beyond what is recorded in this book.

What we have discovered in exploring this issue is that in many cases religion in childhood reacts in unpredictable ways with the other ingredients of development. For some it has been a source of comfort and inner strength. For others it has brought anxiety and fear. Many carry a mixture of negative and positive reflections. When talking of beliefs many relish the rich inheritance that they feel religion has given them, but all describe struggle, and strong reactions that persist into adult life.

Whether within an intense community experience or with a less immersed contact with religion, our contributors describe their religious experiences in childhood as not a mild or negligible aspect but rather a significant and long-lasting influence.

If, as we propose, religion in childhood can have significant consequences, we would suggest that those introducing it to children should take a precautionary approach. Religion, however imparted, will be received by a child in a way that is unforeseeable. The long-term impact is unpredictable.

Some contributors report valuable elements that they have taken into adult-hood from their religious childhoods, like a sense of belonging, support and in-spirational models. Most, however, have also reported significant and negative effects that extend far into their adult lives, particularly in the form of anxiety, guilt and shame. Sometimes our contributors' experiences can carry both the positive and negative. There are those who can feel lonely and abandoned when they depart from the philosophy of a particular church, and this might be a powerful draw for them to overlook profound differences of principle in order to remain part of a community. In other words they have developed a strong need to belong and this overrides a need to agree with a particular church's views. Whether this is a need arising from other influences or life events and exaggerated by religious experience is hard to judge, but it is mentioned by several of the writers in their narratives. Others now strenuously avoid any doctrines or belief systems concerned that their identity and autonomy might be threatened.

Perhaps our advice to be cautious about introducing religion to young chil-dren relates to the concept of God to which a child may be introduced at home or at school. Generally, the God our contributors met in childhood was a God who was all-seeing and all-knowing. It was often accompanied by the idea that you will be judged after death according to your beliefs, behaviour, thoughts and feelings. This was likely to promote the existence of a very powerful, and possibly frightening, force in these children's lives. Equally, to feel that they were eternally cared for, accompanied and loved by a creator God was a power-ful reassurance of security in an unpredictable world. It is interesting that these concepts were not mutually exclusive and that, as children, many contributors carried a belief in a God who encompassed both, although sometimes the con-tributors emphasise that one was more present than the other.

Although we did not ask our contributors to write directly on the nature of the God that they believed in as children and whether the nature of their God changed as they grew into adulthood, it does seem that for many the God that they refer to later in their stories is different from the one that they met in childhood. They make mention later, after much struggle and frequently having accessed professional help, of either a less judgemental and more loving and accepting deity who can love them as they are or else a more abstract and less traditional concept of God, For two of our contributors the move to a position of self-acceptance necessitates a rejection of God. For others there is a struggle towards self-acceptance that persists in which the residue of a religious childhood prevents them fully trusting in their own goodness. We explore the different ways in which our contributors experienced a concept of 'God' more fully in Chapter 4.

We have discovered how individuals incorporate their religious influences at an early age, and that sometimes a superficially similar religious background might have a vastly different implication for different individuals. Outcomes can depend on how parents and other primary carers interpret their own religion in their parenting roles. Other consequences seem to be conditioned by the child's personality. In other words some degree of influence from nurture and some from nature is at play here.

The theme of nurture emerged in the writing of two of our writers, both of whom were brought up in tightly fitting, closed religious communities. Both these childhoods seem to have common elements such as a strong co-operative approach or 'party-line', reinforced at home. Their lives as children seem to be governed by rules and guidelines and strong boundaries between 'inside' and 'outside' their faith communities. However, in one the writer felt in childhood that she was loved, special and admired (if in hindsight overprotected and rather stifled), whereas the other developed a mistrust and internal punishing self-concept from an early age that extended into adulthood with severe anxiety at times of stress. Both describe the over-riding expectation that they needed to conform to expectations, but the long-term effects were different. When we look at different perceptions of their 'God' in Chapter 4, some of these differences can be understood in more depth.

The nature or personality of the individual child seems to be a key element in how a religious childhood is experienced, and how the adult responds to it. This can be seen when Sharon describes her nomadic pilgrim Pentecostal childhood generating experiences of constant change and challenge. The 'spare the rod and spoil the child' philosophy was particularly harsh for an independent-minded, questioning youngster. A daughter with a more conforming personality might have suffered less chastisement for wanting to question and experiment. Sharon took the first opportunity she could to find 'her own way'. By contrast, John Mc developed a strong sense of responsibility for protecting his mother from 'any further sadness' when she was widowed when John was eight years old. His story reveals a child with a conforming nature and his questioning seems to be more of a 'slow-burn'. His struggle comes in adulthood when he has to reconcile his found love for a woman with the celibacy demanded of him if he wishes to remain in the priesthood. He describes how long and difficult this process was for him.

Several accounts reveal how the power of profound internal experiences and interpretations can impact on the child. Each makes sense of them using their own unique patterns of thought and feeling. Events which may be termed spiritual generate intense emotion. Lucy describes her pubescent fall from grace as a traumatic dislocation coupled with severe shame, guilt and loneliness. This became a secret inner anxiety, which seemed to have clouded her adolescence and adulthood. John R describes an adventurous approach with many peak experiences that he identifies as liberating. In one of these he plumbs the depths of his 'own death'. Lindsay describes her fears that God has killed her father and can kill her mother too. From rather eclectic beginnings where she seems to have a number of significant brushes with religion in childhood Catherine recounts a deeply affecting experience as an adult. When her husband is dying in hospital from a brain haemorrhage she recalls how she felt that 'the essence of the universe was Good, not goodness, but Good and that nothing humankind could do could affect or diminish that'. This statement suggests a crystallising of her own religious philosophy, which is different from that with which she has been brought up.

We have been keenly aware of the risks of misrepresenting or interpreting the contributors' words inaccurately. Our task was to define common elements and in doing so we want to make the reader aware that only the full transcripts can offer a real flavour of the reported lived experiences of children growing up with religion. We can give our own overview and acknowledge the limitations of such an endeavour. With the exception of the two co-editors and one other with whom Lucy had a prior friendship, we only know the contributors to this book through this research and we offer our conclusions on their writing from our own perspectives.

The impact of vivid religious and spiritual experiences carries outcomes that may be inhibiting for individual adults. One could look at this from an atheist's perspective and suspect that the outcome of social control is intended. People who are fearful are unlikely to question, disagree or dissent. As a religious person you might feel that the outcomes are beneficial in that they will generate a better world and 'save souls'. These inhibiting and controlling factors may or may not be deliberately intended by those who are communicating the beliefs and expectations. However, we would propose that anyone contemplating introducing religion to children should consider the possible consequences. What we can say from our examination of the subject is that, whatever the intention, children have the potential to be significantly negatively affected by their experiences of religion in childhood.

How children make sense of their worlds varies enormously. Children introduced to the big concepts associated with religion such as 'the one truth', 'life after death', 'good' and 'evil' respond in many ways. Sooner or later, all our contributors found questions, conflicts and struggles with understanding. We have identified that the introduction of these weighty ideas from an early age, with their attendant expectations and threats of punishment are present in the ether of a religious childhood. The impact of these on the individual child can be profound and sometimes disturbing.

We would hope that readers, by engaging with the narratives, will understand their own experiences better, and that whether they be religious people or atheists, in the role of parent, therapist, minister, priest or pastoral supporter, they will be more open to the diversity and depth of the individual experience of a child brought up with religion. Whether religion is imbibed in the form of a rich daily diet or is experienced in a less central or more routine way the outcomes are not predictable. Ultimately we have come to the view that the introduction of religion in a child's life should be undertaken with care for the possible psychological consequences, the examples of which can found in our narratives.

The two of us do not share the same beliefs, as will be apparent from our narratives, and as a result our writing in co-operation has proved to be sometimes difficult, and sometimes an intensely illuminating process for us both. What we have produced in this book is not a compromise of findings. We have included thoughts, ideas and conclusions from us both. We have endeavoured to be respectful to each other and of our contributors' differences without limiting what we have both genuinely found in doing this work. It is in the conclusion where we wonder, amongst other issues, about whether religion can ever be a safe socialising element in children's lives, that we show the greatest difference of opinion, and have chosen to write separately about this particular issue.

Etherington, K (2004) *Becoming a reflexive researcher: using ourselves in research*. London: Jessica Kingsley.
Etherington, K (2009) *Life Story Research: a relevant methodology for counsellors and psychotherapists*. *Journal of Counselling & Psychotherapy Research*. Vol. 9 (4), 225 -223.
Etherington, K (2003) *Trauma, the body and transformation: A narrative enquiry*. London: Jessica Kingsley.
Etherington, K (2005) *'Writing Trauma Stories for Research.'* [Unpublished paper]
McLeod, J (2001) *Qualitative research in counselling and psychotherapy*. London: Sage

2
RESEARCH METHOD

This book explores through a qualitative research method the answer to the question 'How might religion that has been a part of childhood affect the adult?'

Qualitative research follows an exploratory process where researchers 'adopt a philosophical stance that human knowledge is contextualized and local' (McLeod, 2003: 71). It involves seeking information that helps to make meaning from the subjective experience of individuals rather than using a quantitative method of collecting statistical data and representing it numerically. Our intention was to open up this subject and find out from those that had experienced religion in childhood what meaning they had made of that experience. We then wanted to investigate the similarities and differences within those accounts, looking for any significant common factors that might inform our understanding. A qualitative method seemed the most valid for this task.

Since our interest was based on our own life histories we were drawn to 'personal experience methodologies,' particularly the 'heuristic inquiry' which 'requires the total personal immersion of the inquirer in the topic, to the point where a creative 'incubation' brings a new understanding of the phenomenon.' (McLeod, 2003: 83) Our choice was also informed by qualitative research work in the field of counselling and psychotherapy (Rennie, 1992: Bond, 2005: Etherington, 2004, 2009), particularly by the latter who has used life story material extensively in her writing. Etherington identifies the rich source of 'life story research as an important, relevant and appropriate contribution to counselling and psychotherapy research.' She maintains that:

'Life stories allow us to bring together many layers of understanding about a person, about their culture, and about how they have created change in their lives: we hear people struggle to make sense of the past and create meanings as they tell and/ or show us what happened to them.' (Etherington, 2009: 225)

Etherington also exemplifies the benefits of including the lived experience of the researcher in exploring a subject. Indeed in her book *Trauma, the body and transformation: A narrative enquiry* (Etherington, 2003) she includes her own narrative of experience. Her book was an inspiration to begin this research project.

In order to pursue this field of inquiry, we placed an advertisement in *Therapy Today* (the professional journal of the British Association for Counselling & Psychotherapy). We were looking for contributors who were brought up in one of the mainstream religions (i.e. part of a large religious grouping) so that the findings had the potential to be relevant to a broad readership. We wanted to hear from people who had religious beliefs as a relatively consistent influence in their childhood, and who had been subject to those influences in the period from birth to seven years old.

We felt it was very important that the narratives in the book should be reflective, and that our writers should have spent some time exploring their religious influences in conjunction with an independent 'other'. In this way we wanted to locate people who could trace the connections between their religious childhoods and their adult selves. We were also conscious that we wanted to hear considered responses and invite neither evangelising nor unexplored rejection of religion. It was for this reason we chose to advertise in the counsellors' professional journal, as we felt that this readership would be likely to have the capacity for considered personal reflection.

This method of selection had limitations. An advertisement in a professional journal only attracts replies from that readership and our respondents were therefore drawn from the counselling and psychotherapy community. They reflect the demographic of the readership that is, in the majority, middle aged and female. Of the contributors included in the book three are male and seven female. There is one contributor in her 40's, three in their 50's, two in their 60's three in their 70's and one in his 80's. Those under 40 are not represented at all in this study. The reflections therefore are limited to children brought up between 1924 and 1970. The narratives reveal much about the cultural and historic context of their childhoods. World War II was of significance to most of the authors growing up in those years, Wendy describes the separation that was caused in her family, and John R describes his experience of National Service abroad. Others mention the sexual revolution and the women's movement of the 1960's as relevant cultural contexts to their experiences. Sharon's childhood was spent in America where religious attendance increased considerably during and after the war. Peter's emigration to England came about because of changes in the political landscape of his birthplace in the West Indies. Each narrative has its own unique cultural context and our analysis of the narratives must be considered with that in mind.

Our findings cannot reflect the cultural effects on the experience of children brought up in later eras, where religious practices will have been affected by the social and historical contexts of their day. We would suggest that readers can judge for themselves the relevance of this study on those whose first seven years were experienced in more recent decades. Since this book is designed as a preliminary exploration, further research would be needed to draw comparisons with those brought up in more recent decades.

Another potential drawback to the source we used to find our contributors is that respondents who are counsellors or psychotherapists or involved in that field are likely to have experienced being clients in personal therapy and this may make them more inclined to interpret experiences in a particular way which may not be representative of those who come from outside that community.

The most significant limitation of this study is that we did not identify a balance group of those brought up without the influence of religion. Had we done so we might have been able to identify issues that seemed to be exclusive to one group or the other.

We chose to look for religious influences before the age of seven partly as a result of the popular saying allegedly attributed to the Jesuits which communicates in various forms 'give me a child when he is seven and I will give you the man', implying that we are substantially defined by that age. We also drew on Piaget's (1977) four cognitive stages of development, a theory that posits that the way children think about their world changes as they grow up. The ages from birth to two years are seen as the first stage and ages two to seven as the next. This second stage is described as the 'preoperational stage' in which 'children live in a very egocentric world, being unable to see things from others' perspective'.

As Spilka (2003) et al make clear, although Piaget was not writing directly about a child's religious development, the theory does have significant implications. For example, it suggests that 'children are not cognitively capable of understanding the complex and abstract concepts involved in most religions of the adult world.' (Spilka et al 2003) These authors also consider the criticisms of Piaget's work and recognise other approaches to religious development, for example Fowler's (1987) stages of faith development in which the age of six is seen as significant, marking a shift from the 'intuitive-projective faith' stage to the 'Mythic-literal faith'. (Fowler, 1987: 59, 61)

In order to respect the personal impact that an investigation of personal history might have, we asked that contributors made sure that they would be supported by a named person in expanding and exploring their experience. We also wanted to attract those who possessed a readable standard of writing skill and who were willing to co-operate in an editing dialogue with us.

We received 35 responses seeking further information from which we selected ten contributors based on a 500 word sample of their writing matched against criteria including reflectivity, diversity and writing style. Two contributors subsequently withdrew during the process of writing and editing. The book is based on the writings of eight contributors and our own narratives, making a total of ten narratives. One contributor that was selected had a previous friendship with Lucy, but her sample of writing was processed by Lindsay and a decision to include her made on the basis of the set criteria.

Those not selected from the shortlist were notified but no individual feedback was given. Editorial control rested with the two co-authors. The chosen contributors were then invited to submit their fuller stories. These narratives were developed through a co-operative editorial process with each co-editor offering support to a list of five contributors drawn from the list of ten by lots.

The co-operative process began once a first draft of the full piece of writing had been received. No constraints were made on the contributors' writing other than the title of the project: 'How might religion that has been a part of childhood, affect the adult?' and a word limit indication. We were keen, so far as possible, not to influence the content of the narratives to try to make sure that any emphases that the contributors chose to make were not affected by expectations from us or comparisons with each other. Although we as researchers met regularly, we each wrote our story independently before sharing it with the other. We had, however, read the 500-word submissions from our contributors and therefore may have been influenced by them. The eight other contributors had no contact with each other, and those that did meet did so after the first full draft of their story had been completed.

The purpose of the editing process was to develop and refine the writing for publication and not to influence the content. The process involved e-mail, telephone and postal correspondence with some and, where requested, face to face contact. A small group of five of us met up on one occasion. All were invited but half either couldn't make it or decided it was not for them. The meeting was designed as supportive and facilitative to the writing process. At this meeting all those present read from first drafts and the feedback given was designed to encourage and share challenges in the process rather than the content. For some it was a question of encouraging them to lengthen their scripts to extend the details of their experience or to provide specific examples of their histories. For others it was a matter of helping them to make editing decisions to reduce their writing from a much larger narrative to accommodate the restrictions of space. The level of contact between the co-editors and the other contributors varied a good deal. Some contributors preferred to engage very little, others were in touch more. Some contributors did not request or require dialogue on their contributions.

In order to ensure that the relationship between the contributors and ourselves would be transparent we provided two consent forms. One accompanied first and subsequent drafts, and a second and final consent form was signed giving permission to publish. Both the contributors and we, the editors, ensured that the right to withdraw a contribution was reserved at any stage. Initially, one person suggested they might want to write under a pseudonym, but ultimately all contributors decided to write under their own names. Contributors themselves were responsible for the protection of the privacy of anyone named in their stories and did this in whatever way they felt appropriate that would also preserve the integrity of the narrative.

We felt that it was important that, if a contributor found the feelings generated by initial participation or proposed publication overwhelming or threatening in any way, then we should be alerted. Had such a situation arisen we would have considered the implications with the contributor, using the *Ethical Framework* provided by the British Association for Counselling and Psychotherapy, and would have made necessary alterations to safeguard the participants and/or others. While we were concerned that the contributors remained safe in their exploration of childhood, literary considerations also affected the editing process, as our aim was to produce accessible personal narratives to raise awareness of how religion in childhood could affect personal development. This entailed us working with the contributors to maximise accurate communication of their experiences and thus make a serious contribution to the body of theory in this field. In the event, our contributors named their supporters and used them as they felt necessary.

What we did discover, and it is something that Etherington (2005) has written about with insight, is that the very act of writing these narratives provoked some op-

portunities to explore difficult personal development issues. Many of our contributors made us aware of daunting challenges in communicating the content to friends
and family, especially where parents and siblings were still living, or disclosures had
not been previously shared with children or others. Some contributors, and both of
us, found that our thinking and processing was substantially developed in the writing process. This was an interesting side effect of our main aims, and, we understand
from communications with contributors, made the huge efforts involved in produc-
ing substantial pieces of writing worthwhile. This experience is acknowledged by researchers from the social constructionist / constructivism movement as the research
was valued as 'transforming' by a significant number of the contributors as well as
by the researchers. (Bond, 2005)

When the final drafts had been agreed between the contributors and the co-editors all the narratives were shared in the form of attachments on an e-mail to all the
contributors. We invited those who wished to make comments to do so with copies
to all, and advising that any feedback would be limited to content rather than the
writing style. There was little correspondence once this was clarified.

In order to analyse the substantial quantity of written material generated by the
narratives of contributors we employed a system described by McLeod (2003:84)
which involved several stages. Our way of engaging with the data included many
elements of 'grounded theory' (McLeod, 2003:88). We immersed ourselves in the
subject both by writing our own narratives and by studying the narratives written by
the contributors in order to try to engage with subtleties and implicit meanings in
the material generated. Then we each went through the data independently, grouping it according to aspects that seemed to occur in more than one person's experience. Having invented our own categories for the material we then met to discuss
our findings and question our groupings on the basis of evidence from quotations
from the narratives. This lengthy process involved us in coming to agreement on
which were the most frequent re-occurring categories, deciding how we would en-
title these and rejecting those that seemed to be much less significant or possibly
subjects from our own interpretation rather than clearly evidenced. From this work
evolved our findings as described in Chapter 4. However, we struggled to find a
'central or core category' (McLeod 2003:91) generated from the narratives. We were
reluctant to narrow the reported experiences by squeezing data into a conclusion
which would have needed to be unhelpfully vague. In addition we did not agree on
a central theme that could be interpreted as such with sufficient mutual confidence.

Our study falls more into a phenomenological framework in that 'The 'essence'… can never be grasped. But the very process of seeking this essence yields an understanding of the various perspectives and horizons of meaning through which the experience of that phenomenon has been constructed.' (McLeod, 2003: 86) Whether the chosen themes are influenced by our own experiences, and if so, to what degree, will, we hope be for the reader to judge from our own narratives. Furthermore our individual concluding reflections on our experiences of writing this book can be found in Chapter 6.

We designed this research with an open-minded attitude of discovery to provide some reflections on the experience of those who have written their narratives here. Our intention is that this book will be accessible to any who have an interest in this area, or perhaps a curiosity or concern about their own experiences and what effect religious influence in childhood may, or may not, have had on them. In addition we wanted to contribute some informative reflections for practitioners and trainers in the field of counselling, pastoral care, psychotherapy and other associated professions which can be found in Chapter 5. This information, based on the analysis of the data in the narratives, is designed for those who may be involved in the facilitation of clients who may have experienced religion in childhood and who wish to explore its effects.

Profiles of the narrative contributors

Lindsay Smith (Editor)
Lindsay was brought up within the philosophy of her mother's adherence to the Catholic Apostolic Church combined with conventional Church of England practice. She is a retired counsellor, supervisor and trainer most recently working as Head of Programme in Counselling Studies at York St. John University.
Publications include:
The Effect that Listening to Individual Children has on their Learning (2006) (Article) The International Journal for Pastoral Care and Personal-Social Education Vol.24 No.4 December.
Humanistic Counselling Sessions: Demonstrating Key Skills (2009) Co-producer Training DVD. York St. John University.
Lindsay is 58.

Lucy Birtwistle (Editor)
Lucy was brought up in a small Lincolnshire village where her father was the vicar. Lucy has been an accredited counsellor for 10 years and has been practising as a counsellor and supervisor for 15 years. She has a private practice for clients and supervisees. Lucy has experience working in a university as a counsellor and visiting tutor. She has also worked as a counsellor in the NHS and as a supervisor of counsellors and trainee counsellors for several charities including MIND, Survive and Rape Crisis, and still works as a supervisor for a bereavement service.
Lucy is 61.

Peter Madsen Gubi
Peter grew up in the West Indies as part of the Moravian church prior to his move to England.
Peter is currently an ordinand in the Moravian Church and a Visiting Fellow in Counselling and Spiritual Accompaniment at the University of Central Lancashire. He is also a BACP Senior Accredited Counsellor and a BACP Senior Accredited Supervisor in Private Practice. Formerly he was Principal Lecturer in Counselling and Psychotherapy, and Divisional Leader for Counselling and Psychological Therapies, at the University of Central Lancashire.
Publications include:
Gubi, P.M. (2008). *Prayer in Counselling and Psychotherapy: Exploring a hidden meaningful dimension.* London: Jessica Kingsley Publishers.
Peter is 47.

Catherine Hand
Catherine was born in London in 1938 but was brought up in Derbyshire. Catherine's early religious education was through the medium of exciting stories and activities with her mother. She was educated at a religious school in Oxford, and at London University. She taught in secondary and further education, but mostly had a succession of part-time jobs: foster mother, smallholder, nursing auxiliary, veterinary nurse, playgroup supervisor and care assistant. After training as a counsellor in Sheffield she now works in the voluntary sector with women survivors of sexual abuse and people with mental health problems. She is a mother of five and grandmother of seven.
Catherine is 72.

John McCourt

John grew up in a devout Catholic family and attended a church boarding school, then a seminary where he trained for the priesthood.

John is a BACP Senior Accredited Counsellor and a counselling supervisor.

John was a priest, a Local Authority social worker, the Co-ordinator of Therapeutic Services for a Social Services Department, a Senior Practitioner with Barnardo's and a counsellor, group facilitator and supervisor in the NHS.

Recently retired from the Health Service, he provides counselling and supervision in a small private practice and is involved in his local branch of Cruse Bereavement Care.

John is 68.

Publications include:

Working with parents of abused children: a role for Counsellors in Primary Care (2009) Article, Healthcare Counselling & Psychotherapy Journal

The Effects of Child Sexual Abuse on Protecting/Non-offending Parents (1998) Article, Counselling Psychology Quarterly: Vol.11, 3, 283-299

John Rowan

John describes his journey beginning with a baptism into the Anglican Church. He grew up with parents who were members of different churches.

John is a qualified individual and group psychotherapist a Chartered Counselling Psychologist and an accredited counsellor. He works in private practice. John is an Honorary Fellow of the United Kingdom Council for Psychotherapy , a Fellow of the British Psychological Society and a Fellow of the British Association for Counselling and Psychotherapy and a founding member of the Association of Humanistic Psychology Practitioners.

John is 85.

Publications include:

A Guide to Humanistic Psychology (2005) 3rd Edition. London: Association for Humanistic Psychology in Britain

The Therapist's Use of Self (with Michael Jacobs) (2002). Buckingham: Open University Press.

The Transpersonal: Spirituality in Psychotherapy and Counselling (2005) 2nd edition. London Routledge

Jane Simmonds

Jane was born and brought up in Scotland by English parents who were members of the Plymouth Brethren.

Since qualifying as a counsellor Jane has undertaken a combination of counselling work in Primary Care, the Voluntary sector and private practice. She has also worked in counsellor training and as a supervisor. She has recently become interested in work with couples and is currently undertaking further training in Family Therapy. Jane has recently become a grandmother so her energies and enthusiasm are again divided between family and work.

Jane is 57.

Sharon Stinson

Sharon describes her American childhood in a Pentecostal Evangelical family that was constantly moving from place to place.

She is a counsellor, supervisor, spiritual director and occasional writer. After teaching in secondary schools in California and Brazil, she moved to the UK and joined the staff of Acorn Christian Listeners where for 14 years she helped develop listening courses which are now in use in the UK and South Africa. She has published articles and stories with a variety of themes. *The Retreat Magazine* printed her article on how Gestalt groups can be combined with retreats. Her first book, entitled *Jessie's Story*, written for a charity, traced the life of a girl with a brain tumour until she died at nine-years old.

Sharon is 76.

Anni Townend

Anni's narrative begins with a description of her attendance at a Baptist church in the Pennines.

She is a leadership consultant, psychologist and author with over twenty years of experience working with people in organisations. The focus of her work is on helping people to develop greater self-confidence, meaning and purpose, and to enjoy positive and creative relationships, which are truly inclusive, respectful of difference and characterised by courageous conversations that facilitate understanding.

Publications include:

Assertiveness and Diversity (2007). Basingstoke Palgrave Macmillan.

Anni is 55.

Wendy Weston

Wendy's introduction to religion was at aged 3 in a local village church – sticking a religious picture in an attendance book each week. Later she attended a convent school, where she absorbed the Roman Catholic faith. She was confirmed in the Church of England, always asked 'why' and took about 30 years to find the answer which satisfied her. Now she no longer attends church regularly. She works part time as a counselling supervisor. She plays tennis and digs the garden in the summer, and spends happy times with her three granddaughters. Wendy is 70.

References

Bond, T (2004) *Ethical Guidelines for Researching Counselling and Psychotherapy. Rugby: British Association for Counselling & Psychotherapy*

Bond, T (2005) *What does good counselling research look like? Workshop Speech. University of York St. John & BACP Conference 'Creating qualitative research that counts.'* 08.10.2005

Etherington, K (2004) *Becoming a reflexive researcher: using our selves in research. London: Jessica Kingsley.*

Etherington, K (2009) *'Life Story Research: a relevant methodology for counsellors and psychotherapists'. Journal of Counselling & Psychotherapy Research Vol. 9 (4)*, 225-233.

Etherington, K (2003) *Trauma, the body and transformation. A narrative enquiry. London: Jessica Kingsley.*

Etherington, K (2005) *'Writing Trauma Stories for Research.'* (unpublished paper)

Fowler, (1987) *Faith Development and Pastoral Care'.* Philadelphia: Fortress Press USA.

McLeod, J, (2003) *Doing Counselling research (2nd Edition)* London: Sage

Piaget, J Gruber, HE Voneche J.J(1977) *The Essential Piaget.* London: Routledge Kegan Paul.

Rennie, DL & Toukmanian, SG (1992) *Psychotherapy Process Research: Paradigmatic and Narrative Approaches.* Newbury Park California: London: Sage.

Splika, B et al (2003) *3rd Edition The Psychology of Religion : an empirical approach.* New York: Guilford Press.

3
TEN NARRATIVES

Peter Gubi
Catherine Hand
John McCourt
John Rowan
Jane Simmonds
Sharon Stinson
Anni Townend
Wendy Weston
Lucy Birtwistle
Lindsay Smith

Peter Gubi

'Our lamb has conquered': What it has meant to follow him.

Introduction

Religion has been, and still is, a consistent influence in my life. It is impossible to say who I would be without my relationship with God and the Church. It informs all of who I am, and my potential to become that which is divine within me - that which I am capable of. Below are some snapshots of my experiencing that have impacted on my faith and my journey as a human being and as a spiritual being, and which continue to be pervasive issues with which I growthfully struggle at some level. There is no sense for me of regret for, nor criticism of, any of the experiences that follow, nor any of the people who have impacted on my life, nor any of the situations in which I have found myself. Forgiveness has played an important part in that. For however difficult or rewarding the experiences have been, all of them have contributed to my spiritual growth for which I am profoundly grateful. I offer this chapter in the humility that it will speak to the reader as it does, and not with any specific intent in mind.

Early Boyhood

I was born in the early 1960's in Barbados, and was brought up in a religious missionary family in the West Indies. My father was an ordained minister, and my grandfather was a bishop, in the Moravian Church in the West Indies – a predominantly 'black' denomination that historically served the early slaves, rather than the plantation owners. 'Our lamb has conquered – let us follow him' is the worldwide motto of the Moravian Church – hence the title of this chapter. The fact that I was white (being white carried 'currency' and 'influence' in those days, such that many black people kept out of the sun in order to be as white as possible), and that my father was a minister who was famous for his religious radio broadcasts on a small island (similar to 'Thought for Today' on BBC Radio 4), and that I was the grandson of a well-loved bishop who was a Danish-born missionary of a generation that had been oppressed by the Germans and thus was able to relate well to the oppressed descendants of the slaves in the West Indies, meant that I was treated as 'special' and 'important' within the Moravian Church community and within the wider island community of Barbados. This led to an early sense of 'self' as being 'of importance' and 'of worth'. If I am to be honest with myself, it led to some arrogance and sense of inappropriate 'self-importance' too, which I now cringe at. My faith today is governed more by humility, but then, in any group that was formed when I was a boy I had to be the leader, and to be awarded all the badges of office and achievement simply because of who I was, whilst others had to graft for their badges.

My early life also gave me an awareness of 'cost'. I witnessed my mother's depression as she wrestled with the expectations of being a minister's wife. She was expected to hold positions of leadership in the Church which she did not feel able or worthy to fulfil – and as such, she has carried feelings of failure, worthlessness and of being trapped throughout her life. In many respects, the Church seems to have been my father's calling – not hers. As a family, we were 'called' to serve on different islands in the West Indies, which meant that my sister and I had a sometimes disrupted education and no sense of roots – something I still carry in my psyche today. My roots are in the Moravian Church, rather than in any geographically placed community. My mother was moved away from her family and friends on many occasions, and paid a high price with her mental health. Throughout my childhood, I suffered bullying for my minority colour, my father's fame and for my then naïve religious values that I tried to impose on others – for I was taught that it was the duty of all Christians to spread the 'Good News', even if others did not want to hear it!

Our family life began every morning with prayers and a Bible reading from the 'Daily Watchwords' - a collection of verses and readings published by the worldwide Moravian Church since 1730. As a family we would sit on my parents' bed, my mother would read the watchwords, my sister and I would take it in turns to read the Bible passage, and my father would close with prayers written by William Barclay. This ritual gave me a sense of our identity as a family, and a daily dose of 'conditions of worth' for us to live by, in that the prayers indicated what behaviours were 'acceptable and sanctified by God', and those that were not. The intrinsic message was 'this is how you are supposed to be' - something that brought guidance and comfort, along with guilt and inner disharmony at times.

Early involvement at church led to the inculcation of certain values relating to sexuality (discussed more fully further on) and behaviour (e.g. no swearing, respect all authority – especially your mother and father and those older and wiser than you!). It gave a sense of being part of a close-knit community, and enabled the overcoming of innate shyness as I unwillingly endured public performance at an early age through the recitation of poems, the singing of duets and the performance of biblically-based plays at church – even now I hate being on stage or in the limelight, but the experiences have stood me in good stead for when I present papers at conferences or facilitate worship. It also gave me a sense of the worth of black people, a discomfort with overt racism and with disparity of wealth, and an abhorrence of the inhumane way that I saw many people in the white community treat their black 'servants'. Through all this I gained an appreciation that we are all 'God's children who are 'of equal and great worth in the sight of God' – a value I still hold dear. Going to church every Sunday was important because it afforded me lengthy opportunities to receive my mother's cuddles as I sat next to her, or on her lap, during the services. I had a strong sense of pride of seeing my dad 'up there' leading the services. It gave me a strong sense of church being associated with love. This was emphasised further by receiving hugs from people who wanted to cuddle Master Petes as I stood by my dad after the service as he shook hands with his flock on their way out of service. At the times of my mother's depressions, Miss Grig and her family would make us food and show us caring love.

Another abiding memory was that during the hurricane season, the Church building became a sanctuary for those who lived in the shanty town just behind the Church. Just before a hurricane was about to hit the island, my father would go to the Church and do his bit to ensure that the needs of the assembled poor were catered for in whatever way he could. For me this was the gospel being lived out in a very practical way. In a symbolic sense, it represented the security of faith in the storms of life - a sanctuary in which I have been able to seek refuge along my life's journey, as a real and lived experience.

At my school, we had regular visits from Miss Laird, a children's evangelist, who would entertain us with puppets and lively choruses whilst passing on some biblical message or other. I enjoyed her coming. I remember the puppets and the choruses, e.g. 'I am H-A-P-P-Y, I am H-A-P-P-Y, I know I am, I'm sure I am, I'm H-A-P-P-Y'. I can't remember anything of her messages though, but I remember her. Then I passed my eleven plus and entered the top-rated school in Barbados – Harrison College. There I remember learning the Apostle's Creed by rote ('come to judge the quick and the dead' meant nothing to me), seeing the leather belt with horse hair being paraded on its way to the Headmaster's study, and being bullied endlessly for my pedigree but often being rescued from my attackers by Robert Weekes, a boy who went to my father's Church and who seemed to look out for me - an interesting paradox of memories. Robert is still in contact – even though he lives in Barbados and I in England – and, at some level, he is still looking out for me (bless him).

The Move to England

When I was aged twelve, we emigrated to England. My father was unable to renew his work permit as the then Government of Barbados was against non-national white persons working In Barbados (my father was born in the US Virgin Islands), and my father was sometimes politically outspoken in his radio broadcasts. There was also a growing anti-white attitude within the body-politic of the Moravian Church in the West Indies, so my father deemed it prudent that we emigrate – despite my mother's opposition. This event gave me a sense of the importance, and the cost, of having integrity. I remember reading the newspapers at that time which featured my father's plight, and being very proud of him. I also remember the constant tears that flowed from my mother at that time, but didn't really appreciate what she was going through. Instead, I experienced frustration and annoyance at her. It is only recently, since my father has been writing his memoirs, that I have more fully realised the impact of this period in my life on him and my mother. Through these experiences, I learned about sacrifice, love and stepping out in faith, for emigration meant leaving behind the body of my little sister who died shortly after she was born, in an unmarked grave, in an untended graveyard, and moving to a new country with all that that entailed.

For me, as a 12-year-old boy, it was an adventure and I was very much seeing things from my own frame of reference. I still had the security of my loving mother, father and elder sister. I seemed to carry an innate trust of life's journey that was grounded in the love of my family and my God. This was what missionaries did. Go to strange places and serve God. Once in this country, however, I experienced the attitude of the Church towards its 'servants' (in those days) as being very different from what I had experienced earlier in my life, and theologically designed to keep us in humility. It was the mid 1970's, and we were poorly paid and housed in a badly maintained, damp, cold manse – having just come from a hot climate.

Again, my mother felt the coldness profoundly – both of the weather and of our non-welcome – for the British Provincial Board of the Moravian Church did not really want us in Britain and only took us under seeming duress. Any sense of importance that we had carried was constantly challenged. Vicars in England were treated as figures of ridicule rather than as caring advocates of the oppressed, as in the West Indies. Dave Allen featured regularly on television at that time, sending-up the pretences and hypocrisy of the Catholic faith. Whilst being thoroughly amusing, and ultimately doing the Church (in it's widest sense) a favour by outing the truth of the ridiculousness of the Church as the non-Church world experienced it, a consequence of this was that my father stopped wearing his clerical collar which had once been a symbol for good – an action for which he received criticism from some members of his congregation as ministers 'should' wear a dog collar. He also took up a job as a postman to remain financially solvent, as he was paid a stipend that was below the poverty line – for which he was criticised by the Church authorities.

In many ways, my father was constantly being criticised by his congregation, and our 'funny ways' (such as pouring out the tea before adding the milk, and our accents) were often ridiculed, because they were not used to people from 'abroad'. I remember being highly excited when I saw my first flakes of snow, and being constantly questioned and teased about what it was like to live in a mud hut – something I had never lived in. If anything, our living quarters were more substantial and suitable in the West Indies than in this country! My mother's depression worsened. Much of this led to the development of a love/hate relationship with the Church as I struggled to reconcile the 'lived experience of the Church' with the ethos of the teachings of Christ as I understood them to be.

Two saving things for me were that I went to an excellent Church school, where I eventually became Head Boy, and I have always remained grateful to the Moravian Church for my education. It was here that I discovered my capacity for love and for being there for others which has led to my career in counselling. Secondly, there were individuals in my father's Church who did not criticise and somehow stood apart from the general politic of the Church at that time. One particular individual who stands out for me was my Sunday School teacher, Graham Mallinson, whose peace and humility demonstrated Christ to me in his way of being. I am aware of my transference in these matters relating to others (and in those which follow later), but I still have the same love and respect for him now, as I did then and I still see him often. He and his wife also cared enough to take me out on my 18th birthday when I was at boarding school – a simple kindness that I treasured, but again was about God loving me.

My Schooling

My schooling from age 12 to 19, was at Fulneck Boys' School (now called Fulneck School) - a school that was originally set up to educate the children of Moravian missionaries. It was the same school that my father's brother and two sisters (my uncle and aunts) had attended, so there was a sense of continuity and history surrounding my going there. In fact, my history teacher, Robin Hutton (a Moravian) had taught my uncle and had been a boy and man at the school – the Mr Chips of Fulneck – for over fifty years. This, at an unconscious level, personified the sense of 'God as changeless and continuous' – that there were still people around whom, it seemed, had been around forever (in my eyes as a young boy). As I write this, Robin is still alive, celebrating his 90th year, and still active at the school as the archivist – continuity indeed.

My first headmaster there was an ex-army colonel. Each day began with morning worship followed by the reading out of a list of boys who had to leave assembly after reciting the 'Lord's Prayer' and form a queue outside the headmaster's study to be caned for various misdemeanours. The irony of this was not lost on me as a boy ('Forgive us our trespasses as we forgive those who trespass against us').

My sister Anne went to the Girls' School which was situated at the other end of the terrace. Boys and girls were not allowed to communicate with each other, and the Girls' School was run by a very strict headmistress, Miss Mort, – a Moravian - who appeared to loathe and pick on my sister because she was a missionary's daughter. Anne was constantly being told 'As a minister's daughter you ought to know/behave better...' My sister suffered badly from asthma as a child and had to often be excused from games which did not go down well with Miss Mort. Sadly my sister has nothing to do with the Church any more and I wonder how much these early experiences have to do with her rejection of the Church. I seem to have been able to take a different path and did not suffer the same kind of humiliation – or I coped with it differently.

At school, I met two very important teachers who unknowingly impacted on me. One was my music teacher, Harold Jones, a Moravian, who was the organist at Fulneck Church. He believed in, and cherished, my musical abilities, and in his way demonstrated his Christian love in his valuing of me. It is because of him that I undertook a music A-level, and learnt to play the piano and organ. In doing so I could spend time with him, for I had huge respect for his involvement with the Church. He somehow represented the love of Christ that I had experienced in my earlier life, but which felt rarer in my experience of English Moravian Christianity thus far. The other teacher actually never taught me in a formal sense because I never learned German. He was Robin Johnson, a German teacher. He gave willingly of his time to us boarders by organising badminton classes and tennis clubs after school and was on night duty once a week. He was fun to be around and I was able to talk to him when I needed to. He taught me through his way of being that we, as pupils, were worthy of love, were of value and respect. Other staff failed to meet us as human beings. He was a man who lived his Christianity in his encounter with others, rather than talk about it.

A third person who impacted on me was the Moravian minister at Fulneck, Reverend Wilfred Mortimer. Again, I always felt a sense of value and worth when in his presence. He always expressed pride in knowing my father - something I felt greatly too. He was also easy to talk to and someone whom I respected greatly. As a boarder at Fulneck, Harold Jones and Wilfred Mortimer, along with their wives, used to invite me to their houses for tea or take me to classical music concerts – with all the awe and wonder that I experienced there. Because they lived within a five minute walking distance from the school, I could pop in at any time and always received a welcome. At a time when I sometimes felt vulnerable and isolated, I was met by Christ through these Christian folk – an important caring encounter opportunity that Child Protection policies would sadly probably prohibit these days. I was also encouraged to read lessons in Church and to play the organ in Church, thus being included in a community of people for whom I have much respect and whom I felt respected by. Harold Jones also trained and conducted the 'Moravian Singers' - a choir of Moravians from around Yorkshire. Again I felt included and part of something important, and I enjoyed the camaraderie, and the singing. Harold always collected me and returned me safely to the school, and became in many ways a surrogate father.

The Church as 'Sexless'

My teenage years at Fulneck were a time of sexual confusion and development. Because we were not allowed to communicate with the girls, I seemed to receive a message that any involvement with girls (never mind sexual involvement) was somehow 'wrong', shameful and somehow 'dirty'. The messages from my earlier childhood were that sex outside of marriage was wrong 'in the sight of God' – something that my mother seemed to be constantly reiterating. I never saw my sister, nor my parents, naked. As well as these messages, I was aware of a growing interest in same-sex nudity. Before we came from the West Indies I had never seen a naked girl and only occasionally had I seen a naked boy. I had never seen a naked man or woman - neither in the flesh nor in pictures. In this country, whenever we played sport or had Physical Education, we had to have a shower. It was then that I had a regular experience of same-sex nudity and I found it pleasurable.

At that same time, the culture in the school was extremely homophobic (not necessarily overtly, but implicitly among the pupils through humour and teasing), and so I had to keep these feelings to myself. I was also increasingly aware of some biblical teaching that stated that homosexuality was 'wrong', and of some Christian teaching that masturbation was sinful. I was also fascinated with girls, but that was 'wrong' too (or so I thought then). It has taken me years to reconcile my bisexuality, and my pleasure in masturbation, and to see them both as a gift from God - as an embodiment of the divine within me, rather than as something to be ashamed about.

This has been a long and sometimes tortuous journey of recognizing the reality of my body and my emotions, and wrestling with the guilt of experimentation whilst experiencing the pain and rich intimacy of both same-sex and heterosexual love. The way that I have reconciled my experiencing is that I have found God in all of these emotions and relationships, and can see the 'rightness', growthfulness and value of that intense love between two consenting adults - whether same-sex or heterosexual. I have also come to value both the feminine and masculine parts of me, and feel very comfortable with both. Indeed both enable me to be sensitive and caring, yet strong and able to battle when appropriate. In my life and work I have needed the integration of both parts of me in my need for resilience and vulnerability. At such times of strife and tenderness, I have seen the divine nature of Christ in myself.

All of these experiences have drawn me to Person-Centred Counselling. It is this approach, above any other, that values the healing importance of 'encounter' and relationship that is characterised by the unique worthiness and valuing of each individual, demonstrated in the empathic meeting of the other in love and acceptance. It is at times when I have experience of this in my early life, that I have found God. But amongst all the damage that has been inflicted on me and my family, those moments of my encounter with God through others has kept my faith alive, and enabled me to distinguish between what is a distortion of faith and what is true faith. In my last two years at school, in an environment that was largely starved of love, I discovered my capacity to love. For my capacity to love (i.e. to be tender, to be 'there' for the other, to physically hold, to emotionally hold, to listen, to care, to not judge) was valued by many of the other boarders and I was often the one to whom they turned for solace. I did not realise it at the time as I was just simply responding to my capacity to love, but as I had received Christ through my encounter with others, I was enabling Christ in some small way to be encountered by others. This is something that I still hold dear today and is the motivation for my work as a counsellor.

Vocation

Throughout my life I have had a strong desire to be part of the ordained ministry. There has never been a time in my life when this has not been in my awareness at some level.

I have pictures of me as a small boy, aged about four, in my underpants and wearing my father's dog collar, supposedly 'preaching' to a group of assembled teddy bears. At that level, there is something about unconsciously imitating my father and grandfather, for whom I had deep love and respect. Throughout my life there has always been a sense of expectation that I will go into the Moravian ministry and thus follow in the footsteps of my grandfather, my father and my uncle, who between them have given over 120 years of service to the Moravian Church. But because of the anguish of seeing how the Church has treated its servants, the lack of clarity over what my 'calling' is about (is it simply fulfilling expectation or is this really what God wants for me?), and my feelings of anger towards the Church as a political body (something I have now come to understand as me carrying my mother's anger towards the Church, rather than it being my own anger), I have shied away from responding fully to this 'call' – until now.

Instead, my life has been spent in being a secular, rather than a religious, priest. On leaving school I studied to be a teacher. My first degree was in the study of world religions and that course profoundly opened my awareness to other faiths. It also led to deep existential questioning of what life was about for me – and for a time, I lost the 'certainty' of my faith. What enabled me to eventually hold onto it (or come back to it) was simply, that if I was saying that it was all a load of rubbish, I was denying my experiencing and stating that my father's life and work – never mind that of my grandfather and uncle – had been a waste of time. This was too much to do, so instead, I worked on a way of intellectually and emotionally trying to integrate all that I was learning and had learned. In doing so, I reached a place of inclusivity of others' spirituality, however idiosyncratic that may be. However, I realise that I have excluded dogmatism and fundamentalism – those who believe literally that 'I am the way, the truth and the life' - so I wonder really how inclusive I can actually be? On qualifying, I secured a post as Head of Religious Studies and Pastoral Care in a boarding school. There I took assemblies, taught a largely biblical syllabus, and immersed myself fully in the life of the school. I treated and loved the pupils as though they were my own children. I remember one boy, having been upset and having being comforted by me, saying very sincerely and innocently, 'Sir, you are just like Jesus' and another saying 'Sir, I feel more secure when you are here…' - at which I wept because, for me, the essence of me had been met in my meeting of them. After seven years of giving my soul to the school, I left and developed my capacity for loving encounters, which I had experienced as a boy, within the field of counselling. Throughout my life, I have and continue to wrestle with the issue of 'vocation'. What is it that God wants for me, and how can I give of my all in a way that has integrity, is authentic, and which embraces all of who I am? Is the Church enough? Is counselling enough? Is academia enough?

The direction that my life has taken me in thus far encompasses all of the above. I have continued to study and publish research on the interface between religion/spirituality and counselling, leading to an MA in Counselling, an MTh in Applied Theology, and a PhD in Counselling Studies. I recently published a book, *Prayer in Counselling and Psychotherapy* (2008), and my spirituality and faith is very central to my way of being, to how I find meaning and purpose in my life, and to how I live my life and conduct my work. I have found a home in the writings of Brian Thorne, with whom I have trained. I am an officially recognised lay preacher in the Moravian Church and still have a need to belong to the Moravian Church and for community, even though my spirituality is influenced by much more than Christianity. I have developed a Postgraduate Certificate in Person-Centred Spiritual Care and Accompaniment which runs at the University of Central Lancashire where I am currently Principal Lecturer in Counselling and Head of the

Counselling and Psychological Therapies Division. I feel most fulfilled when I am accompanying others on their spiritual journeying. At heart, my life is a spiritual pilgrimage and in my work I meet fellow pilgrims.

I continue to inwardly wrestle with the Moravian Church. As I am, I can be a prophetic voice who writes controversial articles that challenge the cultural assumptions and beliefs of the Church, if I remain outside of the ordained ministry. It gives me freedom to be myself and to share my experiencing and thinking, and generate discussion (at least among those who can understand where I am coming from). On a rational and emotional level my ministry in counselling is immensely worthwhile and richly fulfilling. God is able to work through me in the healing and woundedness of others. I am able to encounter people who have been damaged by, or disillusioned with, the church in a way that they would not encounter me if I were 'inside' the church.

My workshops on spirituality, and the retreats that I am privileged to facilitate enable people who would not otherwise embrace their spirituality, or who have been damaged by their religious experiences, to connect with the transcendent other - that which in my authenticity, I would deem as embracing the love and divine intimacy of God. I can connect, as my ancestors have done, with the oppressed. But to me there is a struggle with authenticity - the struggle of language.

Part of my incompleteness is my reluctance to talk about 'God' because of the bullying that I received as a boy when I did, because of the unacceptability within the world of counselling to talk about faith (and then only if we talk around what we really mean), and because of the difficulty that others bring to the word 'God'. So because I am fearful of rejection and desire inclusivity for others, I sacrifice some sense of completeness which I don't fully understand but know that I regularly experience. And there is an even greater sense in which I 'feel' that I remain incomplete – and regularly experience a place of sadness, fragmentation, and loss - which in my fantasy will only be made whole if I submit to the process of ordination. So, at the time of writing this, I have submitted to the process of being accepted to train for the Ordained Ministry of the Moravian Church in the British Province.

Conclusion

Writing this has been a mixture of pain, pleasure and illumination.

I have always recognized that I am a complex character, and that religion has always been important to me. Not religion that is characterised by a dogma and doctrine that is damaging or exclusive of others. For me these are distortions of religion which I abhor. But religion that is characterised by love is 'the truth' of my faith – 'In essential things, unity; in non-essential things liberty; in all things, love' – the theology of the Moravian Church that is at the centre of Zinzendorf's 'Theology of the Heart'.

In some ways I have found more of the essence of God in Person-Centred Counselling than I have sometimes experienced in the Church. Yet, I have found it in some measure within the Church throughout my life. For me, it has been (and is) about the embodiment of God's love. I have acknowledged how important the Church still is for me and it saddens me that it is in decline and that I do little to prevent this.

Certainly, through my early religious influences, a niche has been carved out in my soul where I experience loyalty and gratitude for what the Church and my upbringing has given to me, however flawed that sometimes has been. I want to acknowledge that over recent years my experiences of the Moravian Church have changed to reflect more of God's love. For the Church in which my family was once ridiculed now embraces me as a valued facilitator of worship. The Moravian Church in Britain is now more valuing of its 'servants' than it has been in the past. In part that has been brought about through a shortage of people putting themselves forwards for ministry. Whatever the reason, the change has meant that God's love is more embodied in the world by the Church, and I am more able to embrace it, and my parents' care during my upbringing, with immense gratitude.

Catherine Hand

Religion in Childhood; CATHERINE'S STORY

It took twelve minutes to walk round the hospital, and I did it twice a day. It was May, and my husband was in a coma. One evening at sunset I found myself exhilarated by the beauty of the sky, and fascinated by tiny snails creeping over the burgeoning plants. It seemed to me that the very essence of the Universe was Good; not goodness, but Good, and that nothing humankind could do could affect or diminish that. Religions and politics seemed small things, and my husband's life or death would be equally fitting. What did matter was that we should love one another, that the nurses should work from love, that everything we do should come from that love.

This experience changed my life; it did not take away pain or grief, nor did it make me a saint, but it gave me a steadiness, and an absolute conviction that, despite all, there is, far beyond our understanding, a benificence.

My mother was nearly thirty when I was born, and my two brothers did not follow until five and seven years later, so my earliest years were spent as an only child. In my adult life I have most often heard women described as strong when they escaped the roles of wife and mother, but I grew up with a mother and a grandmother who believed that the most important thing any woman could do was to bring up her family. They both rejoiced in their children, and my lovingly kept baby book shows how my arrival was welcomed by my parents, relatives and friends, and my first steps and words were recorded.

This did not mean that I was spoilt; I was expected to be polite and unselfish. To this day I remember being made to give a doll I had won in a raffle to a little girl who was weeping with disappointment. I boiled with resentment, and hated the wretched child, and my mother, but did not dare to make a fuss. It was made clear to me that I, as other people, had been put on this earth to make it a better place, and my mother's religious faith was the foundation for her views.

We had what seemed to me a huge King James Bible, with large print and hyphens between the syllables, and many Victorian illustrations, some, like the

Golden Calf, glorious with colour. My mother told me the stories of the Creation, of Noah and of Job, and read me passages which sent tingles down my spine:

"If I take the wings of the morning, and dwell in the uttermost parts of the sea; Even there shall Thy hand lead me, and Thy right hand shall hold me."

We were not always solemn. We read Shakespeare together, my Puck to my mother's Oberon (the part she had played in a school production). We collected frogspawn and fed the tadpoles on scraps of meat suspended on string. Once she declared the day too splendid for me to go to Kindergarten, so we spent it in the fields. The next morning in assembly I asked if we could sing "All things bright and beautiful".

"We sang that yesterday," came the disapproving reply, "when you were not here."

We would walk down to a stream and through the woods and I learnt the names of the wild flowers and one day watched a family of baby mice playing at the opening of their hole. A friend and I picked plantains, passed a piece of stem through the stalk to make arms and dressed them with flower petals. In the winter when it snowed my mother put a teaspoonful of jam into enamel mugs, filled them with milk and left them outside on the windowsill all night to make 'ice cream' by morning. On dark evenings we ate baked potatoes with teaspoons to spoon out the soft insides, tasty with melted cheese.

My brothers were born; at that time childbirth was treated as an illness: a fortnight in a nursing home and a nurse who lived in the house for the first month was quite usual for middleclass women. Although my mother, when not confined ,did the cooking, and let me help, she also did the housework and washed by hand, with the aid of a copper in which the whites were boiled. I was allowed to turn the mangle, with awful warnings about crushed thumbs if I got too near the rollers; the water poured out of the clothes and they emerged nearly dry and contorted into shapes that were almost geological. A girl from a poor family in the nearby city 'lived in'; she wore false teeth and would terrify me by dropping the top set in a ghastly grin. She was devoted to the whole family, especially my mother, and one evening I asked her to come and sit in the drawing room with us instead of retreating to her bedroom, "Oh no, I can't come in there, it wouldn't be right." Indignant, I called on my mother for support, but none was forthcoming , and I thought my mother was unjust.

The Second World War was raging; I was told never to pick up sweets from the road in case they were poisoned, and had a gas mask, which was a favourite play-thing, and an identity bracelet. "In case you ever get lost". I had no idea it was to identify my dead body.

I was told that most Germans were good people, and that we would win the war, and they would be sorry; I imagined they would come knocking on every door and apologise. For some time we had a German Jewish family living with us, but I had no idea of the trauma they had suffered.

We attended the Anglican church regularly: I was in trouble once for answering the vicar's rhetorical question in a sermon, and when the vicar's wife asked me if we said grace before meals, I replied, "No, we just say 'thank goodness'", which was not the answer she expected. I went to Sunday school, I think so my parents could have some peace, but none of this made much impression on me.

There was some ill health: I had a fall, and my leg became infected, I was de-lirious and ill for some time, this was before antibiotics were in general use. My mother nursed me, despite my protests when the dressings had to be changed. I had measles and whooping cough, my father had carbuncles on his wrists, my mother would cover her head with a towel to inhale Friar's Balsam to relieve heavy colds. None of this frightened me; I only remember being panic stricken once, when my mother left me and my small brother alone in the house when she called round, briefly, to see a neighbour.

I was eight years old when we went on holiday to Cromer, in Norfolk. We rent-ed a house in which, unbeknown to us, soldiers returning from the Far East had been billeted, and one had died. My mother, too, became ill, we returned home and she went to hospital: within days she was dead.

Her name was hardly mentioned again. My baby brother stood up in his cot night after night crying, "Mummy, mummy", but nothing was said. I was told she had died, but my elder, three year old brother was not, and years later he told me he thought she had just gone away and left us.

We were not told about her funeral or where she was buried, so a schoolfriend and I searched for her grave. It was marked only by a strip of stone bearing her surname, there was no Christian name, no dates, no text: nothing. Weeds grew over the plot, only a china vase in the shape of a rabbit, which I remembered from home, containing a few dead flowers, showed that someone had once visited it.

We stood and stared, neither of us had any words. We were about nine years old. Utter dereliction filled my heart. I have never been back; I do not think I could find the place again, and I am not sure why I do not try to. We told no-one what we had done.

My father immersed himself in work.

"It was a good thing it was your mother who died," he told me later, "For you would have been so poor."

We no longer visited our grandmother or our aunts and uncles in London, "They would talk about Winnie" I heard my father say.

We were cared for by my paternal grandmother, a bitter and frustrated woman. My salvation was the mother of a friend who always welcomed me, and spending time at the riding stables. I was passionate about horses, and became a very good rider; to this day I find riding an ecstatic experience.

At the age of twelve, a few months after my father re-married, I was sent to boarding school. I was 'too friendly', apparently, so no-one would speak to me for about two terms. I have never experienced such isolation and, as prisoners in solitary confinement do, I turned to religion.

The school, just outside Oxford, was an Anglican foundation, with twice daily prayers and attendance at church on Sunday. The liturgy provided comfort, and the sermons inspiration, schoolgirl fervour considerably aided by the sonerous voice and Brylcreemed black hair of the curate, with whom we were all in love (he later became Archbishop Blanch of York).

The Headmistress sometimes took a chosen few to Christchurch, berating us afterwards if we had not recognised that Psalm 139 on the notice board was Psalm CXXXIX in the Prayer Book. Once some of us went to Magdalen College Chapel; it was near Christmas and in the candlelight the choir sang Berlioz:

"O child of man, lo to Bethlehem
The Kings are travelling, travel with them.
The King of Glory, the King of grace,
Shall guide your heart to its resting place,
Gold, incense, myrrh, thou canst not bring,
Offer thy heart to the infant King,
Offer thy heart...."

We were expected to accept the teachings of the Church and the school, and the emphasis was on sin and salvation. We were never quite good enough, always sinners, criticism, not praise, was the norm. When I came to leave, after seven years, I was lauded for my humility; in fact I had been quite thoroughly brainwashed.

One history lesson, though, did shock me into a question. Henry VIII, we were told, made himself Head of the Church in England, thus breaking away from Rome and forming the Anglican Church. "Were we Roman Catholics before that?" I asked,

"Oh, yes."

"But I thought our church went right back to the time of Jesus?"

"No, we broke away from the Roman Catholic Church because it was corrupt."

This amazed me: I had always inferred that the Roman Catholic Church was the schismatic; a strange, foreign institution which worshipped the Virgin Mary and indulged in occult rites involving incense and Latin: now I was told that this Church was the one that descended from the Apostles. A Church based on the King's desire for a divorce seemed to me to be on very shaky ground, and from this time onwards- I was about thirteen- I took a surreptitious interest in Catholicism.

As expected, I progressed to University. English literature was my first love, and I gained a distinction at A.S. Level, but the History Mistress was senior to the English mistress, and I was her protege. I had played with the idea of studying Sociology, but the Headmistress declared, "No girl of mine will read Sociology." So History it was, though I knew from the first day that this was a mistake but I was far too timid to approach the authorities to ask to change courses.

My three years of study bored me utterly. I was only interested in 'Political Theory' and 'Ecclesiastical Institutions of the Middle Ages', these made me think, and escape into a world of idealism and beauty. I met my future husband and we married as soon as I graduated. As he was still a veterinary student I was the breadwinner, and the obvious occupation to enter was teaching.

My father was delighted: I had married a man who was likely to earn a good salary, and had chosen the profession he thought the safest and most suitable for a woman.

This, though, was the last thing I did that pleased my father. I had hated boarding school, and teaching in the East End of London confirmed me in my left wing politics. Teaching itself I did not enjoy; I was not interested in my subject and did not enjoy dealing with children en masse. As soon as my husband graduated we had our first child and moved to the country where I began the life I knew I wanted. My father was appalled as we eventually had five children, foster children, dogs, cats, goats, chickens and geese, and I became, outwardly at least, an Earthmother.

It was not until years later that I realized that my animosity towards my father, and repudiation of all that he believed in was due at least in part to my anger that he lived while my mother had died. All authority was now anathema to me. I read Freud, Jung, and Bowlby, William Morris and Virginia Woolf. I wanted a career, but was convinced that my duty was to be a full time mother, and I loved that role, and felt that I was replicating the large family from which my mother had come.

At this time I gave up God. The Vietnam War was raging, and I too was raging at a God who would permit such suffering, and the Church's feeble responses. At that stage I was still not radical enough to go on marches, but later became an active member of C.N.D. and a pacifist. The inequality between the rich West and what was then called the Third World gnawed at my conscience, and we became members of an organization founded by Horace Dammers, which advocated simple living.

After a few years of marriage, my husband began to suffer from depression and acute anxiety, and an inability to work with, or form good relations with, his colleagues. He went from job to job, and the family followed him. Eventually he set up his own single-handed practice, and any idea I might have had of a career of my own disappeared as I became his veterinary nurse and gofer. He was an excellent diagnostician and surgeon, but his eccentricity and outspokenness put many people off, and it was difficult to survive financially. He was desperate to understand why he was so different and so unhappy. It was not until after his death and the birth of an autistic grandson that it became clear to me that he had suffered from Asperger's Syndrome. As a counsellor, I am now wary of labels, but do think it would have helped him if he had been able to put a name to his condition, and it would certainly have made me more understanding: I would have demanded less of him. The medical profession, including psychiatrists, were at that time far less knowledgeable about autism and Asperger's than they are now.

At times I was very unhappy: my husband could be a great intellectual companion, and our values and politics were compatible, but he was frequently utterly miserable, suicidal, angry and sometimes violent, though never towards the children. I took my marriage vows very seriously, and did not consider divorce, and I also knew that the children would be devastated if we were to part, as they loved him - we all did - and he was a good and caring parent, especially with babies and young children.

Motherhood had made me, overnight, hypersensitive to the woes of the world. I wanted to find a way to be more effective, and admired some of my friends who were Quakers, so for a while we went to Meeting. My husband and I travelled many miles to attend a Quaker weekend. We arrived at 10:45p.m. to find every-one in bed though we had been expected. This and other experiences led me to find Quakers cold and smug, and I missed music and words. There seemed to be so many aggressively plain, domineering women, with insignificant husbands, and I wondered if you could really call yourself a Quaker unless you were middleclass, educated and a fell walker. Once, in December, the Meeting House had been used by another organization for a party, and a great, glistening, sparkling Christmas tree had been left there. A Friend rose to his feet and apologised for it, bemoaning its presence as inappropriate. I never went to a meeting again.

But my hunger to belong had been re-awakened, and after the birth of my last child I wondered if we were right to be bringing them up with no religious teach-ing or affiliation. Maybe I could do more good and come to terms with my rebel-liousness if I revived my interest in Catholicism? I started to go to Mass and was received into the Church, even though when I replied "I do" to the unexpected question in the service, "Do you believe in all the teachings of the Church?"

I knew I had begun with a lie.

For fourteen years I was a faithful communicant, became a governor of the lo-cal Catholic school, a member of the St. Vincent de Paul Society and completed a course for lay leaders and teachers of religious studies. I was a regular reader at Mass, and found great comfort in the beauty of the liturgy. But I was increasingly angered by the position of women in the Church, and the emphasis on piety, regardless, it seemed to me, of one's conduct in everyday life; above all, the obses-sion with sexual sin when all about us the arms race continued and the first Iraq war began.

I had in fact been accepted and treated with kindness by the congregation and the clergy, but I could not see that. Now it seems to me that, like an adolescent, I was looking for Utopia and thinking in absolute terms: black and white, good and bad: object relations par excellence. I flounced out.

Within months, my husband, on the verge of retirement, took a huge overdose of barbiturates, and was in a coma for ten days. While I was staying at the hospital I had what I can only regard as my vision, and thereafter my life was changed.

Although my husband recovered he seemed to have suffered some brain damage. He became increasingly erratic and angry, and eventually left home to live in sheltered housing some distance away. He started divorce proceedings. I was devastated with grief. I was also poverty-stricken, and had to support my youngest child who was only fourteen, and whose loyalties were torn because of his parents separation. I continued teaching the literature class for adults which had kept me sane for the past ten or more years, but that paid merely pocket money. I had to find a job. It was so long since I had taught in school that I was unemployable in education, nor did I want to return to the classroom. I had no qualifications at all so I took a job in an old people's home.

Over the next seven years I worked in residential and nursing homes, as a home help, and in the community. At first I felt I had come down in the world: how I resented having to don a pinny and serve meals, and to be condescended to by visitors. But it was good for me to have no escape, and to realise that I could either feel bitter, or learn to do the work well, and with good grace. A friend who was a Buddhist gave me an article which explored the difference between suffering and pain. Pain is inevitable, but suffering is caused by resisting or clinging to the pain. I grew to love the old people I was looking after and felt a huge sympathy for their emotional and intellectual as well as their physical needs. The tactile contact: washing and dressing them, tucking them into bed, caring for them intimately, comforted me, alone as I was. I began to feel, not just think.

I was shattered by my husband's desire for a divorce, but knew that nothing would change his mind. I wept for him most days, and had panic attacks when I drove the car. After five years the divorce was finalised, and his mood at once changed, he came to visit, he planned to move closer to my home, he was going to come for Christmas. Nine months after the decree absolute he died of a brain haemorrhage.

The death was dreadful, but final. The children and I mourned him sincerely, but, in a way, we found ourselves relieved, free of anxiety about him and our pity for him. Nothing could hurt him now.

Soon after this I was forced to stop working at such a physically demanding job, and had to have an operation for a hip replacement. At the same time I received two legacies, one from my father who, despite my lack of appreciation for him, provided generously for all his children, and one from my stepmother. She had cared consistently forus all, bearing in silence the knowledge she must have had that I was never able to feel for her the love that she deserved.

I had been a Samaritan for over twenty years. Now, I thought, I could improve my skills. Before my husband's death I had gained the Counselling Certificate at the local F.E. college, and had been accepted as a volunteer at the nearest branch of the mental health charity, MIND, and now at last I could afford to work towards the Diploma.

Almost by accident, as it was recommended and nearby, I found myself a student at Temenos, in Sheffield. In my eagerness, I had hardly given a thought to the approach that I wished to follow, but maybe the sort of God I do not believe in had a hand in leading me to this Person-Centred college. My years there were pure joy. For the first time, it seemed, I experienced unconditional positive regard and cherishing, and found my tendency to criticise and condemn melting away. I found within me a warmth and forbearance I did not know I had. My mistakes were just mistakes, and I could learn from them, and as other people trusted my process I began to do so as well. I felt as if I were swimming in a warm sea, where I would not drown, in my own element, and knew a consistent joy which I have never lost.

Since that time I have worked in the voluntary sector, as I think that the people who need counselling the most are probably the ones who are least able to pay for it. Some of my clients have mental health problems, others are suffering from the tragedies of life, some are women who have been sexually abused as children. An advantage of working in this sector is that I can generally see clients for about a year, so that we can form a deep and trusting relationship without worrying too much about time constraints. There can be no suspicion that counselling is being extended for financial reasons, and the understanding that this is a finite exercise means there is less danger of either of us becoming too dependent. I am aware, also, that I have a problematic attitude to money; I am conscious that my feelings about my father, and the enormous importance of money to him; that he was only able to demonstrate his concern for us, his children, by means of money; has made it difficult for me to be in any relationship where I would feel that I was only available if I had been paid for it. I know I am inconsistent about this: I would be happy to take a salary to work in a voluntary organization, as that would not be taking payment directly from a client; and I am able to survive financially while working as a volunteer.

In fact, working as a counsellor requires and stimulates what I hope is a necessary, not narcissistic, constant examination of one's own attitudes, and a fascination with the ideas and motivations of other people. So my interest in ways of living, philosophies and a spiritual life was further encouraged and fed by the people I met and the books I read.

Thoreau's Walden, with his call for "simplicity, simplicity, simplicity', his transcendental delight in the natural world, his awareness that "our inventions are wont to be pretty toys" and that "most men lead lives of quiet desperation" chimed with my own convictions. One of my quarrels with churches was their emphasis on the heaven that waits for us only after death, while this world is but a vale of tears, and the Augustinian split between things spiritual and material (influenced by his mother, Monica, who encouraged him to desert his partner and their child, embrace celibacy and go to Italy to further his career). Rather I found a kindred spirit in Thomas Traherne: "You never enjoy the world aright till you see how a sand exhibiteth the wisdom and power of God...till every morning you awake in Heaven....till you so love the beauty of enjoying it, that you are covetous and earnest to persuade others to enjoy it ... the world is the paradise of God". Eternal life, I think is not to do with time, but it is a way of being and of seeing which is available to us now, if only, because of our imperfection, in snatches.

I reread the Gospels, taking notice of Jesus's references to the Kingdom of Heaven, which, it seems, is among us, if only we could see it. Sin is, perhaps, a sort of blindness. If, because of childhood trauma or unbearable pain, one is consumed with fear or rage, one is unlikely to be able to bear or apprehend the vulnerabilities of others: no-one could commit acts of cruelty or go to war if one could truly see and feel the agonies of the victims. I am conscious in myself that it is a lack of awareness and love, a neediness, that causes me to do less than I should for others. The doctrine of the Incarnation was meaningful to me: if God could become man and so love the World, if he cares about the 'sparrow sold for three farthings' and told us to 'consider the lilies of the field, even Solomon in all his glory was not arrayed like one of these', surely we, too, should love and care for this world, this life, these animals, birds, plants, rivers and mountains, these human beings amongst whom we live. This world has been given to us to wonder at and to be happy in. We do not know what, if anything, will happen to us after death: We do know that we are alive, here, now, and that what we do affects our whole environment. To concentrate on one's own personal 'salvation' in terms of one's ultimate destination, seems to me to be glorified self-centeredness.

Perhaps Eternity does not mean everlasting life, but a quality of life. Perhaps the Resurrection is a new life when our eyes are truly opened. These ruminations made Jesus a far more compelling and vibrant person to me: someone who was aflame with love, who felt joy and pity and terror and pain to a degree that we can scarcely apprehend, and whose courage was beyond belief. I did not, I do not, disbelieve in some sort of survival after death; in fact at times the longing to once again be with my mother and those whom I love and who are dead is overwhelming, but it seems to me to be a matter of which we can know nothing, and not one on which we should concentrate unduly.

I am content with that.

And what about God? As a young woman I was prepared to be angry with Him for all the suffering He permits, or to disbelieve in Him altogether. But I could never feel that I was alone in the Universe. As I grew, I hope, more mature, I came to think that a bit more humility would help. I cannot cope with even basic mathematics, and know little of science; I understand virtually nothing about the world, its arts, music, languages and cultures; how could I possibly ascertain whether there is or is not a God, or whether He is a concept or a creator? I think we would be better off if, like Keats, we were capable of " Being in uncertainties, Mysteries, doubts, without any irritable reaching after fact and reason". I like the approach of the Orthodox churches, as described by Karen Armstrong in her History of God: "Everything that we can see or understand is only a symbol which reveals the presence of a reality which is beyond all thought".

During this time I also read some Buddhist literature and was attracted by the ideal of disinterested compassion, and of non-attachment in the sense of not clinging to people or objects for my own ends. I also attended workshops and retreats on mindfulness meditation, and mindfulness is, as far as I am able, a part of my everyday life. The practice of counselling has aided this as, in essence, the relationship with the other is an act of complete attention, respect and compassion: 'feeling with'.

However, I was still experiencing a yearning for words, for singing and for a ritual through which I could express my spiritual hunger, and I also wanted to belong somewhere.

One Christmas, my brother and I went to Midnight Mass. Afterwards he said:

"Why did you not take Communion?"

"Because I do not believe what they all believe," I responded.

"How do you know what they believe?"

How indeed? What I do believe is, that, like emotions, one's beliefs are not under one's conscious control, and cannot be summoned at will, nor is their presence or absence an occasion for praise or blame (how often have I heard clients condemn themselves for having feelings which they think they must be evil to experience). So I began, once again, to attend Mass.

The Mass, to me, is a re-enactment and celebration of what is going on all the time: things earthly becoming holy, and the holy, earthly; or rather it is a recognition of the fact that all is, in essence, unity. In some way that I do not understand I can accept that the bread and wine do become Body and Blood, as a foetus is nourished by the food its mother eats and becomes a human child. The Mass is also a sacrifice, an act of love, for any real love entails longsuffering and may make enormous demands of us, "costing no less than everything", as it did of Jesus, and of thousands of others since.

My affinity to the Catholic Church probably relates to my need for a 'mother', and for historical rootedness. I am well aware that, as my mother and I were not able to weather the storms of my adolescence together, I am likely to idealize her, though she is spoken of with great tenderness and admiration by those who knew her. I think I probably played out these pubescent conflicts in my inability to tolerate the human imperfections which are found in any institution, religious or secular; I sought a Golden Age.

My aversion to authority was - is - I am sure a reaction to my father's dominance, and to the unyielding regime of boarding school. Now I know that, although I do not share my father's values, he did the best he could for his children: he used money as a symbol for his affection. His own father had been a gentle, kindly man, a shopkeeper who felt so sorry for his impoverished customers that he would let them pay their bills in kind; a set of wooden elephants used to be displayed with bitterness by my grandmother. My father's childhood was thus overshadowed by the fear of destitution, and his young manhood by the slump of the thirties. I am told that I am obstinate and self-willed (or determined and independent), like him.

Both my parents regarded the 'Roman' Catholic Church with suspicion, and would never have considered leaving the Church of England, though my father only used it for christenings, marriages and funerals.

I hope that I now have an attitude to spirituality, and to the Church to which I belong which is as adult and thought out as I can manage. I know that the Catholic Church seems to encompass literal believers and those who look on its teachings with a more mythical, mystical or maverick attitude. I like to be part of a congregation of people of all ages, races, classes and opinions who come to Mass as naturally as they would eat breakfast or go to work, and do not approve of "making windows into men's souls". To me, one's beliefs are made manifest by one's actions.

There are aspects of clerical teaching which I question: getting to heaven as an aim is regrettable, surely the point of Christianity is to bring God's Love to Earth, not to concentrate on one's own salvation? The 'Just War' doctrine seems to me to be indefensible: pacifism is absolutely intrinsic to Jesus' teaching and life - and death - and I think the Church, and we as citizens, nationalists and timorous people, are too afraid to embrace it. Do we really believe that 'might is right', that victory is always given to the righteous, and that we have made progress as we go from bows and arrows to nuclear bombs, with greater and greater carnage on the way?

With this exception, I am suspicious of certainty, with its dangerous stasis and bloodstained history. Rogers in his 'stages of process', judged flexibility, fluidity and openness as characteristics of the adult organismic self, and his own ideas changed and developed right up to his death. I do not think I would be a very good counsellor if I had arrived at the end of all questioning or change in my life.

Not many clients talk about religion as such, but most are engaged in moral or existential concerns. I notice that those with diagnoses such as schizophrenia, or those whose lives are particularly chaotic or who feel they cannot live up to the standards their families insisted upon, or who suffer from pervading guilt, tend to be drawn to those churches which offer forgiveness, the experience of being 'born again', and a strict regime thereafter. I do not, however, think that this is particularly healthy or helpful in the long term. Many clients, particularly those who are gay, or in some way nonconformists, are very angry with the religious establishment. Most, though, do not seem to find religious belief or practice particularly relevant, but seem to evolve a philosophy of their own, probably influenced by Christianity , as it is still the dominant tradition in this country, and this I personally would regard as healthy.

My own childhood experience of religion, particularly the death of my mother and exile to school, I am sure influenced my reason and my emotions. My emotional need for belonging and comfort was to some extent assuaged by religious practice, and my reason engaged by the impossibility of simple belief. As the child of my parents I have travelled far from their convictions but am grateful for their influence: the moral guidance they laid down and on the whole lived by, and the literary and cultural wealth to which they introduced me. Our life in the country (as a tiny child I was taken to stay on my uncle's farm to escape the Blitz, and I have hardly lived in a town since) also had a huge influence: an ever changing, ever the same world of beauty, of life and death, and, one hopes, an existence as far as possible of harmony and simplicity with the created order has moulded me as much as anything or anyone else.

I do not expect ever to come to a final resolution or conclusion: I know that I am fickle, curious, variable, and hope to go on learning and changing until my dying day. During my life many people, apart from my parents, have challenged and interested me, and I have walked with several saints. Life has been, and is, very good to me, and who knows what will happen next?

John McCourt

My Stories

These are events and memories that have been significant to me as I grew up in a strongly Catholic family, becoming a priest and then leaving the priesthood after 20 years in order to be free to marry. It has felt like a long journey but one I'm glad I made – and in many ways a journey that I am still on.

August 1986

Mobile phones weren't readily available in 1986 and I'd walked to the nearest phone box, not yet having had a phone of my own installed. I was going to phone the two most important people in my life – Jo and my mum.

It was the evening of the day when I first moved into my flat and I wanted to let them know how I had settled in. I was 43 years old and this flat was the first place I had lived in that was my own – even though it wasn't really, as I was only renting it!

Before this I'd always lived either at home, at college, at the seminary or in a priest's house attached to a church. For the last 20 years I'd been a priest but today was the first day of the rest of my life. I made the phone call and walked back to my flat with a light heart and thanked God that the weight I'd carried for a long time was gone – it really was a weight off my shoulders. I'd resigned from the priesthood – a huge relief. Several months before I'd told the Archbishop of the diocese in which I worked of my wish to leave the priesthood and of my intention to resign in the summer. I'd also told my family, close friends and the people in the parish where I lived. This was the culmination of a lot of heart-searching – hence the relief.

September 1953

It was a very different feeling the first night I spent at the boarding school – in a dormitory with 25 other 11 and 12 year old boys. I was 11 and the youngest (and smallest). We'd just started at the school because we hoped to be priests – in about another 13 years! We were only 11 or 12 and you had to be 24 to be ordained a priest. We were all keen young boys from Catholic backgrounds who'd said we wanted to be priests and this was the start of that journey. In those days if a young boy expressed a keen interest in the priesthood his parents were encouraged to let him attend the Junior Seminary – a boarding school run by the church and staffed by priests. This would provide a good standard of secondary education and enable him to progress to training for the priesthood when he became 18 and could move to the Senior Seminary. In effect the Junior Seminary was a grammar school whose pupils were full-time boarders and whose only pupils were boys who wanted to become priests. You could change your mind and not continue with this training at any time, or could be asked to leave if you were judged not suitable. But changing your mind and deciding to leave were not so easy because as the years went on you realized how much others had invested in your dream. No-one said that you would be letting them down – but you felt that you would be. Nonetheless many boys who started with me did leave over the years.

But that lay a long way ahead. This was September 1953 and that first night in the dormitory I remember lying awake seeing the outline of the more than life-size statue of the Virgin Mary at the end of the dormitory and thinking it would be Christmas before I went home and saw my mum, my brother and my auntie again. There were no weekends at home or family visits in 1953. We lived at the Junior Seminary from September to Christmas, then from January to Easter and then from Easter to July without a home visit or visits from family – just holidays at home at Christmas, Easter and during the summer. This was part of the discipline and training – but we were only 11 or 12 years old - excited but unsure what this journey to being a priest would be like. I can remember crying myself to sleep that night. I'm glad that Junior Seminaries no longer exist. They are a thing of the past in the training of priests – and rightly so.

October 1950

I can't remember a lot about my dad because he died in 1950 when I was eight. That's not to say that I don't think about him a lot or have some vivid memories of him or that he's not important in my life. He has been hugely important in my life and still is.

We were on holiday in Llandudno in North Wales in 1950 – I don't remember this but it's what I've been told. My dad was taken ill and had to be rushed from

Llandudno back home to Lancashire with my mum in the ambulance with him. In the days before the motorways this was a difficult journey and I can only imagine what it was like for them to make it in an ambulance going at high speed. In October my dad died in hospital in Manchester from a brain haemorrhage.

The only memory I have of this time is being taken to see his grave sometime after the funeral, which I did not attend. In later years my mum told me – "You grew up in a week when your dad died." She explained that prior to this I had been a very clingy child, needing to hold my aunt's hand to go to school for example. This ceased after my dad's death and apparently I became quite independent. My mum wondered whether someone had told me that I "needed to be strong from now on". I have no memories of this but it would certainly fit with subsequent events.

We were a strongly Catholic family, my dad was from Ireland and my mum and closest aunt (who became like a second mother to me) were teachers in local Catholic schools. I became aware of the supportive role that local priests played in the family after my dad's death and I gradually became involved in the local church, becoming an altar boy. I got to know the local priests, especially the curate – a large, cheerful man who seemed well known locally and who rode through our estate on his motorbike. The clergy and the local church began to assume a big part in my life.

Aged 8 I'm sure I didn't have any real sense of what this loss meant to my mum or the rest of our family – to have two small children (me aged 8 and my brother aged 4) and to have lost her husband aged 36. What I did sense was that I had to make sure my mum was okay and not to upset or distress her any more. I'm sure my mother did not put that responsibility onto me, but it's one I think I put on myself from then on. When I was young I don't remember her talking very much about my dad and there were no photos of him on display in the house for a long time. I used to put this down to her not wanting to speak about him because it was too upsetting. They had only been married for 10 years when he died and initially lived in Manchester – but only for less than a year as their house and all their possessions were destroyed in the Manchester Blitz of December 1940. In 1951, six months after my dad died, my grandmother also died. She was my mum's mother and I saw her nearly every day on my way home from school. Even at my young age I had a sense that my mum had had plenty of sadness to deal with in her life.

Twelve months later I began to speak about wanting to be a priest and the parish priest advised my mum that I should go to the Junior Seminary when I was 11. Her preference was that I attend the local Catholic Grammar School where I had a place and only later go on to study for the priesthood if that was still what I wanted to do. I ended up going to the Junior Seminary and subsequently the Senior Seminary (on the same campus) and this effectively became my home for the next 13 years. What this separation from my mother cost her emotionally I do not know – another major 'loss' that I only really considered as such when I was much older.

I suppose the priests in the Seminary became substitute dads for the dad I had lost – but as a young boy I clearly didn't think of it that way. They were kind and helpful and well-meaning men. Corporal punishment (a cane or a strap) was sometimes used for the junior boys when we broke rules but I don't think this was any different from other boys' schools in the early 1950s, though rightly condemned today as unacceptable. I have no horror stories or memories of abuse such as have been recently reported about Irish Catholic residential establishments and if any occurred in our school I was unaware of it. I was a pious and conforming young boy who tried to fit in and do what was right.

My religious faith and belief in life after death meant that my dad was always included in my prayers. Many years later when I was struggling with whether to leave the priesthood or not I made the 60-mile round-trip to his grave and sat on a bench alongside it for several hours. "What should I do dad, what would you say?" It was massively important to me to believe that he would approve of my decision. I believe he did – and still does.

September 1960

England might have been at the start of the 'Swinging Sixties' but, aged 18 I entered the Senior Seminary – 6 years of Theology, Biblical Studies, Philosophy, Church History, Spiritual Guidance and more lay ahead… preparing for the priesthood. Our remnant of students from the Junior Seminary were now joined by older students, who'd been to university, or held down jobs and had had a more 'normal' life.

Amongst the reading and study, a book stands out in my memory – recommended to us and titled - *A Man Apart*. It painted a picture of the ideal priest being 'in the world but not of the world'; standing apart and being different from others; his clerical status, dress and celibacy marking him out as different. This felt like an 'elitist' idea of being a priest and was not one I was comfortable with even then. The way of life in the seminary at that time seemed geared up to promote and develop this view – an all-male establishment, away from home and family, disciplined monastic-like routines. And sex and intimate relationships? Well, sex was tied in with marriage and since priests did not marry then sex was not going to be an issue. And close friendships with either men or women should be avoided as these could be fraught with danger. And what of sexual thoughts and feelings? They were temptations to be resisted and denied. This reinforced the ideal of the strong, untouchable 'Man Apart'.

But there was another view of 'being a priest' with its roots in being alongside people in local communities, being aware of hardship, injustice, poverty and the 'Social Gospel', where a priest was involved in the lives and welfare of people not 'a man apart' just performing rituals in church buildings. This was a vision of priest-hood that had more appeal. This was a way of being a priest that I could buy into.

A group tutorial one day with a well-respected member of staff – 'Father Tom' a priest who enjoyed an international reputation as a Biblical scholar – brought this contrast into focus. I had shed some of the 'quiet conforming young boy' characteristics by then and remember arguing forcibly how priests needed to be actively involved in local social concerns and be working to address issues of injustice and poverty. Father Tom's comment that I can still remember more than forty years on was 'You're training to be a priest, not a social worker, you know'. This held more prophetic truth in it than either of us realized.

The book *A Man Apart* is long out of print. Out of interest I looked up the title on Amazon. The first three books it came up with under that title were (in order) – a biography of the London gangster Reggie Kray; a biography of the former England Rugby Captain Will Carling; and, finally, a study of the 'British Police-man and his job'. I wonder where the priest as 'A Man Apart' would fit in there?

Anyone not brought up as a Catholic would not be aware of the significance of the English Martyrs to Catholics in this country. How our Catholic ancestors were persecuted for their faith and discriminated against for more than 300 years from the time of Henry VIII of traditional Catholic upbringing. The discrimina-tory legislation still in force today about Catholics and the right of succession to the Crown is a mild survivor of those times. There are many accounts of how 'recusant' nobility Catholic families and ordinary men and women 'kept the faith alive' in this country when being a Catholic was a dangerous business and being a

Catholic priest carried a death sentence – and death by the most brutal means. The priests' hiding holes found in historic houses owned by the National Trust might be of passing interest to visitors but were matters of life and death to our Catholic ancestors. To be training to be a priest in the light of this tradition carried with it a sense of walking in the footsteps of giants. It was a privileged profession one was entering and it carried an awesome sense of duty. Becoming a priest was no light matter – a statement of the obvious really!

I was ordained in 1966.

July 1979

It wasn't often I received personal phone calls from the Archbishop, so it was unusual to get an invitation to see him as he 'had something important to discuss with me'.

Though seen by some as a bit remote and rather formal I had always found him genuinely interested in individuals and liked him for the way he was eager to speak out on issues affecting all members of society - not only his fellow Catholics. Along with the local Anglican bishop he had a national reputation for challenging politicians when their actions brought about hardship and inequality to local regions. I still did not know what he 'wanted to discuss with me.' I soon found out – he was asking if I would become responsible for promoting vocations to the priesthood in his archdiocese, for recruiting, assessing and supporting young men who had expressed an interest in the priesthood, and then seeing them through their training. This was a bombshell. I asked time to think about it, and I would let him know.

I knew this offer was a vote of confidence in me – and of the way I'd worked as a priest for 13 years. What he did not know was that I was struggling with continuing to be a priest – hardly the right person to be promoting and encouraging others to become priests. I had by now worked in two large Merseyside parishes and had wide experience of many personal and community issues. In the course of my community involvement I'd come to meet the person who was later to become my wife. I was becoming more aware of how important she became in my life and how much I was concerned for her well-being. I told the Archbishop of my dilemma and, if he could accept my uncertainty about continuing as a priest, I was prepared to 'give the new job a try for a time'. This was a good example of how hard I found it to say 'No'.

Within 12 months the conflict between the work I was now doing and the increasing doubts I had about my own vocation as a priest became so acute I could not continue in the new job. I sought counselling from another priest I knew and trusted and saw him regularly for most of a year. Decisions I made during this time were to seek training as a social worker whilst continuing to work as a priest. That is what I did.

Looking back it would have been better to have grasped the nettle in one go and offered my resignation then. I hesitated because I feared how others would think of me, how I would be letting people down and how others would deal with my resignation. A prayer that had been important to me for many years was in my mind too – a prayer of St. Ignatius:

To give and not to count the cost,
to fight and not to heed the wounds,
to toil and not to seek for rest,
to labour and to seek for no reward
save that of knowing that I do Your will.

This spoke of doing what was one's duty not necessarily what one wished. Set against this was my own sense of needing to be true and honest with myself. It took me a further 6 years to resign, a delay and indecision for which I feel a sense of shame. I envied those who in similar circumstances seemed able to make clear-cut decisions and just resign.

I resigned from the priesthood in 1986.

May 1992

The day Jo and I walked down the aisle together I later described as the 'proudest day of my life' – and it still is. Family and friends, work colleagues and some priests were there; some we'd anxiously worried would not approve were there with their congratulations and best wishes.

But what was the wait – I'd resigned from the priesthood in 1986? Our wedding was conducted by a Free-Church minister we knew and was in his church – not a Catholic church because I could not marry in a Catholic Church without a dispensation from my priesthood status. I had applied through the bishop to Rome for this. My formal request for the dispensation had now been lodged for over 3 years. I knew they took time and that they weren't often granted so was not too surprised, but I'd hung on and hoped. It is illogical but it was important for me, which to say the least was selfish and something I am not particularly proud of.

When my brother and sister-in-law had married in a Registry Office in 1969 I had not attended their wedding because as a Catholic my brother 'should have' married in a Catholic church and as a priest I felt I could not attend. I regretfully sent my apologies at the time. This was not one of my proudest moments and one I long regretted. On the day of my wedding it was important to affirm again to my brother and sister-in-law how much I regretted not having been at theirs. I'd said it before, but it needed saying particularly on this day.

Two months later my dispensation ('laicisation') came through and a priest-friend subsequently blessed our marriage in a Catholic Church. From not being married at all, I had had two weddings in one year, but the May wedding by our Free-Church friend was our real wedding day!

June 2009

I have been an ex-priest now longer than I was an actual priest. I have mixed feelings about the Church – not mixed up feelings about religion as my personal faith in God and in being a Christian is strong. I struggle with the Church as an organisation but have never felt the need to look to an alternative church organisation. For all its faults it seems right for me to continue to be a Catholic. I feel angry at the Catholic Church but sad about it at the same time – if truth be told, more sad than angry, and maybe some shade of guilt about leaving the priesthood when I know that there is a shortage of priests.

The anger is about having had to grow up away from home and family – as someone 'apart'; the anger is also about the Church's inconsistency in imposing a compulsory celibacy for its priests yet at the same time welcoming into the Church married clergy from other denominations who can continue to work as married priests – whilst my wife and myself and many other former priests and their wives have no such option. It feels we are an embarrassment. I personally have no wish to take up such an option but it would seem only just for it to be there.

The sadness is that this situation is brought about by a Church ruling that could easily be altered. Forty years ago, in the 1960s and 70s, the Church was more open to the world and many changes were taking place at the time of the Second Vatican Council, when 'the windows were thrown open to let in some fresh air' as

Pope John XXIII said. It feels like the windows have been closing more and more in the years since. This is the core of my sadness.

So why do I still go to Mass each week? Because I still need to feel I belong to something that has been so much a part of my life. The Church as organisation has caused me problems but the Church as a hander-on of the core Christian message has given me enormous benefits. Maybe that's part of the reason why I'm a practising Catholic. I need to add that I've always felt better about doing the right thing - and going to Mass is one of the right things for a Catholic to do. I feel I belong – and am happy to do so even if it is in a quiet 'sitting-in-the-pews' way. It goes without saying that there's more to religious belief than putting in an appearance at church – there's personal prayer and Bible reading; living by religious values at home, in work and in society. All these are still important to me as a result of my upbringing and my continuing faith and I'm grateful to my family and the Catholic Church for providing that.

The other part of being a priest, the pastoral work with people, I've done in a different sort of way – through a social work career and presently through my counselling work. The pastoral work with people was always going to be the more important part of being a priest for me - as Father Tom had prophetically said!

It felt strange at first being a member of the congregation rather than up there on the altar conducting the service. The first parish I lived in when I left the priesthood had a parish priest about my own age – Father Gerry; a sociable, friendly man who put you at your ease. He'd noticed his new parishioner and commented on it to me after Mass one Sunday. Taking a deep breath I launched into a brief explanation for my arrival in his parish and my background. After barely a moment's hesitation he shook my hand warmly, hoped I'd be very happy in my new life and how welcome I was in his parish. This was such a contrast with the lack of contact from priests who had been my former colleagues – some of whom had been and continued to be very supportive, but some I knew well never contacted me again. The way in which your name and all reference to you just disappears from the annual *Diocesan Yearbook*, does leave you with a feeling of being 'air-brushed' out of history! The comfort is in knowing that I did good and useful work as a priest, work that was appreciated by the people in parishes I served and work from which I learnt a huge amount.

Back to Father Gerry – after Mass on Sundays, on leaving church he'd sometimes say quietly 'Well, John, how did I do in the sermon today – was it okay?'

It usually was – and often I'd just give him a 'thumbs up' and there'd be a mutual grin! This was a real contrast to the sometimes awkwardly embarrassed response of some clergy when I mentioned my former role. It's been noticeable how this is very unlike the responses and reactions of 'ordinary people' – including from former parishioners who've been universally kind and supportive over the years. Colleagues in my social work and latterly in my counselling work are interested in an understanding way about my background, but in reality have far greater interest in my professional ability to do the job.

What is it that religion does that can make it awkward for people to just treat you as 'an ordinary human being'? That's what I have wanted to be treated as: nothing special, or out of the ordinary, or a freak or an oddity – which the 'exclusiveness' of the priesthood tended to promote......a man apart! I did not seek to be a 'man apart' – I wanted to be a man who belonged to people – and that is what I've now found and I'm glad to be there!

...and what about Counselling?

Given the large role religion has played in my life I sometimes wonder where it has gone to when it comes to my counselling work. Do I simply abandon all the influence and impact religion has had on me when I enter the counselling room? I don't think so. I don't leave it at the door but take it in with me – however well-hidden. This makes me think about how much or how little we as counsellors can or should bring our values and religious beliefs into the counselling room. As counsellors we don't seem traditionally to have asked questions about spirituality or religious belief. In fact there seems to have been a move against it.

One reason may be that we are fearful of being seen to influence clients and quite rightly want to ensure that we respect a client's world-view and so seek to avoid putting our world-view onto them or even give the impression that we might be so doing. The counselling room is no place for evangelism or for preaching any more than it is a place for a laissez-faire acceptance of 'anything goes'. Being non-judgemental is not the same as agreeing with everything and not challenging anything a client says. Equally, enabling the client to explore the significance and importance of religion and spirituality in their lives is not the same as imposing on them one's own religious view-points.

Spirituality, religion and churches do not necessarily all fit together – they may do but not necessarily. People can have an internal spiritual life without laying claim to any religious belief still less a commitment to a particular religious tradition, faith or church. Though we might encourage wider knowledge and awareness of different faith traditions it seems more important to attend to this client and seek to understand what his or her faith means to them personally. All faiths have many variations within them and individual faith members have a wide range of commitment or dissent to individual aspects of their faith. In my own case, it is often thought that all Roman Catholics think, accept and believe exactly the same about all aspects of their faith – this is far from the case as any knowledge or exposure to a group of Catholics will show. This is just as true for other faiths. The person-centred principle of 'the client is the expert' is the guide – the client knows what any religious beliefs mean to them and they can help the counsellor enter their world.

I find it strange that though person-centred counsellors seem to have avoided stepping into 'belief' areas with clients, it is the counselling modality that many person-centred counsellors have seen as threatening – Cognitive Behaviour Therapy (CBT) – that actually explicitly invites clients to explore their Core Beliefs. Clearly 'Core Beliefs' include more than spiritual or religious ones, but they may well include these as key factors making up part of an individual's worldview.

As a priest I did a lot of listening to people relating their distress, fears and how they'd like things to be – which does not sound that different from what I do as a counsellor. It's also one-to-one and has a high degree of confidentiality around it. So what's different? One obvious difference is that faith and religion are not on the explicit shared agenda in counselling. Another is that it is unlikely that counsellor and client share exactly the same belief system – even nominally. Having said that I wonder how much counselling in fact replicates and takes the place of one role that priests have – that of one-to-one listening and supporting, whether in confessional-type situations or in bereavement support or in many of the other personal support situations in which clergy find themselves. Are counsellors perhaps today's 'secular priests'? Maybe in moving from the priesthood to counselling via social work I've not moved very far. But I do thank God that I made the move.

John Rowan

First, then, my own history. I was brought up in the Anglican faith: baptised in a little church in Old Sarum, and confirmed in Chester Cathedral. My mother was High Church, and when I went with her to services there was always incense and processions, bells and changes of costume, little palms on Palm Sunday and so forth, and plenty of stained glass. My father was what he called Broad Church, and when I went with him to services there was plain glass, no processions, a longer sermon and an absence of what he called flummery. His family came from Ulster, and he sometimes used strong language when talking about the Pope.

When I turned twelve or so, he signed me up for a bible reading organisation called the Crusaders, and sent me to summer camps organised by the VPSC – the Varsities and Public Schools Camps. These were evangelical affairs, and at some point you were supposed to 'take Jesus into your life as your personal Saviour', which I duly did. I became an evangelist myself, and at the age of 16 was going around the county delivering talks on 'What is a Christian and how does one become one?' When I was called up into the Army I used to kneel down by my bedside every night and pray. I got the nickname of Rasputin. This led to an odd incident when the sergeant of my platoon at the initial training camp, who had been absent for a couple of weeks, was asked for me to go to a medical checkup. He said, "Rowan? Rowan? There's no one called Rowan in this platoon!" I shyly raised my hand and confessed that it was me. "Oh!" he said, "I thought your name was Rasputin!"

During my Army service I went to India, and met a tea planter who introduced me to a book called *The Story of Philosophy* by Will Durant. It had accounts of various philosophers, including Socrates, Spinoza, Nietzsche and others. I was particularly attracted to Spinoza. He seemed to take me up to a mountain peak, where I could look down on the world and see how it was all put together. He said that God and Nature were one and the same. There was no division between the sacred and the profane. I bought the book of the Ethics by Spinoza, and was very impressed by that. I still quote Spinoza from time to time – 'The effort to under-stand is the first and only basis of virtue', and 'A passion can only be cast out by a contrary and stronger passion'.

It was in India that I had my first mystical experience. I was 19 years old, and in hospital with malaria and dengue fever. I looked out across the verandah at the sunset, which was a very unusual green colour. All at once I seemed to be taken out of myself into a realm which was quite different from anything I had experienced before. I could only label it as eternity. It did not seem to belong to time. It was as if everything stopped. I had been reading about Spinoza for the first time quite recently, and had been very impressed by that. It seemed that there might be a sort of connection. I did not make much of it. But I remembered it.

Abraham Maslow, in humanistic psychology, made a special study of what he called peak experiences, and later, when I came across his work, I identified what I had experienced as one of these. Peak experiences can come to anyone at any time. They are potentially mind-expanding, but it depends on how they are taken and how they are used. Some people just suppress them. Some take them as revelatory, but are then disappointed when nothing much comes of them. I believe now that they are glimpses of spiritual reality. As such, they are genuine, but unless built on consciously, they are only transitory. They are mystical experiences, but as it were in the foothills of mysticism, and not to be confused with the great heights or depths.

The next thing that happened, six years later, was that I discovered Hegel. This was not really a mystical experience, but it is an important link in the chain all the same. I met Harold Walsby, who became my mentor for about five years. He was versed in the philosophy of Hegel, especially as modified by the British phi-losophers F S Johnson and Francis Sedlak. We were out in his car, and he asked me what my fundamental beliefs were – things I could not doubt were true. As I brought out each one he demonstrated to me convincingly that it was self-contra-dictory, and therefore could not be fundamental. Eventually I was left with noth-ing. All my most basic beliefs had been laid waste, shown to be inadequate and false. He then asked me to take for granted Nothing. And he showed that once Nothing was granted, Being followed from that, because this Nothing was. It had Being, the Being of Nothing. So Being and Nothing were one and the same. Yet they were not the same, because they had two different names. So what was true was the movement of Being into Nothing and Nothing into Being, indefinitely.

But that brought into being a new category, Becoming. And so, by carrying on like that, all the categories of logic came into existence one by one, until the whole of it was complete. And then... but to go on would involve describing the whole dialectical philosophy of Hegel. It was a revelation, and an enormous experience for me. I went on to study Hegel for the next fifty years.

In 1967 I was given what I believe to have been about 400 micrograms of LSD. Both set and setting were good. At one point I remember having a sense of strands of force connecting everything and everybody in the universe. I even seemed to see and hear them. This connection made everything into parts of a whole. It was somehow all one. And this seemed to be the truth. It was as if I had now seen the truth, and all other versions were lesser and less adequate. Things I had read, particularly by Jack Kerouac, now made a lot more sense. Zen Buddhism was also around at the time, and I liked that a lot, and read Alan Watts and Christmas Humphries and Daisetz Suzuki and Philip Kapleau. I also read Evelyn Underhill, and was very interested in the connections between Eastern mysticism and Christian mysticism. I had also read Maslow, and labelled this as a peak experience.

In1969 I went to see a performance of *Paradise Now*, by the Living Theatre, a play about the beautiful nonviolent anarchist revolution. I was very excited and moved and taken by it, particularly the freedom and the breaking of boundaries. Two friends (who had also seen the play) and I started a group called B Now, and we had a series of evenings where we would do nonverbal exercises for an hour, and then go into a group fantasy about the Best Society Humanly Possible, and then eat together, the rule being that you must not feed yourself but only someone else. At various points in these group meetings I had experiences which seemed to transcend the present scene and to take me into the space I labelled as eternity. I called these peak experiences as well. I got more interested in humanistic psychology, and went to a number of growth groups of various kinds.

In 1970 I came across the exercise suggested by Marion Milner in her book *A Life of My Own* (Field 1952), where you look at something, such as a tree, and say "I want nothing". When I did that, the tree would somehow come out towards me and be more real. As I practised this, I could see the connection between this and the experiences of unity and eternity I had already had. It seemed like a mystical experience to me. It was about letting go of the need to make sense of everything, letting go of the need for meaning in my life.

Then in 1971, during a group experience, I enacted my own death. I lay on the middle of the floor, was covered up with a sheet, and people started to talk about me as if I were dead. I went through a very powerful experience, cried a great deal, and really had the feeling that I had experienced death. After that I felt a sense of liberation, as if I didn't have to worry about death, because I had already been through it.

In 1972, after being in a number of groups, I had an experience of contacting my real self, very much like what Rollo May (1983) calls the 'I AM!' experience. This I consider to be a mystical experience, and although it was only a glimpse, as the authors of *Spiritual Choices* say (Anthony et al 1987), glimpses like this are very important. The experience did not last, and I could not get it back by an effort of will, but I went to more groups and had the experience again and again. I gradually, over the next eight years or so, became able to contact my real self at will, and to relate authentically with other people from that position. This contact with the real self, which has been described so well by many people in the humanistic and existential tradition, is possibly the most common mystical experience. It takes us into what Ken Wilber calls the Centaur level of experience. This is the level of the authentic, of the existential self, of body/mind unity. All through the next few years, I had many peak experiences, and after reading the important book by James Horne (1978), I called them examples of 'casual extraverted mysticism'.

Then in 1973, during a session of co-counselling, I had the experience of facing the ultimate Abyss. It seemed that this was the Nothingness that I was most afraid of. To go into it would mean losing everything. My counsellor encouraged me to go into it. I went into the blackness of it, like stepping off a cliff into the unknown. Very soon it changed into a bright light, and I was sobbing with the glory of it all. I opened my eyes, and stood up, and felt extraordinarily tall, as if I had grown way beyond any normal size. The phrase that came into my mind was 'ten feet tall', but it was no exact measurement. I felt as if I had crossed some important line. It seemed more than just a peak experience. I would now describe this as an example of Subtle mysticism, because the concrete sense of darkness and light was so strong, and the absence of limits was so important. Earlier I had had intellectual insights into Nothing, but this was an emotional and spiritual experience, something quite different.

In 1975, in a spontaneous therapy session, following an LSD experience the previous day, I had one of the deepest experiences yet, of quite a different kind. I seemed to contact my transpersonal self. It was an amazing experience, which I would now call an experience of the Subtle self. I felt the most amazing love and compassion, which seemed everlasting and very deep. I wrote it up in an article entitled *A Growth Experience* (Rowan 1992). It occurred as part of a whole series of experiences to do with my own therapy which brought to an end my hatred of women, and from that point on I was much more aware of the feminine, and of the Great Goddess.

Then in 1978, by combining deep primal group experience with taking LSD, I got down to the deepest levels of my personal biography, and undid the schizoid level of my biographical unconscious. This meant that I could be with another person intimately for the first time. I would not classify this as a mystical experience, but it was an example of what I consider to be the truth about the relationship between 'deep' experiences in therapy and 'high' experiences in the transpersonal. One helps the other, both ways. Eleanor Merry (1962) suggests the image of a spiral staircase on a mirrored floor. Every step upwards on the stair (towards the higher unconscious, in Assagioli's (1975) terms) is matched by a step downwards into the floor (that is, into the lower unconscious).

In the early eighties, as recounted in my book *The Horned God* (Rowan 1987), I began to take a serious interest in my soul, or what I would now label as the Subtle level of consciousness. I joined a Wiccan group and was contacted by the Great Goddess and the Horned God. I learned a great deal about ritual and its importance for the exploration of the Subtle. The Subtle is the level of soul, just as the Causal is the level of Spirit. There is still a great deal of ignorance about pagan and neo-pagan religion. Something I discovered was that in exploring the Subtle level of consciousness it is very useful to take an interest in symbols and archetypes and myths and images, and to learn the ropes of a whole symbol system. The Tarot came to be my favourite symbol system and I found it quite rewarding, particularly in its connection with the Kabbalah. By laying out the cards, I was able to get in touch much better with my intuition and my creativity. I also came across the work of Ken Wilber (1980), and could immediately see its relevance for me, since it described my own development so accurately. I thought – "If he is so accurate about my progress so far, he may be accurate about where I shall be going in the future, if I carry on with the process of psychospiritual development". I began to meditate regularly, and did so every morning up to and including the present day.

Also about that time I had a number of visions, and was very much involved in symbols and symbol systems. I acquired a deep sense of the downward direction as spiritual, with the help of the writings and paintings of Monica Sjöö (Sjöö & Mor 1987), and wrote an article entitled "The downward path to wholeness in transpersonal psychotherapy", which was delivered at the Transpersonal Conference in 1989, and later published (Rowan 1992a). Also in 1989, with a woman well versed in Goddess spirituality, I co-founded The Serpent Institute as a training centre for counsellors and psychotherapists. The whole course had a structure based on insights gained from Goddess spirituality, and a great deal of the content was also based in this way. We had an altar and a number of rituals, and some of the experiences I had there were ecstatic, including a trip to Avebury, Silbury Hill and West Kennet. There were real experiences of the presence of the Goddess. I also had an experience of being contacted by the Horned God, under the name of Pan. I started to use my transpersonal consciousness in my work in therapy. Out of this work came the book *The transpersonal in psychotherapy and counselling* (Rowan 1993). This later went into a second edition *The Transpersonal: Spirituality in Psychotherapy and Counselling* (2nd Edition) Routledge 2005.

In the early nineties, I was having ecstatic experiences quite frequently at the Subtle level. I was also in therapy, and later in supervision, with Ian Gordon-Brown. Wilber said that people often avoided going on to the next level, the Causal, by a sort of contraction. The Subtle level was so full of symbols and images and powerful and good experiences that it was hard to move on. I discussed this with Ian, and he encouraged me to deal with these issues. So I deliberately set myself to let go of these contractions. I found that it was easier than I thought. I could have experiences of the Causal level through a process of meditation which led me through the levels, one by one, until I could just let go of the joys of the Subtle and enter into the joys of the One, the One without a second, the pure substance of being. And then I kept on having glimpses of the Nondual, and built up quite a store of insights from that realm. I started to write more and more about the transpersonal. In 1993 I wrote a series of poems about the ten ox-herding pictures of Zen Buddhism, which were published in the same year.

Then in 1997, the woman I had been living with since 1978, and who I had started to call my Shakti, became my wife. We had talked about handfasting, and jumping through the Beltane fires, but in the end we just had a normal wedding in a registry office. She had had her own experiences of the Goddess, even though she had not deliberately cultivated them in the way in which I had. Now it seemed that we had sealed and formalised our relationship, which was and is very deep and rewarding. This is an important part of my whole appreciation and understanding of mysticism. Now it seems to me that I understand the mystical realms rather well, with the help of Ken Wilber, who I still find to be a very good guide. I can move into them at will, and come back with things that are relevant and important for me. Recently I came across a quote from an American poet, which said –

Along the way to knowledge,
Many things are accumulated.
Along the way to wisdom,
Many things are discarded. (Hoff 1981)

and that seems to me to say a lot about my own journey through therapy and into mysticism. More and more assumptions have been discarded at more and more different levels, and each time it has felt like freedom and liberation.

I still feel that I have a long way to go, and every now and then something happens which tells me that I have not really gone very far, and that I still have an ego, and a body, and appetites and desires. But I feel that I have at least made a start.

Jane Simmonds

How might childhood experience of religion affect the adult?

April 2008

For me, religion and matters of faith have always been a part of the landscape of my life. There has never been a time I can remember when going to church and thinking about faith has not been part of the warp and woof or my life. It has been pervasive, no less than the fact that I was born a girl.

The Initiation

I have an early memory – perhaps 3 years old. I'm in a medium sized room with bare floor boards and brown painted wooden clad walls. I think Sunday School takes place here. There are a number of adults in the room and someone stands me on a chair. I am wearing a smocked dress – the kind that quite little girls wear and I am to recite a bit of the 23rd Psalm. From somewhere, I remember the words and just say them out. I feel surprised – I hardly know that I knew the words, but they've got into me somehow. I experience the approval of being a good and clever little girl.

I was born and brought up in Scotland by English parents, who were members of the Plymouth Brethren. We lived a long way from the rest of our family, and church became like a surrogate family which provided a strong sense of belonging, warmth and safety. In a nutshell, at 7, I 'gave my heart to Jesus' and at 13, I dressed in a rough black full length gown and 'went through the waters of baptism' which involved being completely plunged into a tank of warm water. By my early teens, I was fully initiated, safe and saved, and believed that others were not.

When I was four years old, we moved house and church congregation. The new 'Hall' was at the end of C. Street. It was a pre-fabricated large hut and as you entered the building, someone would be standing in front of a row of hymn books welcoming everyone to the service and handing them a hymn book. To both right and left, there was a small room where coats were hung up and umbrellas left to drip. As I grew up, this also became the place where I would meet my friends and giggle and share secrets together before entering the hall. There were windows on each side, rough wooden planks on the floor and a large dark brown pulpit facing. In a way, this was my weekly catwalk. Nobody looked as I walked in but everybody watched.

Depending on what service one was attending, the dark brown wooden benches were arranged in different ways. For the 'morning meeting', there was a plain table in the middle with two silver cups and two silver plates on a white table cloth for communion – but known in our group as 'The Lord's Supper'. Also there would always be two red velvet collection bags. The wooden benches were arranged in four banks around the table and facing it. Each family had their regular place to sit and we sat just in front of the pulpit (we called it the platform) in front of the W. family and behind a couple who had been missionaries in Africa – M and B. Ostensibly, no one led the service. It was up to male members of the congregation (the Assembly) to suggest a hymn, say a prayer or give a reading from the Bible. One or two of these men would also give a talk based on an interpretation of a Bible passage. These were not pre-arranged though no doubt some thought had gone into them beforehand. As I look back, some features of these meetings seem bizarre – all the women and girls wore hats (quite elaborate ones with very fashionable matching outfits) and remained silent throughout the proceedings. Only the men were allowed to participate verbally. Some strong messages there then! But I remember these times as very quiet and reverent, with significant periods of silence when all sat with bowed heads. No instrument accompanied the singing which was rich and sonorous and many people sang in four part harmony like a Welsh choir, though there were never any practices. The sound and words were emotional and heartfelt – people sang loudly or softly as the words dictated and seemed to have developed a natural feel for singing together. You stood to sing and then sat down. The prayers were extempore – no prayer book or liturgy played any part in the proceedings, but people seemed to pray about what they had sung and then sang about what they had prayed and those all flowed into the Bible reading and were picked up in the preaching. It always all led to the taking of communion which felt like the climax of the meeting. As a child, I was not allowed to partake of the bread and wine which was passed round silently, but my mother sometimes slipped me a little bit of her bread as I snuggled into her warm fur coat. The whole thing was a different world. I was warm and safe; the meeting was slow and quiet and I was often moved by the words I heard and sang, even though I suspect some of it was unintelligible to the uninitiated. At the end of the meeting, Mr. R. a small man with greasy hair, stood up and gave 'the Intimations'. "Mrs. Brown has been laid aside on a bed of sickness this week, and these are the meetings for the week....We give thanks for the new 'case of salvation' as a result of the crusade which has just finished.... We will be giving out tracts in Cameron Court this afternoon while the Open Air takes place – D.V!" (in translation, "God willing" – since all was deferred to the will of God.)

We all then spilled out onto the pavement in front of the meeting hall and talked in little circles for half an hour or so before going home for lunch and to prepare for the next round. By about 2pm it was time to get ready for Sunday School and I attended regularly each Sunday until about the age of 12. When I arrived, the wooden benches had all been moved to face the platform – and we sat in a designated place next to our teacher – boys on the left hand side and girls on the right. My first Sunday School teacher was Miss E. G., a single lady. When we had sung a number of choruses and participated in communal games and prayers, she took us off to a little dark brown back room and told us Bible stories. I have a strong memory of the story of the little girl, who got ill and died, but Jesus was called and He took her by the hand and made her well and told the parents to give her some fish and chips to eat! There was a tiny little toilet in the corner which was handy for the small children and made a noise so that every one could hear.

Sometime around the age of seven, Uncle Dan came to town for the 'Children's Meetings'. These would take place every evening for a week and the hall would be full of bubbling children who were as excited as if they were going to see Father Christmas. In fact, 'Uncle Dan' looked remarkably like Father Christmas without his reindeer and red coat. He had real, pure white hair, a genuine twinkly smile and a big tummy. He also had a bag of presents and sweets which he distributed liberally if you could answer a question in the Bible quiz or remember the Bible verse you had been taught the night before. He could tell a great story too, and I remember vividly the one he told about the little black boy who was sitting in his bath tub scrubbing his skin vigorously and asking his mother sadly, "How can I make my skin white?" "You can't," replies his mother. Uncle Dan went on to explain in detail how this was exactly like sin which cannot be got rid of how-ever hard one tries. But wait! There is a solution – simply trust in Jesus and give your heart to Him and your heart will be made whiter than snow. Then we sang, "Whiter than the snow, whiter than the snow..." My young heart is touched, I want to be friends with God, I don't want to be bad, so I respond and when Uncle Dan prays quietly and asks who has given their heart to Jesus, I put my hand up. Everyone is happy and delighted and at the end of the week, I am presented with a lovely blue manicure set to mark the momentous occasion. I still have it tucked away somewhere.

I'm ambivalent about recounting this story because as I write I am aware of my own doubts about some of the methods and dynamics involved in it and yet also quite sure that they do not differ very much from the ways in which parents and schools often socialise and deal with the children in their care. However, at a deeper level, my experience is that it was a milestone and a part of the story of how I awakened to the deepest spiritual parts of myself.

Later my teacher was Mrs. S. the married sister of E.G. and mother of my first real boyfriend, A., whom I loved dearly but he was a 'bad boy' (he smoked), and I gave him up with much regret because I believed it holier to do so. Mrs. S. played the organ for the Sunday School. It was an amazing instrument which I learned to play myself in due course. You had to pump the pedals while playing the keyboard with your hands and pulling our various stops at appropriate points to vary the sound. I think I was one of Mrs. S's favourites. As you got older, you graduated to the back of the hall until it was time to leave Sunday School and go to Bible Class.

During these years of Sunday School, there would be a competition each year to learn a passage of the Bible appropriate for every age group. In the autumn, it would come the evening when all the children had to come to the hall and be taken into the small back room individually, in order to recite their passage to the judges. It was nerve –wracking and never very good at making the effort to memorise, I would always feel ill-prepared. In due course, the Sunday School Soiree would arrive and during this fantastical evening, the best performer of the Bible passage would stand up in front of the whole congregation to recite the passage again and later in the proceedings there would be a presentation of prizes to each child. I still have a number of the very nice old fashioned Bibles and hymnbooks with a green and red name plate in the front page telling which passage I memorised that year and how good my attendance had been.

Another part of the evening involved each Sunday School class presenting a kind of tableau they had been preparing for weeks before. It invariably involved learning a few lines like the verse of a poem. You stood in a line on the platform, said your words, while holding up a placard of a picture or a letter. When everyone had done this, it contributed to some significant word like 'salvation' or 'grace'. Once the word was displayed, we would sing a song about it and everyone clapped and laughed.

Another highlight of this evening was halfway through when the 'boxes' were distributed. The dark brown benches we sat on were very clever, as they had a long, fold up ledge on the back of each bench. You could keep your Bible there and of course, when the 'boxes' were given out, you had a little table to put the white oblong cardboard box on. Inside the box, were the most delicious Scottish delicacies – triangular sandwiches filled with spam, a sausage roll, a Gemmels' cake (Gemmels were a local baker famed for fancy cakes) and a chocolate biscuit. While these were being eaten, someone would come round with a huge teapot of hot tea and hand round the china cups (Where were those pesky Health and Safety regulations in those days?). There would invariably be a spill, but no one seemed to mind and it was easily cleared off the wooden floor. This was all the greatest fun and a highlight of the year. All this served to reinforce and affirm 'the Decision to Follow Christ'.

By the age of twelve, I had graduated to Bible Class on a Sunday afternoon. It was run by a most enthusiastic avuncular man called W. K. Again, we sang a lot and then broke up into smaller single sex groups and earnestly discussed passages from the Bible with an adult. My leader in this enterprise was one, Miss J. L. – another single lady whom I loved very much as she was gentle and thoughtful. We discussed the finer points of Bible passages in what can only have been a cupboard with a small window– again painted dark brown and furnished with a small bench to sit on and I can only think that many of my developing teenage ideas were formed there. I wonder what they were. I don't remember specifically but I remember liking to go to the class to meet my friends and talk and discuss things that seemed interesting and important to me.

I guess I learned that sex before marriage was out, women submitted to men, I should obey just about everybody – God, parents, teachers – and consuming alcohol and smoking were pretty wicked. I learned a whole theology about being sinful and needing to be saved, about the Second Coming, what girls did and didn't do, and the answers to all manner of esoteric theological questions which no one but ourselves were asking. I knew and was sure and I learned to be good and compliant, to feel guilty and to try hard. I've since realised that there was no way to ever be good enough. But I think I also learned that I was loved and that I belonged (if I toed the line, which I largely did) and that quite a good number of adults spent significant amounts of time with me – both playing and learning. I was being thoroughly initiated into the faith.

The kind of religious atmosphere I was exposed to was full of emotion, personal challenge and inspiration. There were often calls from the pulpit to repent, re-dedicate oneself, put one's faith into action, save the lost and so on. Although I suppose it could have been, I think it was rarely if ever hysterical or coercive, but one felt better for trying harder, being more dedicated and correspondingly guilty if one was not regularly attending church, reading the Bible, praying and recognising one's shortcomings.

Sometime around the age of thirteen, I came to another milestone as the call went out to be baptised by full immersion. No sprinkling of the head as a baby would do, in fact this was regarded as a heresy which encouraged people to think they were OK when they weren't. One had to obey Christ's command, renounce all former ways and 'walk in newness of life' in a personal resurrection. I don't really remember exactly how it came about that I was sitting on one of the brown benches near the organ, with Mr S. and Mr A., two Fathers of the Assembly. Both of them were gentle and kindly, and their job was to satisfy themselves that I was truly and soundly 'saved' and ready to 'go through the waters of baptism' so that they could take their findings to the 'Oversight.' This was a group of men (always men), totally unelected (usually benevolent but, if push came to shove, probably unaccountable) and the final authority in all matters relating to the life of the group – including whether or not I could be baptised.

Despite being on the young side, as candidates were normally reckoned to need to be fifteen or sixteen before they made this momentous step of commitment to God and the group, I was allowed to go forward on account of my seriousness and good behaviour. I felt proud and honoured, accepted and approved of. Shortly afterwards, on a Sunday evening, I put on a full length black robe in the little back room which had been my first Sunday School room. The material was heavy and black to signify death to the old life and completely covered me apart from my head and hands. The hem contained weights so that it would not float up in the pool indecorously and I mounted the few steps onto the elevated platform where a large pool of warm water and Mr. S. were waiting to receive me. I confessed my faith publically and was plunged into the water. Voices singing, "Up from the grave He arose…" filled my ears as I struggled out of the pool hampered by the now soaking black robe which had become incredibly heavy with water.

I was recently invited to a similar occasion when the 17 year old son of a good friend undertook something similar. As I looked at it from a different standpoint, I saw how the group sang with such gusto, listened with approval as the next generation told of their spiritual journey thus far – as far as they could tell, these young people were now safely in the fold, just as I was many years ago - although there was just one more hurdle to go. If you married someone who did not share the faith, you were considered to be 'unequally yoked' and would probably suffer all the dire consequences predicted and regularly attended to in the next few years' discussions and Bible studies. But if you could successfully negotiate that hurdle, chances of leaving were much reduced.

As well as running the Bible Class, energetic Wallace had around this time, conceived the idea of a youth club called the Maranatha Centre. Unsurprisingly, this name, like our meeting hall (Ebenezer) had a biblical origin – the Bible being a pretty central foundation and reference point for everything that was thought and done. The Maranatha Centre was another pre-fabricated hut at the other end of the town, where we all gathered on Monday nights, Friday nights and Sunday nights. On Monday nights we went to the Centre to play table tennis and games and the helpers fried mountains of chips for us to eat. On Friday nights, there was a youth choir. We practiced and sang lustily for hours before meeting our friends and buying chips on the way home. On Saturday evenings, the choir would often pile into a bus and go and sing at a 'Rally' somewhere. If not, we'd find a Rally to attend or a party to go to. I think what kept all this together was the social life that went alongside it all. I had a large group of friends and as we moved into our teens, despite the segregated classes and prohibitions about sex, there were many opportunities for relationships to form and reform and some pretty steamy parties to go to.

As I write about it now, I can see that I was being effectively initiated into the faith and culture of that particular brand of Christianity, and what more could I want outside of the warm friendships and social activities I was part of? I was busy, involved and absorbing the faith all the same time. If I was feeling cynical about it, I could say I was being gently brainwashed, kept very busy and subtly indoctrinated. I could also say I was being assiduously looked after, trained, taught and my spiritual, social and other needs were being attended to by the adults in my life.

Although I now question some of the implications of all this and smile at the odd terminology which was very familiar to me, my spiritual self was awakened and deeply moved in many ways. During long and multiple services on Sundays, my heart stirred in the singing and I was moved to tears in the long silences. I was inspired to respond to God and motivated to reach beyond to find meaning and purpose. It all pervaded my internal and external life.

I rarely needed or wanted to look outside it, but I grew up with a fear of people who were not part of the group – and that included other people who went to church. I did not go to 'church', I went to 'The Hall' or 'The Assembly'. I was warned about the danger of being drawn away from God into wicked practices such as dancing and going to the cinema – "How would you explain what you were doing if Jesus came back?" All was well while I stayed inside and conformed – which I largely did. What I have described mainly relates to my life up to the age of about sixteen.

The impact

I began, "I'm trying to work out how I 'do' faith."

"What do you mean? Isn't it enough just to be? Weren't you ever encouraged to have a contemplative life like those enclosed monks and nuns who spend their lives in prayer and apparently 'do' nothing much in terms of the outside world?"

In my case, from an early age, I developed an interior life which was quite devout and spiritual. I was moved by the songs and the words, I felt the desire to know God and by the time I was 12 or 13, I prayed for quite long periods on my own and studied the Bible on a daily basis. Often, as I began the practice of devotions on my own, I would be deeply moved or challenged by something that I read. I felt it hot and strong, I learned to study, compare, follow through themes, understand… and believe. I was truly repentant – there was always something I'd done or thought wrong, but I was always expectant and sometimes inspired. But there was another part to all of this. It also became a duty and a chore which if I didn't fulfil it, had the power to blight my day and induce huge amounts of guilt. This was no mere teenage phase – at least if it was, I continued the struggle for approaching forty years until I realised that I needed to find another way of pursuing my spiritual journey. I had a burning desire to know and love God and the forerunner to this was that from my earliest days, either my father or mother would say prayers with me when I went to bed. At that time, I said the same thing every night – I developed a mantra like prayer which went something like this;

"God bless mummy and daddy, Auntie D, Uncle W, (and all the other members of my family and friends that I could bring to mind) and make me a good girl. Amen."

I grew up with some strange contradictions. On one hand, the Brethren church to which my family belonged strongly espoused the reformed doctrine of 'salvation by grace alone.' In many ways, I still find it a wonderful idea that I cannot and need not do anything except accept that I am infinitely loved, forgiven and accepted. Sounds like Carl Rogers ad infinitum. How strange that I experienced and found in myself and others such large amounts of guilt and that there were all these spoken and unspoken rules to be kept – on pain of death, it seemed. For example, church attendance and lots of it, was mandatory. So was the wearing of hats in church which was deemed to demonstrate the women's submission to the men. Women were not allowed to speak or lead in church gatherings – they were always silent and not part of any aspect of church government. It was not permissible to go to a cinema, dance or drink alcohol, especially in a public house, gamble...

"How confusing," she remarked.

No, I wasn't confused. I knew and understood the rules exquisitely and learned how to live within them. Remember, I prayed to be a good girl and I was. I belonged to a large warm and close community and I learned to be afraid of anyone outside it. I had many good and close relationships within; I was saved and safe, certain and right. I sometimes used to wonder at my good fortune. I had been born into this wonderful rightness when apparently others hadn't. How good God was and how favoured I must be. But how scary and dangerous all the people outside were and if I got too close to them, they would surely lead me astray to think and do the wrong things and I would be eternally lost.

Heavy water and the grave clothes

By my early forties, my children were growing up and I was restless and began counsellor training. I was also angry at the restrictions I experienced in my church group. During some counselling, I saw myself squashed in a box, unable to stretch my arms and legs. My counsellor commented that it sounded like a coffin! How I got out of it is a long and ongoing story, but one of the images which occurred to me along the way is a Biblical one – where Jesus calls Lazarus out of his grave and he has to take off all the grave clothes which are binding him up and sticking to him. Perhaps this pictures my ongoing search for an authentic spirituality I can live with. Part of me can't live with it – another, can't live without it.

A propensity to guilt

How would I describe myself now? My spiritual health, my religious practice? I still count myself as deeply believing, or at least wanting to believe and choosing to believe in the Christian God – Christian because it's in me and I'm in it by virtue or the fact that I happened to be born to believing parents, in a historically and culturally Christian society. I became immersed in it and embraced it at a personal level and have never felt much interest in seriously investigating another version – I suspect they all have similar pros and cons. That statement represents a huge journey for me, since I come from a tradition which would see it as seriously heretical, since it holds that It is the only right way and all others are wrong and to be feared.

"You're not helping!"

"I've got it wrong."

A recent small incident got me thinking about how my childhood experience of religion might still be playing a part in my present day reactions.

After supper, my husband, daughter and son-in-law were discussing their plans to buy their first home. It was an animated discussion and I was keen to help them be aware of some of the financial costs involved in their plans. I guess I was challenging some of what my daughter hoped for, and at one point, she turned to me in annoyance and said, "Mum, you're not helping!!" In a split second, I was aware of what I know is part of my default setting which says to me, "You've got it wrong, you are at fault here." As I was saying this to myself, I heard my son-in-law say, "No, it's helpful for us to talk about this together."

I realised again how easily I blame myself or feel I have done or said the wrong thing. Of course, sometimes I have but at other times perhaps I haven't, as when my son-in-law's comment allowed me to see that my being at fault was not the only way to look at what had occurred.

As I look back to my childhood I remember that I received many messages from church which suggested that it was highly likely – even inevitable - that I was somehow guilty of misdemeanour – well actually that I was sinful and even the good things I tried to do were not good enough. "All our righteousness is as guilty rags." A high standard indeed and in recent times, I feel angry to realise that I came to believe that nothing I ever do can be good enough, it is always deficient, unacceptable – and I think I learned it personally at a deep level as, "I am not enough."

A sense which has pervaded deep recesses of my being and driven my actions until I began to take off those particular grave clothes and realised that whether I'm enough or not, I'm all I've got and it has to be enough.

I am struck by the thought we're all a product of our time and that this is true of the specific story I am telling. It came out of the time between the early fifties and on into the sixties and seventies. It was set in a particular place and culture –the west of Scotland and a warm, close knit and quite exclusive religious community.

As I think about my earliest years, I feel nostalgic and appreciate many things I experienced. Most were quaint rather than sinister even though I can't embrace a lot of it now. There were also negative aspects which I was aware of but were not fully formed in my experience till later in my life when I was again part of a different religious community where I felt endlessly and boringly guilty. I've sat in so many meetings in my life – sitting in rows one behind the other with no right of response, no opportunity to say I don't agree, I see it differently, no power to stop or influence what was going on. I developed a huge sense of ennui and resentment at the waste of time for living, doing and communicating.

The second community was a fearful one – fear that someone would disagree, cause trouble, fall away from the faith, be contaminated by outside ideas. And because of fear I think, the leaders in these communities become domineering and controlling and silenc all dissent with disapproval and censure. My experience of it was abusive and I had to leave it or die – a costly decision which perhaps I haven't fully come to terms with.

I also have a sense that in a strange way, it is difficult to really grow up and properly mature in such communities. I'm not sure if this applies to both men and women but I think it has been difficult for me to become independent, self determining and grown up.

Afraid of people outside the group

I don't quite know how it came about, but I know that by the time I was a teenager, I was afraid of people who were outside my faith community. I had somehow gathered a set of beliefs which told me that I would probably be influenced negatively by anyone who held different religious views to me – they would be likely to lead me astray and terrible things would happen to me. My experience was that I would feel distinctly uncomfortable around anyone who fell into this category so I would avoid making friends with them or spending any unnecessary time with them.

I recall an incident from my first job as a newly qualified teacher in a very difficult comprehensive school. There was a lively group of staff, some of whom were very supportive and kind to me as I struggled to establish myself. There was also a newish RE teacher who always sat in the corner of the room to eat her sandwiches. She wore a hairstyle I knew to be favoured by the kind of religious groups I was familiar with. She too was kind to me and took me under her wing – I was very wet behind the ears. I was part of the English department, and one lunch time, a group of the staff I worked with decided to go down to the local pub during lunch time. They invited me to join them. What a dilemma! I wanted to be friendly, but at the same time, I felt awkward and as though going to a pub was slightly wicked, but I agreed to go anyway. The next time I spoke to my friend the RE teacher, she was very forthright in her condemnation of my going. I tell this not to point my finger at her personally, for she just illustrates the voices and messages my childhood was scattered with. The first powerful message was that someone (or Someone) would be watching and noticing every detail of my behaviour, and even my thoughts, with an implication that He would see and take a dim view of any wrong move. I grew to have an instinctive sense that I had got it wrong.

Another incident from my early teens stands out for the same reasons. I was never allowed to go to a cinema until I was 14 years old. I remember being part of organised group discussions before this where my friends and I talked with the help of an adult about how we should not go to dances, pubs or cinemas because if we were there when Jesus returned to earth at the Second Coming, He would find us there and we would have to explain what we were doing there. I remember being so powerfully affected and convinced by this at the time, that no one had a hard time keeping me away form them – I was quite sure it was safer and preferable to stay away rather than explain what I was doing, however, innocent. Consequently, I felt afraid and awkward and was therefore compliant. However, alongside this was a strange ambivalence. Outwardly, my parents kept the rules too, but my mother loved to dance and told me about how she had flouted the rules when she was young, and taught me to 'jitterbug' in the kitchen. I also knew that my father enjoyed a glass of wine on occasions, though alcohol was frowned on. So it came about that I was allowed to go to the cinema with my friends to see Cliff Richard in *Summer Holiday*. I can't describe how enthralled I was but I think more importantly, I began to explode the myth that there was something wrong with it. The power was beginning to be broken.

How to be a woman

Listening to the radio this morning in bed, I heard a discussion about Simone de Beauvoir and her book, *The Second Sex* and her famous quotation that women are not born but develop. It rang some bells for me and led me to wonder how my upbringing had affected me as a woman.

As a little girl, I remember overhearing my mother say to a friend, "Her father worships the ground she walks on." I suspect there was more than a hint of, "She can get away with anything with him – but not me!" I instinctively felt these comments to be true and it felt good to be a girl. I was adored and had a sense of some power with my father. I have no doubt at all that my concepts of God have been hugely influenced by my relationship with my father who I experienced as warm and strong. I have also realised in more recent times that he must have been an anxious parent and was very protective of me, the only and long awaited child. There were also things that we didn't and have never really talked about. I had the strange experience of feeling that I was very prized as a daughter but was also treated like the son and heir. Somehow my father managed to get round those Biblical stories where the sons superseded the daughters and inherited all the wealth. I never felt he wanted me to have been a boy. From quite an early age, my father and I have had an ongoing conversation about money and savings. I have never been an apt student of this but emotionally, I have felt very valued and close to my father during these conversations where I felt like he was teaching me all he knew about how things worked, entrusting things to me, including me in his plans, forming my understanding and somehow preparing me. He has never flagged even though he must have realised I was going to be no good at managing financial matters. But this has been a positive part of our relationship. The less positive side of it is that I remained dependent on his advice and very reluctant to make my own financial decisions or take responsibility for how I managed things. This is still something I am growing into. Did all this benevolence rob me of the drive to achieve more, strive for what was out of reach and take risks? After all, I had everything I could wish for and more so why should I extend myself and reach for my potential? I think it kept me young, domesticated –the second sex, and I still wrestle with the sense of underachievement and wanting more but at the same time, being inclined to be scared to try, take the risk to succeed or fail and a sense of inertia holds me back.

I've mentioned in passing the hat wearing that was part of our religious community. I grew to hate wearing a hat – I don't know whether this related more to its tendency to flatten my hairstyle or the quite explicit explanation that was given to us that this was an indication of our submissive spirit to both men and God. I once had a boyfriend of whom I was very fond, who unashamedly explained to me that if I didn't have a hat on during a service he would be quite likely to be 'stumbled' by looking at my hair instead of concentrating on worshipping God. This was his euphemistic way of giving me responsibility for keeping his sexual urges in check!

But back to dad, me and hats. The hat was only the beginning of a ritual which took place every season. About four times a year in our community, every mother and daughter would go to the shops for a new 'rig out.' These were expensive and fashionable outfits – natty little suits, coats, dresses, and the whole had to be finished off with matching gloves, shoes, bags and the ubiquitous hat. There was a certain Sunday on which we all turned out in our new outfits and admired and were admired by everyone else – quite a fashion parade! But in our house, before this public viewing took place mum and I would come home from the shops laden with bags of goodies and the real ritual for us was that I would try on my new clothes and show them to my dad. My memory is that he would Ooh and Aah with the most genuine approval and satisfaction. We all won on those evenings – mum had done well to search out and pay for the new clothes, dad seemed to delight in seeing me dressed up and I felt admired and beautiful. This last is a strange one – I have always known that I was pretty average in appearance, but I have most often felt beautiful and I put it down at least in part to this ritual which seemed to have the power to override the objective evidence in the mirror and save me from some of the agonies of growing up.

The other ritual which I looked forward to each year was the Christmas present from my dad. He would go to the most expensive woollens shop in Glasgow - Rowans - and would personally select a beautiful jumper or cardigan – one for me and one for my mother. They would be carefully wrapped in tissue paper and an attractive box and tied with pretty ribbon. They were the last and most important presents to be opened on Christmas Day and the envy of all my friends – one of whose mother would promptly go and buy her daughter the exact same jumper, much to my annoyance.

In such ways I learned that women were to be pampered, looked after and admired – I should not worry my pretty head about anything, because the men, particularly my father would take care of everything. It was my job to be attractive soft and fluffy. If I was clever also, well that was all to the good so long as I didn't take it too far by taking the place of the men, thinking for myself or being disagreeable or rebellious. As an adult I have and do wrestle with finding my voice and my personal authority in some situations.

Despite the many sexual prohibitions and injunctions which we were taught from the pulpit and in Bible Class, our community had a curious attitude to our growing sexuality and relationships. One of the key times when boy girl relationships would form (and incidentally when many 'decisions for Christ' were taken) was in the summer when we all went away to Camp. For a week each year about a hundred teenagers and twenty or so adults would hire a school building in a pretty village. We all got on a coach laden with camp beds, food and luggage. We were allocated a dormitory and a dorm leader and this was our team for the week. Each morning 'reveille' sounded early and every team had to appear in the playground dressed for physical jerks led by the adults. After breakfast, there would be morning prayers and a thought for the day after which there were non stop activities, games, dressing up, competitions and lots of sizing up the opposite sex and contriving of conversations. After supper there would again be singing and challenging talks followed by emotional opportunities to 'respond to Christ' which many of the young people did. Then there would be hot chocolate and several hours when the adults would try to get the teenagers to fall asleep, resulting in much chasing of miscreants around the camp site. This was all the greatest fun while people fell in love with God and each other, adults and youngsters all involved together, mostly good-naturedly. My first kisses were experienced just outside the light of the Camp bonfire, largely sanctioned, even encouraged, by the adults, as long as things didn't go too far.

When we got back home, we all kept in touch and devised many opportunities to have parties in our homes where boys and girls got together with the full knowledge of their parents who more or less kept out of the way and provided food but no alcoholic drinks. This was the Sixties, we played Postman's Knock in darkened rooms. There was a curious mixture of theological teaching and pragmatic recognition by the adults that largely worked for us all. I had no sense now or then of sexual repression, but remained curiously naïve while also experimenting with my sexuality in the most delicious and yet limited ways. Some years ago, I revisited my old haunts and discovered that many of the relationships formed in those days blossomed into marriages which have lasted for more than thirty five years.

There was, however, the unplanned pregnancy, and at the time, it was the most dreadful crisis. One of the girls became pregnant – a girl just a few years older than myself. It was the most salutary lesson and served to demonstrate to us all what could happen to us. The public shame was palpable and mothers warned their daughters privately and in the most serious terms. In true two sided fashion, I remember my mother telling me that it would be the most dreadful thing for the family if I were to become pregnant before marrying, men's private parts were pretty ugly anyway and I should certainly not entertain the idea of a black man! But if the worst were to happen, they would not abandon me. On a bleak Sunday morning, the girl and her boyfriend were 'read out' of the meeting. This involved the little man who gave the 'Intimations' intimating that this young couple could no longer participate in 'the breaking of bread' until such times as they had seen the error of their ways and shown their intention to repent. They duly got married quietly despite the fact that the boy was still very young, had their baby, and as far as I can remember, remained married. Eventually, they were reinstated as members of the community, though what the experience was like for them, I can't imagine.

All this part of my experience came back to me this morning as I lay in bed listening to the radio - a largely contented old married woman of thirty odd years and in my head also off with Simone De Beauvoir, wondering about her sexual exploits and the impact of her book on feminist thinking. My early experience served its purpose to keep me safe and conventional and I don't regret the solid family life which produced two happily married daughters who have charted the stormy waters of growing up reasonably well and who are both about to produce my first grandchildren. I value it immensely, and realised the other day that in this individualistic Western society that I am a part of, a part of me chooses not to jeopardise the community which is my family with any personal unresolved conflicts or regrets any more than I am going to throw over a deep seated belief in God. The disruption to me and all those around me would be completely out of proportion to any personal gain I might hope for. I am still wondering how exactly to be the woman and person I want to be.

As a woman…

Do the men in my life want me to be sexy, attractive, warm and cuddly but not the part of me that is driven, dominant, aggressive and wants to achieve? I have always felt that it is my place to care, be loving and kind. A good and obedient daughter who did not cause my parents much grief. I was supposed to be an obedient and submissive wife, who loved my husband and family, cooked and cleaned and put my own desires on hold. I had everything I could wish for, so why should I want more? I should also be a wise and self-sacrificing mother. I did desperately want to have children – I also wanted to be married. I think some of my dreams got lost before they were properly formed; my potential in some ways unfulfilled and my drives weakened by having everything. I've found it hard to think for myself, to speak up. I often feel guilty and as though I've got it wrong and will be censured. I've felt stifled and silenced – sometimes by kindness. I needed more challenge and freedom to fail, encouragement to take risks rather than keep safe.

I do want to love and be loved and do what is worthwhile. I want to build and strengthen my family and friendships. I want to express myself sexually but I'm not so much interested in sex as communicating, connecting and personal intimacy with the other person. I want to fulfil my potential, but don't always know what that means and find myself expending a lot of energy and hard work on the wrong things. I want to have a voice and stop giving away aspects of my personal power and authority.

And what does the Lord require of you? To do justly, to love mercy and to walk humbly with your God.

Sharon Stinson

Growing up on a Fault Line

Looking back on my early life, I grew up in a highly charged religious atmosphere with a right-wing bias. I am unsure what effects the 1933 earthquake had on my family, but I carried the aftershocks within me for most of my childhood. I have grown up feeling the San Andreas Fault plates slowly moving past one another since my birth in Los Angeles in September of 1934. In reality, the biggest tremor was created by my father's recovery from tuberculosis. It was a metanoia—a shift to go in a completely different direction; that's the term used theologically, borrowed from Greek.

What does a highly charged religious family look like in the 1930's in sunny Southern California? This is my story, that I want to use to unearth and identify some of the turmoil within me that forced me to break away and come to my own metanoia as an adult. Both my parents and God sent out waves in all directions to create the feeling of an earthquake of a highly unsettling and corrective nature. Even during a time of being playful and silly, my father would shift gears and demand a stop to 'this nonsense.' Sunday found us in church for four to five hours plus additional meetings during the week. Sternness came across in the way I was disciplined. 'Spare the rod and spoil the child,' said the Proverb. As a rather determined child, I learned about the rod frequently with slaps on my backside, or leather belts used for frequent spankings. As I sit on the fault line, I hear my parents reinforce the Proverb: 'Train up a child in the way he should go'. Mother and Father took this seriously and considered what they taught at home and what the church reinforced were more authentic than the State education system. In such an atmosphere we grew up being told that we were the chosen ones and that we must never 'be unequally yoked together' with non-believers. Having this constantly put into my thinking limited my relationships and screwed up my way of relating to men who were 'outside the fold'. In an atmosphere of certainty, I was to accept that the Bible was the inerrant word of God, in other words, 'It's true because it is in the Bible.' Since it was possible to find chapter and verse to direct our lives, my parents followed the Bibical leading for church attendance, paying a 10 percent tithe on any money earned, and following the Puritan work ethic, but our religious devotion did not reinforce the Gospel teaching to 'love one another' and 'love your enemies'.

In 1933 my parents had good reason for joining the Pentecostals in Los Angeles. Pentecostals - an off-shoot from traditional churches - proudly claimed to believe in the 'full Gospel' which included prayer for physical illnesses. The story of my dad's healing was well known, not only in our family, but in various churches he visited. He witnessed to his healing to unbelievers on street corners in Los Angeles. The story begins when a doctor advised my dad to get away from Texas. He jumped on a freight train and illegally hitched a lift to Southern California where his older brother lived. Fearing God and death, he began to seek help through religion. One night he entered a store front church in East Los Angeles where he heard joyous singing and loud praising. At the end of the service, a large woman dressed in a full length white cotton dress welcomed him. When he told her about his impending death, she called those present to encircle him. She then got out a small bottle of olive oil, put a dab on his forehead, said a prayer of healing, and laid her hands on my dad's head. She quoted a verse from St James' Epistle in the New Testament to validate what had happened to him. Something did happen. Rather than dying, my father experienced what he would call a conversion experience. Being full of zeal, he contacted my mother and insisted that she leave Texas and brings their three year old to Los Angeles. She agreed once she learned that Hollywood was close by. She loved movies and reading about the lives of movie stars. It didn't take Dad long to make sure that my mother had a similar conversion experience to his.

Both now were 'born again' believers, and it was into this revival scene that I was conceived. They gave me names that they found in the Bible: Sharon, from the Rose of Sharon mentioned in the Song of Solomon, and Faith which came into prominence with Abraham, the father of faith. I have always liked my name Sharon but, during my miserable adolescent years, I wouldn't reveal my religious-sounding middle name to my friends.

Once my father and mother had experienced healing for themselves, they turned their backs on medical treatments. When we had aches and pains, they got out the anointing oil and prayed for us. I found release from my earaches when my mother heated some olive oil, dabbed it on cotton wool and prayerfully put it in my ears. On these rare occasions as a child, I felt close to her. The closeness no longer existed by the time I began my painful menstrual cycles at thirteen. I was afraid to tell my mother what was happening to me. Fear drove me to ask for help the second time this happened. Without saying anything, Mother handed me a sanitary pad, gave it to me and then left. Only much later did I realise that my mother was embarrassed by anything intimate.

Sometimes healing worked like magic. One dark night during World War Two, with our windows covered in blackout curtains and no one allowed to walk on the streets because of a curfew, my elder sister and I were left alone with our little brother. My parents joined a group to pray against the invasion of the enemy and cry to God for peace in our country. Then our little brother, David, started fitting. We had never seen him do this before. We didn't know what to do. We couldn't leave him jerking and foaming at the mouth. Then suddenly the front door burst open and there he was, Dad! He rushed in, turned David on his side, found something to depress his tongue and then began his prayer of faith. To my knowledge, my brother never had another convulsion. But how did my Dad get home? When I asked him, he casually said, "When the warden called out, 'Who's there?' I said back, 'Warden.'" He remained a risk taker all his life, not obeying the laws of the land if they interfered with what he sensed was right.

My mother's approach to healing differed from my father's. Not long after she was converted, she quickly learned that Pentecostals didn't attend movies. She found a religious substitute in the dramatic productions of Angeles Temple. Sister Aimee Semple McPherson, the minister, staged larger than life re-enactments of the Christmas and Easter story. Mother made sure that we didn't miss any of these. We sat in awe when Jesus was born. Out came the singing shepherds with angels. Kings came in with their oriental finery to complete the story. For Easter we watched the awful scenes where Jesus was beaten, hanged on the cross and died. The most thrilling bit was when Jesus was resurrected. After each performance ended, Sister Aimee invited the unsaved, the sick, and the lame to come forward for healing. Some years later, Angeles Temple lost its attraction, and Mother shifted her attention to other spectaculars.

In a big circus-sized marquee with fresh sawdust covering the grass, I played with other children while Oral Roberts shouted at us that 'Jesus heals today.' Those seeking healing formed long queues. I sometimes counted how many 'went forward'. At least I was learning to count up into the hundreds. While I liked the 'tent meetings', I was happier when mother switched her devotion to the Humbard Family services. Rex Humbard and Maude Aimee, his wife, sang Gospel music with other family members. Then came the 'practical and no-nonsense preaching' just like Rex's daddy before him. Following the Humbard family from town to town provided nights out for us with exciting entertainment. One member of the family played the saxophone. I couldn't take my eyes off him. From then on I decided that I wanted to play an alto sax and within a few years, it became my instrument.

Secretly I think that my mother wanted her family to become a second Humbard Family. In no way could we come up to their musical standards, and I guess this might have been a great disappointment to her. We played our instruments, but we did it on an individual basis, certainly not as a harmonious family group. My brother played the electric guitar and piano, my older sister played the piano and sang, and I blew on my alto saxophone—which didn't really blend in with the others. My younger sister never found her instrument, but she could belt out a song when she wanted to get on stage. During one church service, she stood up and began to sing: 'Over hill, over dale, we will hit the dusty trail as those caissons go rolling along.' I burst out giggling in the middle of her song. In church we expected a Gospel song, but instead the army marched around the church that evening. After all, a war was going on and a child was reminding us.

During the war years, my dad often drove by the big Lockheed aircraft company that was covered with camouflage. My Uncle Scott got called up and looked so handsome in his army uniform. Then one day my dad got his draft papers telling him the time and day to report for his physical examination. He wasn't a conscientious objector, but for some reason he didn't want to go to war, maybe because he wasn't fit. Many nights he had to sleep sitting upright in bed to help his breathing. So the morning he was to report to the clinic for his physical, he left the house early. By running long and hard, he worked up his asthma so successfully that he failed the examination. He told us with great relief that he had been turned down. "I thank God for this. It is an answer to prayer." Obviously not a healing prayer, but he could return to his job as a butcher in the meat department in Alhambra, California. A few months later, one of the butchers found him passed out in the walk-in refrigerator. "We have to move to the desert," he announced after returning from the doctor. Several hours east of Los Angeles, a small developing town called Twenty-nine Palms was beginning to attract more people, mainly those needing to be cured of asthma and other chest ailments. Dr James Luckie from Pasadena discovered the healing properties of this desert area with dry clean air in an elevation of 2000 feet with pure and clear water. Dad was skinny as a rake when we moved to Twenty-Nine Palms, but by working physically hard outside in the dry heat making concrete breeze blocks, his asthma cleared within a couple of years. "'God has healed me, but I have to admit that this desert air has been a help," he would say. I didn't mind the desert because I had my first little terrier dog for a pet, learned to ride a horse, and got to go swimming during school hours to cool off.

Since there weren't any Pentecostal churches in Twenty-Nine Palms, my father began to invite people to our house on Sundays. Just five miles to the north was a large US Marine Base. Before long several Marines began to show up for these meetings. My dad taught them about the 'prayer of faith' for believers that wanted healing. "We need a piano for our services", my mother suggested. Dad found one someplace, but strong as he had become, he couldn't move it by himself. He asked four Marines to help haul it to our home. I watched as the men strained to take it off the van. "It's going to fall!" I yelled as I watched the heavy load topple on top of one of the men. "It's killed him!" I kept shouting. The others quickly hoisted the piano off the Marine. He didn't move. My father prayed rather desperately, "Jesus save him." After a few minutes, the Marine shook his head and began to stand up. Was it the soft sand of the desert that acted as a shock absorber for him, I wondered? 'You're lucky,' I said hugging the Marine. My father corrected me. "That was not luck, Sharon, that was God."

Once my dad was cured of his asthma, he got itchy feet again and decided to move his family yet again. This time we went to Banning, California where he opened a roadside stand selling local fruit, peaches, apricots and cherries. We moved into half a house, left unfinished by some builder. Dad decided that he could make this 'chicken coop', as my mother called it, into a home. Without previous building skills, he did what he said he could do using his new found physical strength combined with his usual drive and determination to prove everyone else wrong. During this time, he met the pastor of the Pentecostal Church, Johnny Ridge, who appreciated the ministry gifts of my father. Thinking only about myself, I begged Johnny, "Can I play my saxophone in your church?" From then on I sat next to Curtis who taught me to transpose the songs in the hymn book from C to E flat. Once the singing was over and the sermon began, I moved to sit next to Loy Hutchinson. We worked out a way to hold hands so that my parents didn't notice. The services went on for hours it seemed. Those of us who were full of twelve and thirteen year old hormonal energy, rushed outside as soon as it came time for an 'altar call'. These additional prayer times would keep our parents involved for another hour. In the Sunday school bus parked behind the church, we found our special seat, held hands and gradually explored kissing.

In 2003 I revisited Twenty-nine Palms and Banning for the first time since leaving. I drove up and down streets but couldn't find the houses we lived in. In telling my story to my goddaughter, I claimed Banning as my Rites of Passage town,. While living here, I experienced my first kiss; I started menstruating, and I learned to drive my Dad's Model-A Ford. The door to adolescence had opened. Even though I was only twelve, my dad said that he was proud of me for learning to drive. A year later we would be on the move again, this time to another state. No one else in the family knew how to drive, so while Dad drove the hired van with all our worldly possessions in it, I proved to my family that I was up to the task by driving all the way from Southern California to the middle of Utah. It wasn't until I turned eighteen that I finally decided to get my first driver's license even though I had never been stopped by a policeman.

It was predictable that no matter where we lived, my parents would surround themselves with born-again believers. Perhaps there was an undeclared 'loyalty system' functioning which stated that they should worship only with those 'filled with the Spirit'. In time I could recognize these 'saints' because they had a style of praying and used Biblical language to communicate within their exclusive group. The Pentecostal movement started in the 1906 Azusa Street Revival in Los Angeles. This revival began mostly in black churches with members longing to live pure and moral lives. In order to live as holy people, they needed to be 'filled with the Spirit' and 'speak in tongues'. Always as a child, I heard people in church utter unrecognizable language which would be followed by someone interpreting, which usually began with a familiar phrase: 'Thus says the Lord...' These were called 'gifts of the Spirit', or God breaking through to speak to his chosen believers. Learning to imitate seemed natural so my little playmates and I played church. I don't remember ever having a doll or playing house. Rather I would gather a little group of children together, sit on the porch in front of the house with them and we would play church. I would drag out my dad's large guitar, much larger than any of us children could manage, put it on a tiny lap and begin strumming.

No chords, no music. We made up songs or belted out choruses we remembered. One of us would make up a testimony and tell how God had saved us from our sins. I frequently 'spoke in tongues' by saying over and over 'unda lay pronto'. A giant Authorized Version of the Bible would be opened and we would pretend to read verses. What fun I had imitating my parents and taking charge of the others.

A few years later I would learn about 'backsliders', those who once believed and then 'fell from grace'. Unbelievers would be damned to hell while true believers would be going to heaven. In Sunday school I saw pictures of hell as a place of continual torment where souls burned in hell fire. The pictures of heaven put before me were beyond my grasp since I didn't fit the 'good little girl' category. But the teaching, reinforced by the pictures, told me that heaven and hell existed as geographical places. I certainly didn't think that I would end up burning in fire, but neither did I see myself floating on a cloud or sprouting wings. What was going to happen to me? Other images that were more down to earth but moving toward the same end were the narrow path and the wide path. Daily I seemed to get in trouble and couldn't avoid the conflict of the wide path. The rigid standards set for me didn't suit my nature, but only intensified my struggle. I kept slipping off the edge of the narrow path while still believing in God and goodness. I desperately wanted my mother and father to listen to me and love me for my uniqueness. Instead I got scolded and spanked. The stern God always seemed to be communicating out of my stern parents. I needed to make church a place of fun. Since I loved music, I sang with great gusto and learned to harmonize as an alto. I memorized numerous key Bible verses. I learned the names of the books of the Bible by heart. None of these kept the San Andreas Fault from causing inner earthquakes.

The 1933 quake must have sent out shock waves even in my infancy. Within days or weeks after I was born, my mother bundled me up and presented me to 'the flock'. Her good friend Sister Iris had given birth to a boy about the same time. For our first year or more we were passed around from person to person during the church services. Once I could crawl or stand holding onto the backless benches in our store-front church, I began to scoot without being harnessed as long as I didn't make too much noise. From this perspective, I watched my mother and other women 'dance in the Spirit'. When the Spirit 'came upon them' they would stand and twirl around in the aisles with their eyes closed. I gawked in amazement as they moved closer and closer to the hot fat-belly wood burning stove. I watched to see who would get burned, but no one ever did. I also entertained myself when a train roared by on the tracks just outside the wooden structure called Pentecostal Faith Church. That tuneful whistle from the steam engine spurred me to climb up on a bench and look out the window. Even above the loud noise and rumble of the freight train, many of the preachers could still be heard. Sister Mabel Lindsay had the best lungs. Mother said that the trains were not a problem to Mabel because she was preaching 'under the anointing'. God wanted us to listen to the preacher, not to the noisy trains.

My mom and dad were friendly with Sister Mabel. I liked her husband John who didn't attend church. He spent his time digging and planting in his vegetable garden. If I ate my dinner really fast, I could go out and be with John. I liked being close to him better than being inside listening to God-speak. Suddenly, he died. My mother told me that I must come to the mortuary to see John in his open coffin. I resisted, but she insisted. When we walked into the strange smelling mortuary, I panicked. The place seemed spooky and the music eerie . Mother held my hand and guided me into a special side room to 'view the body.' As we got closer and I could see a coffin, I pulled away from her and ran looking for someplace to escape. I could not look at dead John. Many years later in a therapy session I relived this experience where I finally faced my fear and was able to say my farewells to John. Perhaps this dear, accepting man was my inspiration for trying to grow vegetables when we moved to Banning and for feeding and collecting eggs from my few Bantam hens in our yard in Rosemead.

After John's death, I didn't attend any other funerals until two of the teenage girls who were members of the church had a head-on collision and were killed. No one ever discovered why their car was on the wrong side of the road crashing into a big lorry. At the funeral, I stayed clear of the girls' father who wore a bright yellow tie. He proclaimed loudly that "My girls are with Jesus now and it is the best place for them to be." Not knowing exactly why I reacted against him, I felt anger and then guilt bash me about. Wasn't this father a holy man who knew his daughters were in a glorious heaven? If only I could jerk off his yellow tie and kick at him. Once again my emotions were held in tension between what I was taught and what I was experiencing.

Since my parents considered the church their real family, our blood relations were almost strangers to me and classified as 'outside the fold.' On rare occasions we had visits from my aunts, uncles and cousins. I no longer even remember their names. I trembled when my dad's parents made a rare appearance with their stern faces. They ignored me. They still look forbidding in the two black and white photographs that I have of them. My father's older brother and his wife made me take off my shoes when I visited them so that I wouldn't mess up their light coloured, deep woven carpet. I did get to know two of my mother's brothers when we visited the place where my mother grew up. I was eight years old when my mother decided to go to Oklahoma. My sister Doris and I loved the Southern Pacific Railway because we had freedom to run up and down the aisles. Mother packed fried chicken legs, cornbread and cupcakes for the trip. Then Doris, age three, ruined our freedom. She said in a loud whisper, "Niggers, Sharon," pointing to two passengers. The next time we passed them, the woman grabbed Doris and said, "Y'all call us nee-groes, not niggers. Hear me?" For the rest of the trip, Mother made us sit in our seats.

Being on a farm in Elk City, Oklahoma, allowed me to run wild and release my pent up energy. If I leaned way over the wooden fence, I could just manage to scratch the pigs' backs with a wire brush. I had never seen a butter churn before. My grandma let me try to turn the wooden handle that dipped way down into the milky liquid. In my exuberance I would get carried away and have to be corrected. "Now Shar'n don'tcha curdle that butter, ya hear me? That's enough now." My two uncles used to squirt me in the face with warm milk as they pulled down on the cows' teats, something I didn't have strength to do. Then one day, Uncle Ray asked if I wanted to climb up into the hay loft in the barn. Eagerly I scrambled up the ladder and buried my face in the hay. 'This smells wonderful,' I said throwing clumps of new mown hay into the air. Before I knew what was happening, my uncle pulled me down on top of him with his trousers unbuttoned. Instinctively I knew something was 'nasty'. I hit and kicked until I was free and then slid down the ladder to find my mother. "Ray tried to do something naughty to me," I cried. My mother's reply was "Go find Grandma and see if she wants your help." A year or so later when Uncle Ray came to visit my family, he was sitting in the car waiting for the church service to finish. Escaping from the long meeting, I jumped in the car with him. Once again, he pulled me onto his lap with his trousers unbuttoned. I fought him and screamed until I escaped out the car door. I never told my parents of this incident. Later Uncle Ray died an alcoholic leaving behind several wives and children .

Before we left Elk City, my grandma drove us to Oklahoma City to visit Grandpa. The day was hot and humid, and Doris and I hated being told to stay in the car. We jumped back and forth from the back seat into the front and took turns honking the horn. Time passed slowly until we heard a loud scream. I looked at the hospital building and saw someone in a second story window. "That's grandpa, I know it is! What's wrong with him?" Even though I questioned my grandma and mother when they finally arrived, they dismissed me as being silly. Years later I made inquiries into my family history and discovered that my alcoholic grandfather died of syphilis in a psychiatric hospital.

We never had alcohol in our home when I was growing up. As Pentecostals the moral code wouldn't permit drinking, not even beer. Neither did I ever catch my father looking at another woman with 'lustful eyes.' I do remember catching him fondling my mother's breasts once, and my confused mind went wild imagining 'sinful' things. I knew one of his sins though. Before he was saved, Dad used to roll his own cigarettes which he had to give up because he learned that 'his body was the temple of the Holy Spirit.' He told us in his testimonies in church that he used to throw his tobacco and papers over the wall each evening, and then the next morning climb over and recover them. Apparently he managed to break the habit before I was born. When I was about six, I remember having a nightmare in which my mother and father were arguing. My dad stomped out of the house and went to buy himself a pack of cigarettes. This dream bothered me for days. Our home was a place of no smoking, no drinking, no going to movies, no reading comic papers on Sunday, and no books with sex in them... The code had to be followed by anyone 'in the fold'.

What we could do was eat rich foods. Out would come the potato salads, corn on the cob, fried chicken and sweet iced tea whenever we had a social event—which was often. After the first course, we had to wait for our food to settle a bit. Then out came the desserts. We feasted on slices of apple pie, chocolate cream pies, or my favourite, peanut butter pie. After this we would need another time to digest the high caloric food. Dad would divide us into teams to play soft ball or pitch horseshoes. Finally it would be time to make ice cream in a six-quart wooden bucket with a metal container in the centre for the cream, sugar, and flavourings. I was always eager to turn the handle, especially before the cream began to harden and be too difficult for me to manage. 'Let me put more rock salt around the crushed ice. The ice is starting to melt.' Where there was action and people, I pushed my way in.

I made lots of friends as an extrovert, but I didn't make any friendships that lasted once we moved to the next town - from East Los Angeles, to Garvey, to Rosemead, to Alhambra, to Twenty-Nine Palms, to Banning to Ogden…. Did I sense that there wasn't any value in connecting with others because I also felt disconnected from my parents most of the time? I can remember names of a few high school friends, but I have had no contact with any one of my childhood play-mates. I acquired my father's competitive spirit and was always eager to play games both inside the church and outside. Easter egg hunts created great excitement once we had listened to the true Bible story, of course. I especially liked to roll down the grassy hills after I found the coloured eggs so that I could turn over and over again getting stains on my new cotton homemade Easter dress. Inside church we learned how to play games using the Bible. "Everyone close your Bibles until the chapter and verse is said. Whoever finds it first, raise your hand," the teacher would say. If he said, John 3:16, I would raise my hand immediately because I knew it by heart. Many of the verses that I memorised as a child have stayed with me. On other occasions in our competitive learning we would have the red team against the blue team. "Add up my points. Let me see how many ticks I have. I have been here every Sunday, brought my Bible, memorised my verses, and put my pennies in the missionary offering. Do I have more points than anyone else?" I cried out to be acknowledged and In desperation found ways to make my demands heard.

The need to prove myself, to win over the others, was strong. My parents didn't see me as a winner, as far as I knew. "Train up a child in they way he should go and when he is old he will not depart from you," said a much quoted proverb from the Authorized Version. The firmer my parents training, the more I had to fight to survive as the second child who didn't feel that she belonged. All of my siblings had names that began with D; not me. My older sister was ladylike and my ador-able younger sister had olive skin and brown eyes. Then there was me; the only redhead with blue eyes, and a tomboy. My mother doted on my brother, and when we got in trouble, he invariable blamed me. I remember when we dug a foxhole in the desert so we could have a secret place. In this hidden place we tried to smoke. We got a brown paper bag; cut it into little squares then got some dried weeds in the field, crushed them and pretended they were tobacco. Both of us coughed and burnt our throats. Finally, I stole some real cigarettes out of a parked car. When we got caught, my brother immediately said, 'Sharon made me do it.'

'Training up a child' went hand in hand with another Proverb: 'Spare the rod and spoil the child.' My parents took this quite literally using various objects for spanking—me more than the other three. Dad would use his belt; mother favoured a wooden spoon or coathanger. Once she grabbed a wire hanger and chased me as I ran away to escape punishment. She swung the hanger and hit me in the eye. That was the only time that I heard my mother apologize to me. She had scared herself and had tears in her eyes. From then on, she would say, "When you father comes home, he will deal with you."

Making sure that each of their children had a 'personal experience with Jesus' fitted my parents 'train up a child…' approach. To insure that this happened, at least once a year an evangelist would come to conduct 'revival meetings'. The flock enjoyed being renewed on an annual basis and others could get saved and have their sins forgiven by being washed in the blood of the lamb. Hearing once again that God loved me so much that he had sent his Son Jesus to die for my sins sounded like good news. Then the good news would have a bit of damnation attached to it: if I didn't accept Jesus I would have to face eternal punishment and hellfire. Feeling this threat as a child, I walked forward to kneel at the altar for the evangelist to pray over me. This became the annual pattern, until my rebellion.

The Pentecostal church did not believe in infant baptisms or christenings; instead we were dedicated. To be baptised, we must wait until we were of an 'accountable age', so I could account for myself by giving my consent. My father took those of us who were newly saved out to the river where we were dunked under the water. I have proof that this happened. My mother gave me an old 3X4 black and white photograph with Dad and me in the Weber River both dressed in white. When I saw this photo as an adult, I couldn't believe it. I had completely forgotten my river baptism at age thirteen. If this was to be such a significant spiritual experience, a religious rite of passage, I wonder what kept me from remembering.

As a young adolescent moving from sunny California to live in Utah, the State where 68% of the people were Mormons, my tensions mounted. The plates in my San Andreas Fault moved close enough to begin to rub against each other. Living among Latter-Day Saints I didn't observe them struggling with their attitude to God and church. What was wrong with me? My father quoted St Paul: 'we are saved by faith and not by good works.' If this was true, how come our home was full of discord and animosity while my close friends' homes were so loving and accepting? My father enjoyed saying that LDS stood for Lost Dead Sheep. I preferred being with my Mormon friends, yet I was not free to join them when they went to see a film or go to a dance. What if my parent's found out? What if a 'blue bolt' from heaven were to strike me dead while I was in the cinema? The Pentecostal morality code was effective in keeping me in check even though I tried so hard to get away from it. In the 1940s and early 50s we did not have television, but on special occasions we got to see feature films at school. I dare not tell my parents that I had been to see a movie, except when we saw the *Song of Bernadette*—since it was about a miracle of healing.

During my first years living in Ogden, Utah, I came across a writer of Christian romances named Grace Livingston Hill. I wasn't afraid to openly read her novels of gentle love with a high moral content. I then proceeded to devour book after book of hers taken out of the local library. Hill's father was a minister so the themes of her novels fit my family's spirituality exactly: good and evil; God's ability to restore; and the Bible is clear. Maybe I was attracted to her since in her dozens of Christian Romances she included attitudes of defiance, hard-heartedness to God and deception. I could relate to these.

Not long after we moved to Ogden, one of my teacher's commented, "My, you look so like Southern California." Not understanding her, I asked one of my classmates what she meant. I looked different and my clothes were homemade and light cotton. Feeling the pain of being an outsider, I rushed home to press my mother into taking me shopping. "I can't go back to school with these dresses. I need a sweater and a wool skirt. Utah has snow in the winter. We're not in Southern California anymore." Even though we had always lived simply and Mother sewed my clothes, she took me to one of the less expensive stores to choose my new outfit. At school the next day, several girls came up to inspect the label on my sweater. I sensed that I hadn't passed the test. Not the right brand! To be accepted as one of the in-group, I should wear Janzen sweaters, Pendleton skirts, Joyce shoes, and Vera scarves. This was one of the many painful lessons that I would have to learn living in this state with a dominant religion with well educated and socially adept followers.

Having a father who pastored a Pentecostal Church on one of the main avenues in Ogden, my sense of shame intensified. I wanted to flee from being associated with my parents' religion. None of my close school friends shut me out of their homes and I always felt accepted, but I carried the burden of being different. I desperately needed friends and became inordinately attached to a few of them. I became a clinger in order to survive. One day Bill, the boy who played first position saxophone in the band, asked me to join a little dance band that he was forming; we would play during lunch hours at school so pupils could dance if they wanted to. A few months later, he asked me to take dancing lessons with him. I had to make up stories and lies so that I could join something that my parents believed was wrong, dangerous, and immoral. I continually argued with my mother and father. One Sunday evening two of my friends stopped by to see if I could go to their Mormon Ward with them—their places of worship were not called churches. When my dad said that I would be going to church with him, I said 'I don't want to go to church with you, I want to go with my friends.' My dad grabbed me firmly by the arm and jerked me into my bedroom. 'You will go to church with me and you will respect me.' I answered back, 'How can I respect you when you don't respect me?' He pushed me down on the bed, removed his belt and spanked me. My dread was that my friends would be able to hear me crying. I was fifteen years old.

The Pentecostal Church had so few people that my father needed to continue working as a butcher. On the street in Ogden that most people said was to be avoided, he cut meat for the poorest of people including blacks and prostitutes. He felt more at ease with them than with well-educated and financially secure Mormons. Then in 1952 he got the bug to move again, this time it was to Denver, Colorado. I refused to go before graduating from Ogden High School in June of 1952. For the few months before I graduated, I moved in with an elderly woman who lived in a run down house on the other side of the tracks. At least I had a few months freedom to make my own choices.

Just prior to graduation the saxophone quartet I played in performed during the special assembly for those who had achieved. One of the cheerleaders apparently said, "If I were a girl, I wouldn't play the saxophone." After this degrading comment was passed onto me, I went home and looked at myself in the mirror. My sexual confusion and insecurities were such that I took these words to heart. A year after that, I sold my sax and bought a flute. It was not my instrument. It would take another forty years before a group of friends in England bought me a new sax. My fingers immediately felt at home when I held it.

On June 5th I wore my cap and gown along with 500 others in the class of '52 students. When I walked outside the doors of the school in my cap and gown, I spotted my mother and father sitting in their car waiting for me. The 900 mile drive to Denver was sheer agony. Leaving behind friends, school and my adopted city, I climbed in the car feeling angry and hurt. What I had achieved didn't seem to interest my parents. Curled up in the back seat, I couldn't talk because of the pain and resentment that I felt. After some time, my mother turned around in her seat and said "Stop that crying. You'll just have to forget about this. You are moving with us and that is it."

In the mile high city of Denver, my dad's business venture went bust. We lasted only six months before moving back to Utah. The churches in Denver were too large and grand for my parent's type of worship. Once again we packed up and moved back to a small town near Ogden. I put my energies into finding a job and within a few months Western Union Telegraph Company rescued me and sent me off to train as a telegrapher in Idaho.

I quickly discovered that moving away from home didn't mean leaving the trappings behind. Since we had moved so many times in my childhood, uprooting didn't seem unusual. Even now, I find it strange to hear friends talk about a sense of rootedness. I know people who haven't moved once in their life time and who keep in touch with friends they went to school with. I can count up to nine different towns we lived in before I left home, and this included three different Western States in the US. I don't know how many houses we temporarily lived in, nor do I have a record of their addresses. After all, we were pilgrims and before I became disillusioned, I could sing with the loudest of the Pentecostal worshippers:

A pilgrim was I, and a wand'ring. In the cold night of sin I did roam,
When Jesus the kind Shepherd found me, And now I am on my way home.

So many words from the old songs are embedded in my memory, but I sang them without knowing that they were reinforcing my parents understanding of God, church and religion and seeping down into my psyche. I wasn't on my way home, but in desperate need to get away from the restrictive scene and get a dose of what the Pentecostals called 'sin'.

I left home at seventeen. Shrugging off the influences that had wrapped around me proved difficult. My San Andreas Fault kept moving dangerously close to major quake. I looked for an escape route on the wide path not giving a thought that it might lead me to destruction. I wanted to taste some of the forbidden fruit. Would a blue bolt really strike me if I went into a cinema? If I puffed on a cigarette would I feel free and satisfied? What did beer and wine taste like? These little no-nos were beckoning me. Away from home, I began to notice men and they noticed me. The ones I valued began to teach me a new way of relating. My fault line began to shift and move away from the danger zone. I started feeling safer. The earthquakes didn't open up the earth and swallow me. Fire and brimstone didn't rain down on me. So like a prodigal daughter, I left home and went into the 'far country' to explore real living.

In the far country my work transferred me from town to town, each one enticing me to have a look into the forbidden areas. My job with the telegraph company brought me in contact with new ideas and a wide range of interests - especially meeting men. In Wyoming, where oil and minerals were being unearthed, I met geologists who came from all over the US. John from New York enabled me to understand the difference between my native intelligence and acquired knowledge. Guy let me know that I was loveable and someone he wanted to be with. Frank wanted to marry me and scared me away with his proposal. I fled with a friend back to California. She encouraged me to attend San Jose State University where in five years I acquired a BA in English with a credential to teach secondary school. Learning outside the Pentecostal box let me see a world that was much bigger and exciting. I spent six years heading up the Humanities Department in the American School in Brasilia, Brazil where parents and pupils from thirty different countries showed me that America wasn't the only country in the world even if I had been raised to believe it was the best.

On August 1, 1980 I boarded a flight to England with only two large suitcases— my worldly possessions. I moved into uncertainty without fear. I had no job, no income, but hope. For two summers previously (1978-79) I studied for my MA on a one-off course for English teachers at York University with New York University. Geoffrey Summerfield unknowingly enabled me to be healed more fully as he suggested to the twenty secondary teachers an unusual course in writing out of our life experiences. "How was affection shown in your home?" "How were you disciplined as a child?" I unearthed a creative force within me that released me to write tirelessly out of my pain, hurts and misunderstandings. The release I felt from bringing so much to the surface gave me the courage to return to California. I needed to check out as an adult who I was with my family. I lasted with my family two years with a lot of blood, sweat and tears, but I found a way through. I let vulnerability have a chance. I told my mother of the burden I had carried all my life: "I never believed you loved me." I challenged my brother to look more closely at how his leadership was making it difficult for those around him, including me. During these two years I saw more clearly how my perspective of God in all things differed from my family's way of thinking. I was appalled by the right-wing American fundamentalism that kept showing pictures in black and white. My biggest discovery was that I did not have to carry the weight of guilt and shame for much of what happened in my past.

For thirty years, I have lived in York, England. No longer do I have the itch to keep on the move, I'm a settled pilgrim. Here, on this small island, I have found that God is in all things. I continue to believe in healing, but unlike the Pentecostal Church that focussed solely on physical healing, I have experienced through diverse therapies, especially Gestalt therapy, emotional and psychological healing. The sacred/secular split doesn't make sense to me anymore. My friends have become my family.

It has taken years before I could see that the conservative foundation stones that my parents placed under my feet did not destroy me. In a strange way, they were a gift to make me determined to find a better way, a freer way. 'Everything is useable, nothing is wasted,' said a wise man.

Sharon Stinson
6 November 2009

Anni Townend

Footsteps: A narrative inquiry into the impact on personal development and adult life of an early religious upbringing

The Baptist Church stands on the top of a hill in the Pennines. In my childhood it was coated in dark black smoke churned out by its neighbour The Brickworks. Both looked down on a small mill town, also very blackened by smoke from the many mill chimneys. Every Sunday, for as long as I can remember, I went to church, "twice on a Sunday" – once to the whole service and once to Sunday School. When I was old enough I walked there and back, it was the best part of going to church. It gave me a feeling of happiness and possibility, like walking in the fields every Saturday close by to where my father's mother lived, and contrasted sharply with the feeling once inside the church which felt heavy, dreary and dark. There was never any question our family not going to church, and when we went on holiday we always found a church to attend, if a Baptist church was not to be found then a Methodist would do. It is what we did.

Punishment for wrong-doing in the eyes of the Lord was a big feature of my early childhood, and that the Lord was watching my every doing and knew my every thought. Punishment was meted out severely by my parents who believed that what they were doing was "for my own good". The ultimate punishment I felt was that I would end up in hell and not go to heaven. Thus it was that I was brought up to be God-fearing like my mother, and her mother and father before her. Suffering for our sins was very much a part of this, and that Christ had died for us to save our souls. Living in fear and suffering were part of our "daily bread".

Both my grandfather and my mother sang in the church choir – they were very 'proper' and held their heads high. My grandfather was the church treasurer and a deacon, and was the epitome of a Baptist - upright and teetotal. My mother was a Sunday School Teacher and some years later became a church deacon. Every Sunday we went back to my grandparents before lunch when occasionally my grandfather did a recitation which was always arousing in a way that the sermons never were. I learnt that we were all born in sin, and that Christ died for our sins. Every night we read a Bible story, we prayed, and asked God for forgiveness for our sins.

Everything that we did was given meaning through the Bible; Scriptures; parables of God; Psalms; Hymns; Bible stories and the Lord's Prayer. We knew right from wrong, mainly we learnt what was right from being told what was wrong. As I grew older so did my wrongs and the "wrongs of the world". It was wrong to do anything that might be construed as work on a Sunday and, or that might involve others working – such as shopping. Equally, if not more so, anything that could be seen as playing or having any fun and games was strictly forbidden. Sunday had been designated as a day of rest and a day for worship, for God's will to be done and for serving others.

I did not believe that I was "born evil" or that I was "born to suffer" and knew this deep, deep inside of me from a very early age. From when I was about three years old I had a strong sense of innate goodness within me. This feeling separated me from my family and I felt different from them. I was nevertheless God-fearing. I was especially fearful of punishment for getting things wrong, making mistakes and of getting hurt. By the time I was a teenager I mistrusted and disliked myself so much so that I didn't need others to punish or judge me, I did this to myself.

It was not until my early teenage years by which time I was at a girls' Quaker boarding school that I fully appreciated that other families operated differently to my own. The discovery that other families did not go to church twice on a Sunday and that they appeared to live happy and healthy lives was huge. I distinctly remember the feeling of surprise and delight mixed with apprehension that I had survived a Sunday when I stayed for a weekend with my friend's family without going to Church without being struck down by the hand of the Lord. Furthermore we had spent much of the day in our pyjamas and the rest of the day enjoying a walk - casually dressed and having fun – on a Sunday. This experience was only marred by my discovering that the crowd gathered on a bridge had witnessed the death of a young man who had jumped to his death. I wondered if, after all, it was God's way of showing me what might befall people who don't go to church and do "his bidding"; was this in some way a warning?

It was only during this time that I began to understand fully the enormity and extent of what had been, at the time, a particular religious upbringing. At Quaker boarding school I met and mixed with girls from other religious backgrounds whereas up until I was 10 years old I had been immersed in the Baptist faith; I also discovered through attending twice weekly Quaker "meeting" the power of silence and of connection with others in silence. Although immersed in the values and beliefs of the Baptist faith I had never been immersed in the water which sat in the basement of the church awaiting those who chose to give their lives to the Lord. This is not to say that I did not dabble, and sometimes "put my toe in the water". I was curious. I wanted to know what it would be like "to give my life to Jesus" and to "suffer the little children to come unto him", and to this end pursued the Scriptures. As a child I attended Bibles classes and won a number of trophies for my knowledge of the scriptures, and every year received Scripture Prizes – in the form of a book token.

As a teenager, having experienced a number of visiting ministers preaching about their missionary work in far away countries and thanking the congregation for their contribution by way of financial support, and prayers for doing "God's work", I seriously considered the possibility of becoming a missionary when I was grown-up. I did "give my life to the Lord" on more than one occasion, taking Him into my life, seeking absolution and redemption, but it never lasted.

For the most part what I found did not stack up. Indeed it only added to my confusion. I had been brought up to totally mistrust anything that could be considered superstitious, and yet, on further enquiry into the Scriptures, I discovered page upon page, text upon text, of superstition. The more I grew up the less certain I became. I was frightened. It was as if every step I took towards Jesus took me away from him. The answers that I received to my questions did not satisfy my curiosity. Some questions simply could not be answered, and what was asked of me was to "trust in the Lord Jesus". This, for me, proved to be a step too far.

And yet what would become of me if I rejected totally the Lord Jesus Christ? Would I be thrown out of family and home? Would I be struck down? Could God read my thoughts? Did God know what was going on in my mind? Would I be found out, like Doubting Thomas? And would I eventually "come round", "see the light", and be a better Christian for it?

My early religious upbringing was my only upbringing, I knew no different. My experience was one of somehow being fitted into a mould into which all of me would not fit or for which I was quite simply the wrong shape and size. No amount of shaking of the head at my wrongdoings, or worse being slapped or hit was going to "knock me down to size". That is, nothing was actually going to destroy my spirit which throughout my life, for as long as I can remember, has felt like a strong thread running through me.

It was this inner spirit that I reached into when I turned 20. Away from the familiar environs of Polytechnic life where I was doing a degree in communication studies, and abroad in Italy, I had an experience which would change my life forever. This experience combined with my early childhood religious upbringing put an end to the soul searching of previous years and marked the beginning of my journey to myself. I was gang raped.

During the experience I knew what I had to do; I fought and I struggled; when this did not work and I was physically exhausted I talked, I listened, I appealed for compassion and to their "better nature"; I looked them in the eye and eventually I escaped. I had survived. Had I believed in God then I would most definitely have said that the white light in the room and the guiding voice was that of God himself. As it is I felt pure terror, I was blinded by fear and I drew on this inner spirit, this part of me that knew what to do. I experienced a compassion for myself and the perpetrators "for they knew not what they were doing," and a passion for survival that saved my life.

I emerged from the experience even more determined to save myself. I feared that I would be judged as "having asked for it" and worse that I deserved it for having "turned my back on the Lord". The experience had been my punishment for all my wrong-doings. Deep inside me I knew this could not be true, that it was a lie, and that I had to find my own truth.

This was the hardest Lesson (sic) I had ever had to learn, to listen to myself, to trust my intuition – to trust myself. Had I done this earlier I would not have chosen to go into the situation that resulted in my being gang raped. I had chosen to ignore my inner voice, to go along with someone else's decision despite my own misgivings. I knew this at the time and that I had a lot of getting to know myself. There was no turning back. What I did not know then was that the course of my personal and professional life had been set.

The search that had been for "Who or what is God?" became a quest for "Who am I?" Whereas previously I had been trying to make sense of the Scriptures I was now, in my early twenties trying to make sense of myself and of my experiences. I had a desire to be set free, to shake off the trappings of religion and in particular some of the early childhood experiences which trapped me into fear, fear of myself and fear of others.

I enrolled on a self-defence course, determined that never again would I be beaten or hurt. I hoped that I would never be put to the test, as although I had learnt the moves I knew that I myself had not moved. I was stuck.

The movement which helped me to shift and offered me a different way of seeing things was that of feminism, in particular the writings by women about women for women. Books such as *Our Bodies, Ourselves – a Book By and For Women* by the Boston Women's Health Book Collective became my new Bible; a source of information about my body, my sexuality, about relationships. The women wrote of the things which I had never been allowed to talk about - indeed that I even feared to think about in case God could "read my mind" - including sexual feelings, masturbation, lovemaking, contraception and abortion. There were pictures of women's bodies, the anatomy and physiology of reproduction and sexuality; chapters on childbearing and parenting. This book, in particular, was a celebration of women, of our bodies and our feelings, and for the first time I truly rejoiced in being a woman.

I embraced feminism and women's rights. Throughout all of this I had a growing awareness that much of what I did, and how I went about it, was in reaction to my upbringing and to having been brought up to be God-fearing. At the same time as connecting with my body I also enjoyed escaping from my body, and sought "spaced out", out-of-body, experiences. To no avail, there seemed to be no escape from my fears and uncertainties. The judgments always returned the next day with a vengeance, chastising and punishing me for what I had done. Slowly I began to realise that I was doing this to me, and that I disliked myself; I was hurting and punishing me for who I was.

I had completed my degree, was working in a Wholefood Collective shop and training to be a child psychotherapist. Talking to my supervisor and lecturer, Dr W., was the first time I had spoken to anyone about my childhood, and what had happened to me in Italy. He advised, what I already knew to be true, that I had some "work to do" on myself. At about this time an advert was put up in the shop window by a woman, M., who casually suggested that I might be interested in "it". "It" was a co-counselling workshop with John Heron.

The co-counselling workshop was the first of many that I participated in with John Heron who always provided a well facilitated, wonderfully safe environment, in which I could express my anger, beat and kick cushions, shout and scream words which I had never dared to utter out loud, and hardly dared even to think; and howl and cry. I knew that I was saving myself, creating spaces within me in which I could breathe freely and express myself honestly. I was listened to, held, stroked tenderly and loved for who I was by people who had seen and heard me ranting and raving. I was not sent away. I was not labelled and locked up as mad and bad. I was me. And in turn had witnessed them doing the same, I too had held the space for them to be themselves in.

A door also opened up for me with my parents, from whom I had felt distant and estranged. For the first time there was the possibility of my moving towards them, of allowing myself to be seen and heard by them, and also to see and hear them for who they were. It was a beginning of getting to know each other differently. I had found my metier for which I was very grateful and trained as a facilitator with John Heron. As well as facilitating co-counselling workshops for men and women I facilitated women only co-counselling and sexuality workshops – advertising in *Spare Rib*. My parents and I grew closer, and they continued to be hugely supportive of me and my "lifework".

I had loosened the grip of my Baptist upbringing. I had rejected a religion that I perceived as being made up by men for men, one in which women seemed to have a "walk on" part and in which men had the "upper hand". A religion that espoused love but that seemed to me to practice fear much of the time. Whilst many of my friends were travelling to Poona to experience Bhagwan Shree Rajneesh and to become Sanyassans, my travels took the form of an inner quest.

Together with some women friends we formed a Matriarchy Group with the purpose of exploring women's spirituality. We studied the writings of women who themselves had researched female archetypes and Goddesses; including *Descent to the Goddess – A Way of Initiation for Women* by Sylvia Brinton Perera, *The Moon and the Virgin* – reflections on the archetypal feminine by Nor Hall; *Goddesses in Everywoman* by Jean Shinoda Bolen and *Not in God's Image* edited by Julia O'Faolain and Lauro Martines.

We practised some of the ancient rituals that we read about, bringing what we were learning from our reading into our circle of women. We turned inwards, to our inner knowing, paying attention to, writing down and sharing our dreams with each other. Ours was an inner journey. We listened to ourselves and to each other; we read and told stories. One in particular stands out for me, a collection of stories gathered by Anne Cameron from the Nootka women of Vancouver Island, Canada: Daughters of Copper Woman. The experience of this group was liberating for me. I had found a new language that I understood and that enabled me to describe my experience of myself and my spirituality. I felt connected to myself and listened to my own body rhythms at the same time as feeling connected to the wider world and to all people on this earth.

For the first time I had a sense of myself as "I am" in relation to everyone else's "I am". I read Anne Dickson's book *A Woman in Your Own Right* and attended her wonderful workshop where I learnt about assertiveness, self-respect and respect of others; taking self-responsibility for the choices that we make. I realised that my lack of inner self-confidence was at the root of my non-assertive behaviour and that I had much to learn about developing self-confidence, and to unlearn. I had learnt that it was selfish to think of oneself, to put oneself first in any shape or form. As a child I had severally been told that I was selfish. It was made clear to me that to think of myself or to ever put my own needs and wants first was wrong in the eyes of God. Indeed to 'speak from the "I"' was not something with which I was familiar. I had been told that "I want never gets". And so it was that I began to learn about my needs and wants. Firstly I learnt to identify them which took time and only then to experiment in expressing them clearly. I began to find my voice, and to articulate my thoughts, ideas and feelings without fear of being ridiculed or derided. It was also the beginning of setting my own boundaries; through paying attention to myself I became more aware of, and more responsible, for taking care of and liking myself.

It was at this point that I was introduced to Transactional Analysis (TA) initially as part of a two year Diploma in Humanistic Psychology and later on I did more training in TA. At last here was a theory and practice that could help me to make sense of my early childhood and my religious upbringing in the context of the choices that I had made as a young adult. Deep down I felt that I was fundamentally flawed, that even though I did not believe that I was born in sin, there was a "fault" running through me as in a rock. After my experience in Italy and despite all the work I had done on myself I felt that I was "damaged goods". Even though I had loosened the shackles of religion and had chosen to tread a different path I was nagged by self-doubts, anxieties and fears; negative thoughts and feelings.

Eric Berne, the originator of TA, author of, *What Do You Say After You Say Hello?* believed not only that damage could be healed but also that people could make new decisions about themselves and others, through a process of self-awareness and – most importantly – positive recognition. People could choose to change their Life-Script. He suggested that positive recognition was the fastest and most effective way of bringing about change. Berne's Ego-state model provided me with an analysis of the structure and function of personality that helped to make sense of my feelings, thoughts and behaviours. I understood that I was replaying much of the past in the present; thinking, feeling and behaving in ways that I had learnt as a child, often responding or reacting to situations either by doing what was asked of me or doing the very opposite. I spent very little time actually in the present, in the here-and-now.

Berne's theory of Life-Scripts was further developed by Claude Steiner author of *Scripts People Live*, who suggested that we are all born: "I'm OK: You're OK" and by Tom Harris who wrote, *I'm OK – You're OK*. I took great comfort in this theory which affirmed my inner knowing that I was born OK, and not born a sinner, all wrong and evil. I recognised that underpinning my lack of self-confidence was the decision that I had made early on in childhood that had led me to adopting the Life Position: "I'm not OK: You're OK". That I could re-decide to be: "I'm OK. You're OK" was utterly liberating. I had a choice!

Central to my childhood and religious upbringing were discipline and being disciplined; being obedient and doing as I was told, without asking questions and, or answering back. When I was disobedient I was told that I deserved to be punished – "Let this be a lesson once and for all", and it was always "for your own good". I asked difficult questions and I wouldn't take, "No for an answer". This meant that I got into a lot of trouble a lot of the time. I was described as "difficult" and "temperamental". I was angry, "It was not fair". And I was frightened, hurt and troubled. I think that I probably teetered on the edge of the: "I'm not OK: You're not OK" Life Position, and certainly flipped into the: "I'm OK: You're not OK" Life Position as a strategy for dealing with feeling "not OK".

Analysis of my favourite childhood fairy story The Little Mermaid helped me to identify my chosen Life-Script and the kind of messages that I had internalised about love and life. Written by Hans Christian Anderson in 1836 the story tells the tale of the youngest of six mermaid daughters, who at the age of fifteen, like her sisters before her, is given permission to rise from the bottom of the ocean where they lived in their father's castle and see the earth. The Little Mermaid must first have eight oysters attached to her tail causing her to suffer, and her grandmother's message to her is: "Pride must suffer pain".

The Little Mermaid rises to the surface of the ocean where she witnesses a big storm that destroys a ship, on board of which is a Prince who she rescues and falls in love with. She returns to her home and yearns to be with him. She will give up anything of herself to be able to live on the land and agrees to sacrifice her voice in exchange for legs knowing that every step she takes will be agony and that once she is on land she will never be able to return to her family. She is willing to do all of this, even if only for a day, knowing that when the Prince marries she will die, and will have to sacrifice her own life. And so it comes to pass that by day she lives at the Prince's side and by night on her own, in secret, she bathes her hurt, sore feet.

When the Prince marries she is raised above the sea, into the air, where the spirits tell her that because of her suffering and striving she will, after hundreds of years, obtain an immortal soul and be in the "Kingdom of Heaven".

I recognised myself in The Little Mermaid who had to sacrifice herself and suffer in order to get what she wanted, that there was "no gain without pain". I had learnt that to be loved and to love involved pain and sacrifice, and that indeed "love hurt". Like The Little Mermaid I learnt to hide my hurt from others and to suffer on my own. I also evolved a bargaining system based on "doing good deeds" that I hoped would somehow result in my being spared further hurt and suffering and that things would be all right. It went something like this: "If I do x, y, z then all will be well." At some level I think I was seeking to pacify God, in case he existed. Sometimes it worked, sometimes it didn't, and I grew more unsure of myself.

This sort of bargaining could have been the beginning of Obsessive Compulsive Disorder (OCD). If I thought, felt or did something then I would be saved – from hell and damnation, further hurt and punishment. It would take a hold of me whenever I was feeling vulnerable and anxious and prey on my mind. I did as a child and young teenager adopt various ritualistic behaviours, including touching something so many times without interruptions; counting up to a given number (high) without breathing and surviving. My questioning mind which had got me into so much trouble as a young child served me better as a young teenager and adult. I questioned what I was doing and why I was doing it. Interestingly at the age of fifteen, the same age as the Little Mermaid rose from the depths of the ocean onto land, I was diagnosed with depression and for a while was prescribed antidepressants at boarding school. I was troubled by anxious thoughts and found it difficult to quieten my fears no matter how many rituals I made up and performed mentally or physically.

As a child I had learnt that it was wrong to hurt other people, and yet I hurt. I learnt that, "honesty was the best policy," and yet people were not always honest with me; that it was wrong to tell lies, and yet when I told the truth I was not always believed. I had learnt that it mattered what other people thought, and that it was important that they thought well and highly of us. It was also important that we kept up appearances at all costs, lest people thought less well of us. Doing the right thing even if I did not want to do it was necessary. Indeed sacrificing what I wanted to do for the right thing, and for the greater good of others, was all part of doing the right thing by God. This is what was expected and required of us to be good Christians. Suffering was all part of it, just as Jesus had suffered to save our souls, so too were we born to suffer. These messages and more were drummed into me non-verbally and verbally from as early as I can remember - often prefaced by, "Don't" – "Don't do that"; "Don't think that"; "Don't say that"; "Don't feel that".

Mary and Bob Goulding, TA therapists and co-authors of *Changing Lives Through Redecision Therapy*, suggested that there are twelve injunctions (communicated non-verbally) all beginning with "Don't" upon which the child makes a decision about their Life position. In particular I recognised the injunctions: "Don't Be – don't exist", "Don't be you"; "Don't feel" and "Don't think" that had led me to feel less than, to compare myself with others and to find myself lacking. I understood that some of my behaviours that were not only addictive but also self-abusive were part of my living out my Life-Script. It was time to make new decisions, to make different choices that were life affirming and life giving.

I went on to co-facilitate the Diploma in Humanistic Psychology and was thus given further opportunities to experience a wide range of different therapies, including Gestalt therapy, Encounter Groups, Massage, Re-birthing, Body Work, Sweat Lodges and other Native American Indian traditions. All these and more helped me to increase my self-awareness and most importantly my self-belief and belief in others. I continued to work with individuals and groups, and also to do some "Train the Trainers" in both Counselling Skills and Transactional Analysis.

I was in my late twenties and for the first time wanted very much to be pregnant and to have a baby with my partner of several years. I was ready to become a mother. I was thrilled when the home pregnancy kit indicated that I was pregnant. Three months in to the pregnancy I started to feel unwell and knew that something was very wrong. A scan revealed that there was nothing in my womb, and I was asked to come back for a laparoscopy. I was very frightened and turned once again to *Our Bodies, Ourselves* and diagnosed my symptoms as those of an ectopic pregnancy. I feared the worst. I wanted desperately to talk to my parents about what was happening but feared their reaction at a time when I most needed them, that this was my "just deserts" for having "had my cake and eaten it". I was not married. I had obviously had sex, and I was pregnant.

In my vulnerability and frightened state of mind and body I feared that this indeed was God's wrath for my wrong-doings; for everything that I had ever thought, felt and done that would, in the eyes' of the Lord, be considered sinful. Although close friends and my partner were supportive I felt on my own, lost and frightened. I was in unknown territory. My parents, I imagined, would find my being pregnant and unmarried really hard and yet they were wonderfully supportive. For the first time I was able to fully experience their unconditional love for me and it was a true gift. My recovery from the removal of my ovary, fallopian tube and baby was slow and difficult. My relationship with my partner did not survive our grief. At the time I felt betrayed not only by my partner but also by my body – as if "it" were separate from me. How could this happen to me after all I had done to let go of anger, shame, guilt and fear from by body?

Slowly I gathered myself together again. A year later, almost to the day, I had a second ectopic pregnancy with my new partner. It was devastating. Thankfully this time the surgeon was able to repair my fallopian tube and to keep my ovary. I had been spared, and there was still a glimmer, a possibility of my getting pregnant, of having a baby somehow... in the future.

Once again there was a gathering of myself together with the help of my partner, friends and family. Together with a small group of women friends we held a ritual to help me mourn and grieve my losses. I dug two small holes in the ground beneath a huge tree that stood outside of my kitchen window. In each hole I placed a stone, covered it with earth and cried. The ritual was both a letting go and the marking of a resting place for them, and for me.

It also marked the beginning of a new stage of my journey both in my personal and professional life. I stopped facilitating co-counselling, body and sexuality workshops for women. It was too painful. I was much changed – outwardly as well as inwardly. My face had changed forever – I had a sad look about me was how a friend I hadn't seen for sometime accurately described me; I had lost a huge amount of weight and was very thin. I had my long, wild curly hair cut short.

I decided to do a two year part-time Masters in Management Learning. It was an energetic shift from my heart, body and spirit into my head which I enjoyed. At the same time I moved from the North of England to the South. Away from the moors, my home for most of my twenties, and away from the Pennines and dark Satanic mills of Yorkshire, the home of my childhood.

The hope was that I would get over and somehow forget what had happened in the previous two years; the fear that I would never recover from the losses and a deep down sadness. I did and I didn't. I enjoyed the challenges of the Masters, of thinking and writing, and working with others. The desire however for a baby did not diminish and the feeling grew inside of me that if I could find a way to somehow bypass my remaining fallopian tube and place the foetus in my womb then all would be well...

Lo and behold (sic) along came IVF, as if in answer to my question: "How do I bypass my remaining fallopian tube and get pregnant in my womb?" And so it was that my partner and I began the IVF process and I conceived F., who is now a young woman.

As well as there being support from many medical practitioners and scientists for IVF it was viewed at the time by many as unnatural and as interfering with the order of things. There were those who judged it as not, "God's Will", and that it was wrong for men to "play God" in the creation of life. Furthermore just as women's right to choose whether to have an abortion or not was considered wrong in some quarters so too women's right to choose to get pregnant if it was not "God-given" was also considered wrong. Women would be able to have babies without having sex with a man, they would be able to "go it alone" and thus flout all religious law and order. It was, and is, potentially dangerous for women undergoing a new treatment involving vast amounts of hormones that nobody really knew much about, especially the long-term effects. Plus, of course, there was no guarantee that there would be life, or lives, at the end of the IVF cycle and therefore much criticism, and concern for the rights of the foetus by those who felt that lives were being created only to be quickly aborted. I am not sure that a huge amount of thought at that time was given to the feelings of women – who like me in years to come - were not successful in conceiving with IVF. These and related issues were explored at the time in books such as *Test-Tube Women and Birthrights*.

On moving to the South of England I commenced weekly psychoanalysis for several years. This regular weekly opportunity to explore, through Jungian psychology, my dreams, my innermost thoughts and feelings was a huge support in my life throughout most of my thirties and into my early forties. In particular it provided me with an opportunity to reflect on and get clear about my parenting and being a mother for the first time, and helped during the break-up of the relationship with my partner. I moved to live on my own with F. R. my dearest friend who I had known from my student days came to help out with decorating. Gradually and over time our friendship turned into a relationship, and his relationship with F. became that of friend and father.

The desire for another baby combined with the desire to feel more secure as a family prompted our decision to get married. Neither of us considered ourselves then, or now, the marrying sort, but at the time celebrating the change in our friendship of many years into a partnership felt very important. I got pregnant easily and felt a mixture of delight and fear; and with the fear came the bargaining with God. It went something like this, "Surely this time, God, all will be well, I am married now, I am with the man that I truly love; please forgive me and let everything be all right". I was not pleased to be thinking in this way; it seemed that as soon as I felt vulnerable then the bargaining would start up again dragging me down and down into a bottomless pit of fear, feeding my self-doubt. God did not look kindly on me. A scan revealed that indeed I had a third ectopic pregnancy. How could this be? How could I bear a further suffering and loss? I did and with the support of R., our parents, sister, and friends I came through the experience – I "pulled myself together" again. Once again my fallopian tube was repaired and the ovary saved. There was still hope.

I would prepare for pregnancy, look after myself even better. I had already given up smoking prior to conceiving F., I had dramatically reduced my alcohol intake and at this point decided to stop drinking all together. I was aware through the Jungian psychoanalysis that I had a tendency towards addiction and that I could easily have had either a drug or alcohol problem. It was time to stop and the relief at doing so – one day at a time – was huge. It is many years now since I had my last drop of alcohol. It is not something I can ever return to, knowing myself as I do. Other times I smile – I have become teetotal just as my God-fearing grandfather would have wished for me. He had been given to thinking that the sherry trifle made by my grandmother had not sherry in it but "essence of sherry". I wonder if he knew really, and loved my grandmother all the more for making it possible for him to enjoy her delicious trifles.

Thus it was that R. and I began a long, gruelling four years of IVF treatment ,and went through a series of miscarriages. Hopes raised and dashed over and over again. I turned forty, felt depressed, utterly disheartened and still there was a glimmer of light, of hope that somehow I would be successful. And I was. In the spring of 1996 I conceived S. naturally, with the help of a new and what was then revolutionary, and controversial, blood serum treatment. It worked. I believed in it, and most importantly I believed in myself. There was no bargaining with God. I trusted my body. Finally I had let go of the feeling of being "damaged goods" and of being punished for my wrong-doings. I truly believed that damage could be healed and was greatly helped in all of this by the psychoanalysis. In the winter of 1996 I gave birth to S., now a teenager.

My experience of co-parenting with R. and of bringing up our two daughters has been very different from our own religious upbringings, mine Baptist and his Jewish. Our children have received some religious education at school and have asked questions of R. and me about our parents' religious beliefs and our own. We have always been honest with them; we do not believe in God nor in any "after-life"; this is our one precious life to live – and it gives me courage and a huge sense of relief. Our daughters have been into church and a synagogue a handful of times, they have never been to Bible classes or learnt the Scriptures. They have learnt to live with respect for themselves and others; they are loving, kind, compassionate and generous.

We have consciously made some very different decisions from our parents in our daughters' upbringing. The three most significant choices we have made are: to always look for ways to say, "Yes"; to see ourselves as being alongside them, as a parent and guide; to never ever physically abuse by slapping and, or hitting them. Thankfully I have upheld my decision and found it easy to do so. Not least because I found turning a "should/thou shalt" or "should not/thou shalt not" into a "could" opened up possibilities for me in all areas of my life. I am responsible and it is up to me to choose. My experience of taking self-responsibility and of realising that I can choose to do things differently has been hugely liberating for me as a parent. I have also felt my parents' regard and respect for my parenting grow, and it has been a healing process for us all.

My journey has been about a different "seeing the light" and "living in the light". It has been and is about living with possibility and uncertainty, knowing and "un-knowing"; of having courage and compassion. As my grandmother used to say: "You can only do your best" and what I like to think is that she also meant: "Be your best self, be who you truly are, be real." It has become my life's work. I am a psychologist and work with people helping them to develop positive self-esteem, to connect more strongly with themselves – spiritually, emotionally, mentally and physically – and to build relationships with others that are assertive and inclusive of difference. I sometimes reflect on my journey and that whilst I do not abide by any religion, I am in some strange way following in the footsteps of my great grandfather and great uncle who were ministers in their church, believing in what they did and guiding others along the way. I have found my path through connection with myself and with others, and that whilst my path is different I walk alongside my ancestors, leaving footprints of my own.

Background reading

Arditti R., Duelli Klein R., and Minden S., *Test-Tube Women*, London, Pandora Press: (1984)

Berne E., *What Do You Say After You Say Hello?*, London, Corgi Books: (1979)

Brinton Perera S., *Descent to the Goddess*, Canada, Inner City Books: (1981)

Cameron A., *Daughters of Copper Woman*, London, The Women's Press: (1984)

Dickson A., *A Woman In Your Own Right*, London, Quartet Books: (1985)

Goulding M. and Goulding R., *Changing Lives Through Redecision Therapy*, New York, Grove Press: (1982)

Harding E., *The Way of All Women*, London, Rider and Co. Ltd.: (1986)

Hall N., *The Moon and The Virgin*, London, The Women's Press: (1980)

Harris T.A., *I'm Ok – You're OK*, London, Arrow Books: (1995)

Lee R. and Morgan D. (Eds.) *Birthrights*, London, Routledge: (1989)

O'Faolain J. and Martines L., *Not in God's Image*, Fontana: (1974)

Rich A., *Of Woman Born*, London, Virago: (1977)

Shinoda Bolen J., *Goddesses in Everywoman*, Harper Colophon, New York (1985)

Steiner C., *Scripts People Live*, New York, Grove Press: (1990)

Strasser F. and Strasser A., *Existential Time-limited Therapy*, Chichester, John Wiley and Sons Ltd.: (1997)

Strasser F., *Emotions*, London, Duckworth: (1999)

Strasser F. and Randolph P., *Mediation*, London, Continuum: (2004)

The Boston Women's Health Book Collective, *Our Bodies, Ourselves*, New York, Simon and Schuster: (1973)

Townend A., *Developing Assertiveness*, London, Routledge: (1991)

Townend A., *Assertiveness and Diversity*, Hampshire, Palgrave Macmillan: (2007)

Yalom I.D., *the gift of therapy*, London, Piatkus: (2002)

Yalom I.D., *Staring at the Sun: Overcoming the Dread of Death*, London, Piatkus: (2008)

Appreciations

A big thanks to my readers who have helped me to fine tune my narrative - Sabine Young, Stephanie Parry and Anthony Landale and to my family and friends all of whom have been interested in and supported me throughout my writing; and a special thank you to Lucy Birtwistle and Lindsay Smith who invited me to contribute, to enquire into and to tell my story.

Wendy Weston

Early Years

I was born on a snowy January night in 1940 in a Cambridgeshire farmhouse. My father was a Royal Engineer in the war in France. He had insisted, against her wishes, that my mother, who was pregnant with me at the time, join his family for the duration. She would have preferred to make her own plans, but found herself in a small village within a rather unfriendly extended family (my grandparents, my father's unmarried sister, Uncle Oz, an invalid, and two or three elderly aunts who visited from time to time).

My grandparents took an active part in the life of the village church. My grandfather and in turn his son, and his grandson, my cousin, were churchwardens: my grandmother and my aunt would "do the flowers".

We attended church on Sundays, regular as clockwork. I remember feeling special as I sat in the pew with the tall churchwardens staff with its highly polished shiny brass knob on top. I loved looking at the pictures in the stained glass windows, loved watching the organ (in those days a boy had to pump the bellows up and down to make it work, while Madge or Mary played). And the little village church of St Marys became a familiar and much loved place to me. I have happy memories of Harvest Festival, when huge marrows and hundreds of apples and tomatoes decorated every surface; of Easter with the overpowering smell of daffodils and primroses decorating the donation box by the door of Sunday School when I collected my weekly Sunday school stamp, with a picture and a text. The church was a happy place for me, and together with my grandmother reading Enid Blyton's "Bible Stories", (my mother told how I would sit on granny's knee, tears rolling down our faces at the death of Absolum, reading "Absolum, oh Absolum my son") was my first, very positive, introduction to "religion".

My mother did not have an easy time growing up: nothing dramatically traumatic - just ordinary run of the mill stuff for 1914. Her father, born in Sheffield of very poor parents (he and his brother took it in turns to wear shoes to go to school I was told), decided that in order to better himself he would learn shorthand and become a clerk. He met and married in Sheffield, and once my mother was born they emigrated to Montreal. Here he worked his way from clerk until he became a director of the company. But while they were still young, and my mother was about 22 yrs old, her mother was diagnosed with TB for which there was no cure in those days. Until her illness she had been a lively woman with many friends and interests, watching all the early Hollywood greats, and entertaining in the afternoons. My mother remembered sitting aged 4 watching the old black and white films.

Once diagnosed with TB all this changed. In those days TB patients were sent to a sanatorium. At first this was fairly near, and visits were possible, but later on they were recommended to send her to a different sanatorium, far away, and after that my mother saw her mother very rarely. To cope with his two daughters an aunt was brought over from -Sheffield, and my mother was left at home while her sister was sent to boarding school – a permanent sense of resentment to her as she would have liked to have gone too. I do wonder if this made it harder to mother us in her turn.

I am beginning to link the fact of my mother's confusion and difficulty with emotional mothering with the lack of care given to her while her own mother was ill. She never encouraged or praised, and none of us remember being cuddled or kissed. What she remembered of her own mother was watching all those wonderful early Hollywood films and also how important it was to look good and pay attention to dress: not of cuddles, and love, or at least she never said so. I don't think she felt understood by her parents, and once her mother was ill no-one had time for her. All her energies and emotions went into her love of ballet and drama (she told me all about the great Anna Pavlova). She wanted to become a ballet teacher, but her father (brought up as a strict Methodist - no dancing or stage shows) said NO WAY. So she went to McGill, her local university in Montreal and read English, intending to go to England and join RADA. But she met my father on a boat train, and that ended her acting ambitions. (Why did she join a bank instead of RADA when she never, ever got the hang of our Imperial currency? I'll never know). Her father meant well but had little empathy for his two young daughters, and always got it wrong, as when he gave her bike away to a little girl who hadn't got one, and my mother always remembering her sense of injustice at this - "now I haven't got a bike".

This lack of mothering I think made it difficult for her with her own three daughters. None of us were very confident girls and I think now this resulted from our parents inability to praise us (they wouldn't have seen the point, and would have thought it would have encouraged us to "show off" - the bane of my life as I never knew what showing off really was, and I always "put myself down" instead). It is only now with my grandchildren that I can appreciate the importance of encouragement for them to be themselves - I was never good at this with my own sons.

(Why am I going into all these details about my mother? What relation could it have to my religious experience? I ask because I wonder whether I felt unloved and so really responded at a deep level to the amazing message that God knew me, cared about me, listened to me which I absorbed in my junior years.) When the war ended and my father came home, we moved to Surrey, and I found myself attending a day school convent. I was one of the lucky ones, as, talking to other people who also went to convents, have memories of unkind and vindictive nuns and these prevented them having a positive "God experience" as a result. But my nuns were not like this, and I was very happy at St. Anne's. The nuns laughed a lot, they worried about me, they cared for me (I remember being fed extra potatoes because I was such a skinny child) and I knew at a deep level that I was loved. I was very happy there and learnt about God with the other girls as they had their Catechism lesson (I was not a Roman so I was given other work to do, but I was all ears, and learned their lessons as well as they did). When I was 9 yrs old my mother had a third daughter who died aged 13 days. My father (she told me) would never mention Jane's name, never talk about the baby at all, treated it as if it had never happened. I don't know how my mother coped at all. It was my first experience of death but I don't remember feeling sad. The day after Jane died all my class were taken into the chapel, and although no one said anything I knew we were there to pray for my dead sister: Roman Catholics believed she would go to Limbo -where unbaptised babies were suppose to end up in those days. But for my mother life must have been extremely painful and confusing, far from home, no relatives or friends nearby and a husband who did not know how to grieve or even to acknowledge death. My mother did have a "religious" upbringing, which sounded un- loving. Her grandparents on both sides were preachers: one was a quaker who travelled the Yorkshire Dales with a horse and cart preaching as he went, and who" went to bed with his long white beard carefully brushed and left outside the sheets" , and on the other side her grandfather was a Methodist. She remembers terrible Sundays as a child when she was not allowed to do anything: only read bible stories and go to church. In my memory, she never attended a church willingly in her adult life. If there does eventually prove to be "a religious gene", then I have could have inherited it from both my great grandparents;

my two sisters also have strong religious/spiritual lives. When I was about 14 I had my first negative experience of "religion". My best friend next door was converted by Billy Graham - an American Evangelist who took London by storm and I remember my parents talking about how weird this was, and how angry her parents were when she steadfastly kept to her beliefs. It felt very negative all round to me, I didn't understand her at all, felt left out, and cross. But she persevered with her new faith eventually marrying a Baptist minister. She joined a different church, an evangelical church which had a Sunday school (Covenanters– Sunday school for older boys and girls, and was strictly segregated). She persuaded me to join with her and it was here that I learnt of a very different, punishing God. Here I learnt to feel guilty and a failure in God's eyes because I couldn't believe everything they said. I am happy to say this is no longer the case, although, for many years I had twinges of fear when listening to a really zealous, fundamentalist evangelical preacher.

They taught that God had pre-ordained who should be saved, and yet somehow it was my fault if I couldn't believe. – the height of unfairness I thought. They taught of a punishing God and although I accepted that God hated sinners, my overwhelming view of Him/Her up till then, was of a God who loved us , and wanted the best for all of us. I knew that we spoil his/her plan by being selfish and greedy (sinning). This new church view disturbed and confused me, and, I think, put back my emotional development for many years. Their beliefs somehow made it more difficult to believe that " "it was OK to be me". And since then in particular I have struggled to maintain my belief that God has a plan for me, a purpose; I believe it is true, but never knew what it was. But I could see that God wanted my converted friend and "all those evangelicals" but not me.

I understood that she believed that she had been "chosen" by God. But I never felt wanted in a similar way, just felt "left out". Although now, writing this, I realise that by the time I was eleven years old I already had a fairly mature understanding of the goodness of God and my friend next door, who had no formal religious education at all, maybe responded positively to Billy Graham because of her need ? She was fallow ground waiting to be seeded perhaps?

From the age of 15 I explored many different spiritual dimensions. I never stopped wondering "why" - don't understand those of my friends who never seem to see the question. I was confirmed in C of E, I joined a group of Theosophists, I read up on Quakers, and Buddhists, and at 21 attended a training college run on Methodist lines. By then I had given up attending any church at all. I was a bit of a religious rebel by 21, and as I went to a teacher training college run by an elderly fanatical Methodist woman who was determined to ram her brand of spirituality down all our throats , I was able to be even more rebellious... By the time I left college I was more or less agnostic.

My "Billy Graham" friend and I both left college at the same time, and obtained our first teaching posts in the same area and decided to share a flat. This was a good experience for a while. But when she joined the local Plymouth Brethren church and began praying for me, I was staggered: angry, confused, cross, uncomprehending at first. Do you know what it feels like to be prayed for in this way? I had never asked to be "won over", indeed, I had argued against her new found born-again theory which was very new to us at that time in the late fifties. I knew her theory of becoming a Christian (I couldn't not know it as she tried very hard to convert me), I was obviously not "good enough" as I was. I was angry all the time , while simultaneously feeling guilty (although I'm not sure what about). I met her friends and I made my own.

Two years later , time for us to part. She went to train at LBC (London Bible College), and I went to inner London to teach children with disabilities. I had always wanted to do this, but alas. Could I discipline these children whose behaviour was worse than any I had met in Barnsley or Croydon.? I could not. I think I lasted all of 19 days before miserably walking out. I was miserable. No job. No religion. No boyfriend. I began to see an old friend who was solid C of E but who didn't proselitise all the time, and I began to give myself another chance: if there really was a God who cared about me it was now or never: I had to know. So I went along to St. Martin's in the Fields, Trafalgar Square (where Austin Williams had recently retired). I was very wary of "being converted"as I had always believed (since my convent days) that if I "gave in" to God he would send me into the African jungles to be a nun: my worst nightmare. However, I laid out my fleece*** ("If you want me God ,you'll have to prove it" I prayed one day) and to my total amazement, there seemed to be an answer. At the end of the service a vicar announced they had a desperate need for a pianist to play at some local alms houses nearby . I was a pianist. QED. So I played hymns on Sundays for quite some time, and valued the simple services taken by some amazing vicars who took the services on a rota. I learned to grow back into an Anglican . An added motivation for me to become "converted" (which I never did really – I have difficulty with the "conversion" bit.) was that I had recently begun to "go out with" the man whom I would marry. He was a Christian, and I knew that he would only marry me If I was Christian too. I suppose this is not a very good basis for belief. What a dilemma...

Anyway. I read as many relevant books as I could get hold of (CS Lewis, Eric Fromm, G.B. Phillips,......) and eventually took the leap of faith which I think is necessary for everyone taking this journey, beginning an attempt at a relationship with God. Thus began a new phase of learning - about God and myself.

The next 20 years passed more or less conventionally. I married, we had two boys, we were active in our local parish church. He helped run the Youth Club, I ran the Sunday School, we both sat on the PCC. These years gave me a much needed solid base. My husband had a clear understanding of church doctrine and an old fashioned sense of duty. But increasingly I felt we lacked a joint purpose. And we all lived happily ever after. Except we didn't.

Twelve years into a marriage (in which I was feeling increasingly restricted unfulfilled and irritated), at 39 , quite unexpectedly, I fell in love – with a woman. Total and absolute shock horror (mine that is). I could not believe it had happened to me. I had never even had an affair, never even flirted with either sex, my husband was my first partner. I never thought myself capable of such a thing. I had never knowingly met any gay people, and yet here I was, in the 1970s when gay people were almost invisible, knowing that I was "in love" and this with a woman. One of my male friends had once come out to me, and I still remember how horrified I was when he did so. And now it was me. I learnt at once how devious I could be. To watch every sentence so that no one should ever guess the dreadful truth. And this in itself was shocking as I had thought myself to be honest and trustworthy, but here I was keeping important parts of my life secret from my husband, my sisters, my parents. I felt I just had to keep this shameful thing secret. And yet I was very happy at the same time. I was 39 years old. Well, we both thought "we must be the only married lesbians in the world" – how ignorant, how ridiculous, but that is what we thought. We found a group in London called Sappho, a group where women who loved women got together to meet and to talk, mainly to talk. Several of us set up a support group for married lesbians. Sappho was home to Jacky Forster, a feminist dedicated to supporting women and she gave us all confidence and help. Sappho was very important to me for a long time, sadly it did eventually end for many reasons, but it fulfilled a purpose during the 70's and 80's when there were few places for gay women to meet outside a disco. Eventually my new love and I agreed to end our relationship but by then I was well and truly sure that I was indeed gay.

Life was exciting yes, and I made many new friends. But I also felt isolated. I felt I could not share this " new me" with my old friends. On the one hand I felt empowered and happy, and on the other hand so ashamed, guilty and wicked. Where had that come from if not from centuries of condemnation of gay life styles from all the major religions. Why was I so terrified to tell anyone? Where had that come from? When all we felt for each other was a compassionate love. But I wasn't to know that every Christian church would condemn us as "wicked." Particularly the Roman Catholic Church. I met several RC lesbians who were vitriolic about their former church, would never go back: had given it up forever. And although there was a group called "Quest" for Roman Catholic lesbian women it was not well supported at that time and most RC women I met were very damaged by their experiences, and wanted nothing to do with an organisation that had so demonised them.

It took 7 years before I decided we must plan separate lives. I took on my first full time work with local government and within the year my husband had moved to a new home and I moved back into the old one getting it ready to sell. The old married life was over, our two sons were at university, still I had not told my sisters what was going on, our foster daughter (who had stayed with us for a couple of years) had left us for the next phase in her life, and I was on my own again.

I needed a church when I left my family and moved into London. I needed a spiritual home after 15 years at a single parish church during my marriage and I was lucky to find St. James's in Piccadilly. The rector at that time was Rev. Donald Reeves who welcomed everyone (straight, gay, transsexual, black, old, young etc etc.) He and St. James's was as inclusive as it is possible to be. The church was attended by many lovely people, and oddballs, eccentric people, including myself. Two of us helped to set up a monthly lunch group where Christian gay people could meet (it's still there, extended to include bi, trans, anyone withan alternative sexuality). I think we did pride ourselves on being better than everyone else, in a humble sort of way you understand, but Donald provided a wonderful space where all spiritual ideas were discussed and taken seriously. "Alternatives," an organisation exploring spirituality of all kinds began to meet on Monday evenings, bringing in new ideas. However, I digress.

It had taken me nearly 10 years to end my marriage and to leave home – (you will see I have difficulty making decisions!) I enjoyed my new work but six years later as I was in the process of buying my own home, redundancy struck. I was in the second year of counselling training, and had to take a rapid decision: get re-deployed and give up the counselling training, or accept the redundancy and see what happened: I did the latter and with lots of help eventually set up a local bereavement service for the Borough I worked for - it was the only London borough without help for bereaved people at that time.

I threw all my energy into this, becoming co-ordinator, trainer, supervisor, a real one-woman band, but I did eventually obtained my diploma and accreditation with BACP. When I had begun my training I knew virtually nothing about the different therapeutic approaches. What lucky star directed me to Metanoia I shall never know. But I do know that I was extremely distressed/disturbed at finding myself lesbian, and at leaving my husband and boys (then aged 15 and 17), and of being unable to tell any of my family or friends about this. The first therapist I worked with was also a tutor at metanoia, so I suppose it was a natural step for me to go there when I decided to train.

Metanoia was my nearest counselling training and I joined their person-centred course. At the time the course was teaching pure Rogers, probably more so than any other college at that time. Metanoia means change and it has certainly changed and enriched my life. Two of the women tutors who had help set up Metanoia were partners; this felt very empowering to me: two lesbian women, competent and at the top of their field: where else could I feel so at home? Up till that time (I now realise) I had needed rules to know how to behave. I learned these from parents, schools, churches, society. I was a born conformist – a frightened little thing, scared of stepping out of line or being noticed in the wrong way. I only felt safe when following these rules: I was good at maths, music, tennis – I knew where I was because all these disciplines had their own rules. But socially rules can be very restrictive. At last at Metanoia I learnt a new way of managing my life: there were rules, but we called them boundaries, and boundaries make sense to me, indeed, I would if I could teach the whole world how to manage their lives bu using boundaries! (If only my adult children would ask for my help I could teach them too – but my experience is that young people think they know best about everything; sometimes some of us learn better before it is too late).

While I was dealing with my knowledge of myself as gay my sister was also changing partners. We talked for hours, but only about her. I could never breathe a word of what was going on for me: what stopped me? Shame / guilt / lack of confidence /? Actually it was sheer terror, and I don't even know what of. I had internalised the oppression that gay people have lived under for centuries. I still have great difficulty accepting myself as "OK". If I'm honest, I still wish it had never happened. Well I don't really, but life would be much easier as plain old hetero. I was always scared of rejection , and indeed when I did finally come out to my life-long Baptist friend, it proved to be the end of our friendship as she couldn't deal with this knowledge at all, didn't seem to want to discuss it – just knew it was wrong, and our regular correspondence and visits gradually ended.

It is still difficult for me to "come out" and I'm nearly 70. And of course because "being gay" is invisible (unless you choose to dress and act camp), no-one will ever guess. This means that every new acquaintance, at work, at home, needs to be told anew. For me this is always difficult.

I think that if I had not left my family I would never have had the motivation or energy or time to have trained as a counsellor. And this work has given me such satisfaction and variety I would never have had it different. My part time work has included work with bereaved people, telephone work for a helpline for a national newspaper, EAP work, private clients, regular work for an NHS trust, and supervision of other counsellors. I have never worked so hard or been so busy as during the 10 years following my redundancy. And I have enjoyed every minute.

I first qualified 15 years ago and during that time the three parts of my life have slowly become integrated into the person that is now me: my spiritual, emotional and intellectual life are all in agreement - comfortable with each other. I am happy with the answers I have wrenched from life, and I have a rough idea of why I am here - it may not be right, but I am happy with it. I don't know God's plan for me – why should I, how could I? but I am happy that there is one. And if God is proved not to exist, well, it makes no difference to how I behave. I fail of course all the time, but the Christian "Love your neighbour as yourself" combined with Rogers six core conditions are such a good rule to follow. There I go again: rules, I just can't escape! It works for me. I feel grounded and safe believing that love is the ultimate reconciliation for us all, and that Rogers' conditions work with everyone who wants to change their lives for the better. They work best I think within the counselling hour, but ultimately they work anywhere in life.

Roger's six conditions are grounded in love, compassion, care and understanding for others – who can ask for more? They seem to be a practical example of what is meant by "Love God and your neighbour as yourself". I don't think I would have survived counselling training of a different discipline; A spin-off of Rogers' person centred way of working is that ideally the therapist her/himself is changed in the way they think and therefore act in their whole world. Just like their clients. I found the first year very difficult to understand - I never believed that I could complete the training. I tried hard to give up, to leave after year one. It is extremely hard work learning to love yourself, to trust your feelings, to give yourself time and attention. For some of us I think it is a life-long quest. Fortunately good friends encouraged me to stay the course.

"Self-love runs the risk of being no more than self-deception if it is not solidly anchored in self-knowledge. The counsellor needs to cultivate the capacity to listen to herself, especially when such listening threatens to be painful or confusing. Not only is such an ability crucial to the development of self-awareness but it is also a basic aspect of the congruence or authenticity which will subsequently be offered to clients"

It is a long journey, becoming a counsellor. Life is long: where does the journey end?

When I was a small child, and an adolescent, I remember listening to grown-ups telling me to do what God wants, telling me to be good. And I remember wanting to cry out – "HOW DO I DO THAT?" I never could quite figure it out, because I never knew how to do this thing, even when I wanted to. Here in the Person centred way of being , I found the answer. I feel my eyes pricking even as I write this: it has been such powerful stuff for me. And I am not in the habit of admitting when I am deeply touched.

I was lucky not to have chosen to train in psycho-dynamic theory, because although I would have "fitted in" very well, the person centred way of working has proved more beneficial for my personal growth; not to have to have other peoples rules to follow, but to trust my own "actualising tendency" – for which I read "God". For me, congruence was both difficult and exciting - when I finally grasped its concept . I have the feeling that I am more easily able to hold my clients and allow them their doubts and uncertainties because I am able to hold my own as a result of an integration of my early understanding of the nature of God and of my discovery of Rogers' 6 conditions of worth.

The principles of person centred counselling resonate with the principles of my type of Christianity. Instinctively I recognize that this a natural way for me to work; I feel at home working this way. I see Rogers unconditional positive regard equating to "Love your neighbour as yourself" (Matthew 22 v 37-40) in the New Testament. So I have been affected by my early RE. I believe I have free will, and that a desirable choice of action for me (best in my own interests) is the one which Christ would choose (best in God's interests) because what God wants is what I want, and because what I want is also what God wants – what a minefield, what a standard to set myself. God has no "body" on this planet other than the one that belongs to you and the one belonging to me. This belief, this understanding, keeps me sane, and hopeful. It is tough. Not easy. It makes decisions both easier and harder at the same time. Harder because the compassionate response to others is rarely the easy choice for the person responding.

So I am, as an adult, affected by my early religious experiences. They gave me a deeply secure feeling of being loved, a knowledge that "I'm OK, you're OK", that "I am known", and this causes me to behave and feel differently from someone who may have grown up with no such religious understanding.

I hope I am affected positively (as I believe we are all affected one way or another) by my early childhood experiences. I may have discarded many basic Christian doctrinal beliefs – I could never go to the stake for belief in the virgin birth, transubstantiation, trinity, God as male only - but none of this is important to me. What is important is that I know that (for me) compassion forms a framework for a worthwhile and satisfying life. And it can do so for anyone who chooses the challenge.

REFERENCES

Mearns @ Thorne, "Person-Centred Counselling, page 24 SAGE Counselling in Actn
"Games people play", Eric Berne pub. Thomas Harris
Judges 6, v 37, a story of testing God
Matthew 22, v. 36/40
Carl Rogers 6 Core Conditions:
Empathy
Unconditional Positive Regard
Congruence
Psychological contact between therapist and client
Incongruence or anxiety of the client

Experience of a minimal level of the therapist's acceptance and empathy by the client.

Lucy Birtwistle

My Story

I was born in 1950 in a small Lincolnshire village where my father was the vicar. He had four rural parishes. His father had been a vicar as had both his grandfathers, great grandfathers and back beyond that. I had uncles who were clergy and we often holidayed with relatives in other vicarages which usually were large, cold and old fashioned, as well as exciting, having huge gardens. Portraits and photographs of clergy hung on the walls of our vicarage, and with my two brothers and sister I roamed in our overgrown garden. My mother was the youngest of five sisters and her parents were regular and active churchgoers as were her siblings, one of whom married a clergyman. My early years when we lived at our old vicarage seem relatively happy as I was keen to learn and couldn't wait to go to school. I was keen to please too, and believed that as the daughter of the vicar I was a bit different, though not sure how. I had to be good. I remember that was very important to me. There was also something about being respectable as a family, being above gossip. As part of the family at the Vicarage I felt that I lived in a goldfish bowl.

I had a strong sense of responsibility for others. I looked after my younger brother and sister with all the seriousness of an adult when I was still only a small child myself. I was in hospital for my fifth birthday, having had my tonsils and adenoids out, and recall how, on the journey home, I looked after my younger brother as though caring for him was the most natural thing in the world. My experience of being separated from my family for ten days whilst in hospital seemed to fade into unimportance.

I know that I feared harming others even accidentally - at my primary school I fell against another child in the playground and knocked his head against a wall and felt overwhelmed by horrid feelings that I would now call fear and guilt. At the time they seemed to be about getting into terrible trouble because I had done something awful to someone. I needed to be very careful and on my guard otherwise feelings with no name could overwhelm me. To help me I had an imaginary friend who lived down the drain of the downstairs toilet called "naughty Perry" and I can remember the conviction with which I could attribute all my wrongdoings to him-"It was not me —it was naughty Perry" I could say with sincerity. I would go to the drain to tell him off for his misdeeds and then feel at ease. I don't know when naughty Perry started to fade and go but I don't think that he was around much after I started school.

Around that age I could take myself into an altered state of awareness by saying "I am here now – not in a minute – I am here now". Colours would sharpen, I could float somewhere above myself and I had a wonderful feeling of peace and stillness. I could stay there for several minutes-or so it seemed-and I could do it at will by just saying the words. I could do it alone or in company and when others were there I could see and hear them and I really cared for them, they held no fear for me. The length of time I could do it for got shorter and by the time I was ten I don't think that I could do it at all. I once tried to tell my older brother because I wanted to share it and find out if he could do it too, but I couldn't find the words and I became embarrassed and we both ended up laughing. I do remember when I found out that I could no longer do it and I felt sad as if I had lost something rather special. I would stand and say the words and nothing would happen.

I loved being in my father's churches-they were very familiar and safe to me, and I played in the churchyards either on my own or with little friends. We would hang around the gravedigger, an old man called Percy who had been in the First World War and had a fascinating jagged scar all round his neck. His wife had a goitre so they made quite a remarkable couple. Being in the churches was special too because it meant that sometimes I could have my father to myself-he appeared happy to hear my non-stop chatter - he didn't say much but that didn't matter. When I asked him if he minded me playing on the graves, he said that when he was dead he would like to think of little children playing on his grave. Perhaps the Stations of the Cross was my strongest memory of being in Church. On Good Friday, dad would place Church prints of the stages of Jesus' journey to the cros-saround our village. He would take a short service which consisted of visiting each print and at each saying a prayer and reading from the Bible. Sometimes we would sing a hymn. Few people came - once or twice it was just me and my dad. That was really special. Neither of us could really sing, and we had no organist, but there was no discomfort between us.

There was a question that seemed really important to me when I was about 7 or 8 and I didn't know why - I really wanted to know whether Jesus' mother loved him because he was her son or because he was God's son. I asked my Dad and he looked a bit surprised but he gave me a respectful answer. I don't remember what it was now.

Going to the village school, going to Church, being at home was a seamless experience. All were fairly untroubled. My dad was in each-he was often at the school as he took assemblies and RE lessons and popped in from time to time. My mother was at home except for the time that she was in hospital for several days, and what I mainly remember is my resentment that my little sister was cared for by a friend in the village and was not at home. I can see me looking through the friend's gate and seeing her pram in their garden and feeling angry.

I took what I heard in church literally. I didn't know that there was any other way to take it. I was confused by some of what I heard and later, when I was old enough, read. Words that sounded so important and sure. Words that were so old and strong. Words said by my dad and my mum and by everybody that was in my village world. Words that talked of awfulness and sinning and the need to be forgiven - "I am not worthy to eat the crumbs that fall from your table. "I have not done those things which I ought to have done and I have done those things which I ought not to have done". I can see myself sitting with some adult in the congregation - being looked after - too young to sit by myself, perhaps sitting also with my older brother- and wondering what it was that I had done that deserved such words. I thought "I haven't murdered anyone." I knew that was the very worst. But there must have been something I had done that was bad. Had I done or said something that I shouldn't have? With effort I could always find something that fell into that category. I needed to try harder, that was clear. After all I knew what would happen if I didn't. The picture on the wall at home told me all about the sheep and the goats and the Day of Judgement - If you were good enough you went upwards and if not then it was down to the flames of Hell. It was about being saved and you could tell from the wispy smug expressions on the faces of the saved and the terror on the faces of the unsaved exactly who had managed to tread that narrow path in life. I really hoped that I would be good enough to go to Heaven. Hell was a very real place. Dad's books in the study showed me about Hell. I was both fascinated and frightened by one in particular. He had a large and heavy copy of *Paradise Lost* with prints of etchings by Gustave Dore. There was Satan, dark and fiery and terrifying. Time stood still as I looked through it and found myself transported to another dimension, no colour, very real and yet silent.

At this time I could walk away from Satan and Evil and my own unworthiness and be good enough to feel fairly safe-to turn from the books or leave the services and be a child absorbed in the next thing that took my interest. I was a lively and curious child with a strong sense of excitement-a side somewhat at odds with the serious part that was also evident. At the same time I was perhaps growing a little more afraid of doing wrong and, unsure what was wrong, leaving others in charge of telling me-others would know better. I had no way of knowing for myself. Once I could read I also read a Bible passage each night following a set of instructions and explanations in a little book that my father had given me-I felt watched and knew not to cheat by skipping a night, but sometimes I would read several in one night so that I could have a few nights off. When I was very little my father would say prayers beside my bed with me. Sometimes my older brother was there and we would whisper behind dad's back - I'm sure he knew but he continued quietly on.

The move to a New Vicarage just opposite the church coincided with my move to the local High School in the nearby town. It was only 5 miles away but it was also a world away. I was young for my year: having passed the Eleven Plus early I had missed out on lessons at my primary school and I struggled with schooling for the first time. Life darkened. I was not doing well. I was not sure who I was-I was not different in a nice way anymore - my dad did not come into school. I said nothing as I felt myself slipping. I felt scared of school, particularly of the authority it represented. I still went to church. It would not have occurred to me not to. I went through the rituals but it did not feel as if there was any overlap between my life out of the village and what church was saying. I don't remember turning to any words from church for comfort when I was at school, or feeling that what was said in church could help me-it just didn't seem relevant. The fact that I was young for my year in a group that had some street- wise girls in it and that I was the only one from my primary school in that class, gave me my first real impression of being very young and out of my depth. Now I felt different because I did not know what they were talking about either in the playground, or, sometimes in the classroom in lessons. I wanted to get home and go over to my friend who had a horse and go out with her and forget about school.

School did get sorted. I stayed down for a year and found with my year group more confidence and more friends. I had caught up on the work. I was keen to fit in and remained a good girl. I still felt awed by those who stood against authority - wondering how they could do it - where they got the courage to do that from. I was also more prone to "what if…" thoughts that seemed adhesive… reality and fantasy had an unclear boundary sometimes and I looked to others for guidance… anybody would know more than me.

Now it all goes a bit hazy. What I do know is that boys started to become really important. Not that I said anything -what was there to say? Sex was not a word that anyone mentioned- and I think that I mean "anyone". Not much on TV and acute embarrassment all round at home when it was. I imagine that was pretty standard for the early 60s in a small village. Any mention or portrayal of sex on television at home and the air would chill as some attempt was made to find a diversion.

I guess that I had been masturbating for a few years. I did not know that was what it was. I didn't know the name until many years later. To me it was an experience of pleasure and it was secret. The fantasies had changed over the years but I don't recall particular or growing unease. What I do know is that sometime in my early teens, at a level that I had no awareness of, I started to believe that this innocent and normal part of young womanhood was evil. It had to stop. I made a promise to the all seeing and all knowing God that I would never do it again. And I broke the promise and did.

Immediately afterwards I left the vicarage and walked down the lane behind the house. I felt condemned. I felt abandoned. God had never been more real or more angry. I had stepped into a different world. There was no undoing this sin. I had broken a promise to God. I could not go back to a time before I had sinned. Even the hedges and grass were now threatening, the sky too awful to look up at- this was an angry and unfriendly world. This was my eviction from the Garden of Eden, alone.

There had been so many words about God yet now I had no words to express myself, no language to explain what I felt, nothing that could put into a form what had happened.

I believed that the awfulness and terror that I felt at this time had given rise to a unique feeling that no-one else could know-it stood apart from everyone else's experience. I was in an isolated and very lonely place. I felt as though I had dropped a level, I had fallen down into something that I had not experienced before. I returned to the Vicarage and tried to act as normally as possible as I did not know what to say or who to talk to. I guess I also hoped that these feelings would just go away.

I tried to give reasons for my evident change to my parents but I was too ashamed and lost to find a way to tell them what had really happened, and so slowly I accepted that the help I badly needed would never be possible. My change was attributed to adolescence and I learnt to hide the depths of the despair I felt. Very gradually, after many months, the darkest days eased. I took what comfort I could from diversions and when heavily involved in some sporting activity or a book or film, I was able to forget how awful I was for a brief time. However, something was always waiting to pull me down- away from the shared world to the guilty one where there was nothing to celebrate and where my deeply shaming secret remained as raw as that first day. I learnt to be careful to avoid strong feelings wherever possible and the most successful way seemed to be to distance myself from myself by investing in others' lives and their well being. This also suited my barely conscious urge to keep on the right side of God by putting others first. I learnt to try and read others' needs and felt that I should meet those. I kept to a fairly narrow path, doing what I could to keep safe-safe from judgement and from criticism, safe from authority, and always anxious to get things right. I continued to carry my belief that even my thoughts had to be "good". I remembered the Bible passage that talked of God knowing what was inside the head of a lusting man.

I seemed to lose any remaining trust in my instinctive self- after all that instinctive desiring side was what had got me into so much trouble. Spontaneity could not be trusted. Likewise, how could I now trust my own judgement? I had been wrong and bad and I believed that I was someone who could not be trusted. God's words in Church had always told me that I was bad and needed forgiveness, now I felt it. I prayed earnestly for forgiveness and waited for the ease that would signify that I had been heard. It never came.

Over the years and with effort I managed to keep an outer life that looked successful-I achieved enough at school to go to university to study Law. I guess that Law appealed to my desire to get things right. My inner life remained a guilty and shaming secret, one that I didn't have words for, only feelings, and one I had become fearful of, and so frightened and ashamed of that fearful feeling that I had to be careful not to "touch" it, just as I had to be careful not to touch my body, except in a functional way.

At university I felt outside the 60's rebellion that was prevalent in universities at that time as young people discovered their identity and their power, and started to flex their muscles. I was daunted by the experience of leaving home and moving to a big city. I do not remember, either, being able to access in a way that felt relevant the feminist movement and its message of equality and empowerment. I had come to accept that authority in the world would lie with men and that I would find safety only within a conventional home environment.

I didn't really enjoy studying law but I didn't think that was relevant - it was a matter of getting on with it. It was during my 2nd year that I found that I could not keep my anxiety at bay by distraction and was referred to a psychiatrist. I again had no words to explain my feeling of distance, of unease and heaviness. With exams looming I returned to tell him that I was feeling better and that I needed to concentrate on my exams- I remember the not unkind but rather smug young face saying "I thought that was what would happen", and my sense of how small it had all been to him. I knew that nothing had changed and the demons would return when the fear of exams had eased.

I left university, went to law college and then to train as a solicitor. I don't feel as though I made decisions: I did what others in similar positions were doing - I went with the flow of what seemed to be expected of a young person doing the sort of course that I had done. I married another trainee solicitor whom I had met at university. We had been friends for two years before we went out, and I recognised in him a person that I could love and trust.

18 months after we married in 1974, my father died from cancer and heart failure. He had also had his leg amputated as a result of a blood clot. His dying took 6 months. That time is full of stark memories: The Hospitals, seeing him sitting silently staring into the fire and tapping his artificial leg with a stick, and perhaps most vividly, in his wheelchair taking Midnight Mass knowing that it would be his last Christmas. When I went up to take communion I timed it so that it would be him who gave it to me rather than his assistant. The only time that I cried openly was when he was very ill and I left him on the Monday morning to go back home to go to work and somehow knew that it would be the last time that I would see him. I have little conscious memory of finding comfort in a faith that I still acknowledged through church going. I was very caught up in the trauma of life and the belief that I had to try and sort out all that went with his death. My mother was in a state of shock and unthinkingly I took responsibilities that I could have shared more.

I remember praying beside his body before it was removed from the house to try and reconcile myself to the fact that he was no longer there. I kept telling myself that it was now just a shell and that he had gone.

During my father's illness, I did have some comfort from a small statue of Jesus that we had always had on the landing of my parents' house and talking to it as I went past-words that just asked for help. In my confusion with fear and chaos coming closer I did not know what I wanted or needed. I believed that I had to be "strong", which meant I had to keep the powerful feelings that were surrounding me at bay. I could be relied on to look after others and my own feelings were my own weakness. Phrases abound in various forms in church settings about the importance of putting others first though I don't remember that they ran through my mind in a conscious way. From today's place I do recognise that being good and not hurting others was firmly fixed. I am aware that there was a sort of mantra in my head that ran "it is better that you are hurt than that you hurt anyone else". I had to avoid guilt at all costs. That was not something that came in small doses-it arrived in an overwhelming fashion no matter what the cause.

I know that I sunk again, to a yet deeper level of loneliness and abandonment after my father's death. His death affected me greatly. I became more evidently anxious and the more I tried to avoid the feelings of grief that were swirling around me the more I felt myself sinking. I was one of the few women solicitors in my city at that time and had little by way of role models in that strong male culture to show how to be a feeling person and a competent one. I suspect that I was trying to be a middle-aged man to fit in. Of course it couldn't last. I started to have panic attacks – the worst being when I was appearing in court. Somehow I managed to carry on, although afterwards I told no one, not even my husband. I was ashamed of my weakness and hoped yet again that the horrid and unnamed, and therefore unspoken, feelings would stop. When they didn't I became adept at avoiding, so far as I could, situations that could trigger them. As I wanted a baby I believed that if I held on at work as long as I could then I could leave work without anyone knowing about my anxiety. I did not associate my anxiety with my father's death. I just felt that once again I was being assaulted by feelings with no name. After the panic attack in court, my fear that "it" might happen again deepened and I began to lose faith in my ability to speak publicly. I feared that my voice would not come or if it did it would shake so much that my terrified "child" would be seen, others would be horrified and they would turn away and I would be rejected. This was the start of my lifelong struggle to speak in public again, to believe that anxiety in public need not be shameful and could pass.

My first pregnancy ended in a late miscarriage. Although I tried not to grieve too openly, for a short time after I had lost the baby I had a sense of peace, as if at least now it was OK for me to feel sad and show it.

I left work in 1978 to have my first child. Black clouds had descended after I left work and had to manage unstructured time but these lifted with the birth and I felt more happy and excited than I could remember. I said to myself that this was what I was born to do-to be a mother. I also remember saying to myself that I need never be alone again. I was kept active and busy with the births of 2 more children. There was less time to think of myself and although storm clouds were never far away I could avoid my inner life more successfully. I was ashamed by my awareness that whilst I presented a calm and confident exterior I was hiding a frightened and confused child. I also had to work hard at avoiding mention of fathers or death as these words could propel me into sobbing with hardly any warning. With little success I sought help in the '80s with the anxiety that sometimes threatened to engulf me and stand in the way of my enjoyment of my children. At times I became very scared of my thoughts – I remember that I looked in the mirror one time and wondered who I was and what I was capable of-could I be trusted with my children?

All this time I was involved with one local church or another. I believed that if I found the right church then I would be comforted and reassured by what was familiar. We went as a family, my husband's Methodist upbringing fitting in quite neatly to the places we chose to go. In the settings we were in I said and did in an automatic and familiar fashion - I tried hard to believe what was said, and became more involved hoping that it would do for me what it appeared to do for others. I think, with a squirm, that I was quite proud of my churchgoing as if it marked me out as a good person.

Once my youngest child had gone to school I worked as a complaints investigator, originally for the Law Society and later for a secure mental hospital. Then, 15 years ago, out of curiosity, I started a listening skills course. I went from that course on to the Counselling Certificate, which I loved, and then on to the Diploma. I was excited by how life was starting to make sense for the first time: by that I mean that I was starting to understand myself and so lose some of the fear of myself and my thoughts and feelings. On the Diploma I recognised that I was deeply ashamed of my vulnerability and my anxiety level was "off the scale" at times as I waited to be "unmasked". My deep and unresolved grief for my father, which had been buried beneath my desire to prove myself as strong, was starting to emerge and be respected, even understood. At the same time I was also excited by the new friendships that I was making and the challenges that they presented to my existing and known world. Everything felt heightened and possible, perhaps there was more to me than I had believed there to be... and then... everything that was familiar and safe started to feel threatened. I slowly disappeared into a terrifying void in which all I could feel was a great sense of my own worthlessness. I had begun to see myself as two, one was on the ground and the other was above- they were held together by a thread which was becoming thinner and I knew what was coming. I knew that the thread would break and I would float. When it did become too thin to hold us together, I was above the ground with no connection to the other me, the reasoning me, on the ground. For three days my tenuous hold on reality snapped. At this stage, yet again, another, still lower, level seemed to have opened up beneath me and out of these depths an inner critical judge appeared in an overwhelming form condemning me for the questioning that was starting to challenge my familiar safe world. I could clearly see that part as male and uncompromising. I felt totally alone and terrified that I would be rejected for stepping out of some prescribed line.

I knew from when I first started my course that at some stage I would turn to look at my religious beliefs, but somewhere inside me a voice kept saying "not yet". I was fearful of doing too much too soon - what I had relied on for security was already being challenged and I couldn't risk that deepest challenge of all, of questioning God.

Now I was turning to Him for comfort and finding none. I did find comfort with family and friends, and understanding and sense making in my therapy, and I was able to continue with my course, neither surrendering to the old familiar patterns nor allowing the new to unground me to the extent that it had.

I completed my course, able for the first time to talk of my father and his death, having mourned for him during the course as though he had just died. My church-going remained in tact but something was starting to change.

I gradually left my work as a solicitor and started to work more as a counsellor. I worked in various places and set up a private practice. My energy seemed to be in that part of my life-my work, my family, friends. Life was full and demanding. At last I knew that I could share myself and be understood and that I was not alone with secrets that could not be put into words. I struggled on with my relentless fear and shame of wrongdoing but this did not stop me as I continued to discover the growing strength that came with thinking for myself, trusting in those thoughts and expressing them. I started to read more widely and less fearfully.

Around seven years ago I started feeling something new, a tension inside my head whenever my mind wandered to my regular churchgoing. My head felt heavy ,as if something was pushing from the inside and struggling to get out - I was almost there but "it", "something," was just out of reach but getting nearer. It came one Sunday as I left church and walked through the door I knew that I would never come back. Then outside the church came what I had been unable to reach and it was a question: the words were very clear - "Do you believe this?" ("this" seemed to centre around a virgin birth and Jesus' physical resurrection from the dead). And the answer was even clearer - "No".

The struggle was with putting the question into words - there was a bodily effort to find the question that was my question; as if I was treading through deep mud and yet had to keep going, knowing something was out there that could not be ignored, would not lie down. The impact of that moment was huge. The certainty that came with my newly found question and answer, and my ability to find words to form a question, provided me with strength to move from the church. I could not belong nowhere so the move had to be gradual-it had to have some connection to the familiar and there had to be no obligations. I went to the Minster so that I could be anonymous and yet retain some links with a church. I also knew at this time that I had to separate God and Jesus and that I could not doubt both. I still don't know why this was so important at that time but it was. I could feel safe enough if I could concentrate on one and feel some comfort from that thought but if both were there-joined –then I felt scared. I moved from one to the other. That gradually stopped being important.

I suppose that I knew that the place that I was heading to was Quakers. I had always known about the existence of the Society of Friends - the children had been to a Quaker secondary school and I had Quaker friends. When I was at my old church I became interested in the ecumenical movement and chaired the local group of churches, the Quakers being one of those churches. There was a very special moment when I went on an outing with that group to see the Quaker tapestry and read the words woven into it and realised that I was reading my own thoughts beautifully expressed. I then read more about Quakers and started to breathe a sigh of relief as I realised that here was a place where I could doubt in safety with others also doubting. I did not have to shoehorn myself into a creed or believe what I was told to believe. I could - and should - think for myself. Nothing was beyond limits. The word "God" did not have some sacred meaning that could never be expressed or explained and I began to form my own awareness of what it had been for me and what if anything, it had become now. I was more than a little uneasy to discover that the picture of God that I still held was the child's one of a bearded old man in the sky – he (very male) carried a stone tablet, the 10 commandments, scowled and had the narrow judgement of a vindictive village gossip. He was all-seeing and all-knowing - there was no privacy of thought or feeling and all had to be pure. Even now, at times, I can sense the power of that judgement in my fears that I can never be enough and that my actions do not stand up to scrutiny-and that the implications of all this are enormous - eternal. "Who is there for me when I transgress?" Even the words that come to mind belong to a different age.

There became a time when I had to show myself that I was no longer afraid and tell him to bugger off out of my life, he'd been a rotten little shit and I wanted no more to do with him. I had to be that angry and my language had to be that strong. I then needed to replace him with some other image otherwise he would sneak back. Sometimes I believe that God is music - a force that plays all the time and for all time and when I am in tune with the music I can move through everything that life holds and through all the awfulness. I do not have to learn the steps: I have always known them if only I can trust myself and let go of fear. It is not a pain free life that I ask for but perhaps I still seek an accompanied one.

Fear and Comfort seem to have been the twin arms of my faith. The comfort and accompaniment were there if I was "good". The comfort can still be very seductive as it promises an eternal presence through this life and beyond - "behold I am with you always even to the end of time". It manages my fear of abandonment. To assert myself as an individual feels, at this point in my life, to place myself in opposition to the beliefs and Creeds that I was brought up with and to stand apart. I no longer belong with my ancestors, all those clergy who seemed to be so certain and for whom the established church appeared enough.

About four years ago I decided that if I was going to take issue with the teachings that I had accepted for so long I had better go back to the source. So, not one to do things by halves, I set myself to read the Bible from beginning to end. I was horrified by the violence attributed to God's vengeful nature in the Old Testament. Though some of the passages were familiar, I was struck, as if for the first time, by the violence. I was reading them differently: I knew that they told of a very distant time and culture and yet these readings were an unchallenged part of my heritage and my early experience. I longed to get to the New Testament but I had promised myself not to skimp and I don't break even those silent promises! I got two thirds of the way through the Old Testament whilst I was on holiday in France with my husband. (I was also reading other books - my holiday reading did have some balance!)

We were staying in a fairly isolated cottage, doing holiday things, part of which has always been to explore the history of an area, and part of that was to visit local churches. I was enjoying these excursions although I remember one particular church in which one of the rich stained glass windows made a particular impression. I think it was of the three kings at Jesus's birth, and one had gloriously coloured robes and was kneeling with his back to me. The robes had an oriental look.

Over the next day or two, I could feel my spirits start to sink. I was dropping away from contact with my husband and with what was around me. It had been many years since I had felt this parallel world descend. My limbs started to freeze slowly and moving around felt difficult. A silence grew in my head. The owner of the cottage had asked us to look after some geraniums. For part of one day I took off all their dead leaves and carefully watered them - I still see myself doing that and knowing that that was all I could do. I kept looking at them and feeling the only good thing that seemed to be within reach, and that was some sense of satisfaction with how they now looked. I did not know why this had happened and I struggled unsuccessfully to use my therapeutic skills to find a connection, a way back. What came through to me was that I would have to go back. I had left something essential untapped in my own therapy. But for now I was scared - very scared. I had been lost in this world for a very long time in my teens and had spent many subsequent years avoiding anything that could re-activate it. I had looked at it in therapy and thought that it was settled-how come it had happened here and now?

My husband said that we would stop visiting the churches and that he thought that I should stop reading the Bible. We decided to do more where there were other people around and not take the walks that we had planned. Over the next few days I started to re-connect with what was going on around me.

That experience shook me. I can still feel unease sometimes when I am in unfamiliar places, particularly in awesome places such as the Alps, or when I see a great many religious pictures or artefacts in a short space of time. A recent holiday in Italy surrounded by beautiful paintings and sculptures, mainly religious and mainly sited in churches, showed me again how easily I can be swept back into a troubled state. The intensity is slowly easing, however, as I learn to fear the feelings less and share them more.

My most meaningful spiritual experience came on a short train journey about three years ago and it came through facing irrational anxiety. I find travel alone challenging but was giving myself a particularly hard time on this occasion before I left the house - that I should be uneasy about a journey that I had taken many times, that was so short and so simple seemed ridiculous. I decided to take a few moments to meditate, something that I do regularly, and try to accept that this was how it was for me. When I got on the train and sat down I was overcome with a sense of peace and connectedness that I had never known: not only was I a part of every one on that train but I belonged with the carriage and the whole train. With such a sharing and belonging what was there to fear? I had nothing to prove to anyone and a deep trust in myself. I have not had such an experience again.

What value can I find in my religious heritage? Some of my musings seem to contradict each other.

I lived in a village in an area of the country where there was not a lot of natural beauty - a flat countryside and a rather dull local town. Many of the village churches, however, are beautiful, and majestic, and sometimes awesome. They seem to capture the past and still to be a focus for the present, for the villages as they are now. The past is very present to me in a church, and in the graveyard I am fascinated by the stories that the gravestones tell. I grew up in one of the most interesting houses in the village, an old vicarage, and I passed a lot of my time in another fascinating building, the church. There was nothing dull or uninspiring about either. The church spoke of a life that was not mundane-that had another dimension-where miracles happened and angels appeared. It was full of little jobs that I felt pride in being able to do - I could put the cards telling the number of the hymns into the hymn board, and when I got older I could ring the bell. I had fun in church and a part of me still wants to be around old churches. When I visit my father's grave, outside the priest's door of his village church, I feel warmed by the sight of the church. I am unhappy going to any services. I don't know if I am afraid, but I am reluctant to enter the struggle to keep alive, away from the sleepiness that the so familiar words seem to induce.

Having been introduced so young to another "dimension", an insubstantial world where thoughts were known and judged by a being who lived in the sky with his son, his angels and his special dead people, I guess that I have gone on trying to make some sense of what that was really about. Without something to lay over it I could not leave it alone and it would not leave me alone, so my spiritual quest has not felt like an option. To be freer of my past I had to find out what it had been about. What I had been believing.

I am left today wondering about a faith that talks of virtue and goodness and our inherent unworthiness, that urges us to strive for perfection, and has so little to offer by way of how to achieve those impossible goals. I did not know what I was being asked to love -was it a person? An object? Outside myself, separate from myself? Only the fear of being judged had an essence that I could get hold of, that had a form, that I could put substance to and create a reality from, and that was what came alive for me. If I could believe that "it" was on my side it was a formidable ally, but I could not invoke that comfort from a place of imperfection. How could I believe that I was loved just as I was when so much told me of my sinfulness?

That life has a numinous quality, an otherness, I know, and I believe that it is my early life that has given me such certainty. For me conventional Christianity is not my path. It does not lead me closer to wonder. Jesus is my comfort only so long as he stays an amazing and human example of spiritual wisdom and love in action. Although I had hoped that Quakers would be my home, I think now that it may be a stepping stone to somewhere else, further away from Christianity.

I ask myself if my faith (and some of my development) stayed at what I now believe was an infantile level for so long partly because I was introduced to so much so early, and took what I heard as literally true –I did not know about metaphor or ritual or that I may have been offered a bridge to a world of sensing and mystery and that the rich language intended to convey passion and wonder. I guess that my father's experience was very different. I have an image of him putting on his vestments in his vestry before a service with chatter around him and feeling as though he had left me and was doing something meaningful-he was in his own world and it held real significance for him. His movements at the altar through the service likewise held him in a world that was separate - reverence is, I suppose, the Word. I didn't know where he was but he was somewhere else.

For me, religion as I received it stunted the first attempts at releasing inner desires and brought a lack of trust in my own instincts and wants. I craved safety and had a desperation to get things right, as there seemed to be some unnamed punishment for getting things wrong, even when done innocently. I became ashamed of, and distanced from, my body and my needs, trying to avoid an awareness of them. I avoided strong feelings wherever possible as feelings became something to be feared- they had become externalised, as though they were separate and were to be pacified by actions that would not upset them too much otherwise they could overwhelm me. Authority also rested outside of me, and at times I still invest authority figures with disproportionate power, just as I can recognise an over developed "authority" part of myself who needs to get things right.

In writing this, I have chosen to identify what, in my religious upbringing has, so far as I am aware, formed me. I do know that other experiences, and particularly other significant relationships which I have not explored here, have played their part, and that my view of God was created from many factors and influences. Who I was born as also gave me a particular view of the world - as far back as I can remember I have been trusting, curious and fearful. Also I would probably have benefited from hearing informed religious discussion when I was growing up, hearing that others whom I respected held differing views and were not afraid to question what I believed was unquestionable, and encouraged me to think more widely and for myself. Despite being a teenager in the 60's, there was a narrowness to my world, particularly my early world. My attachment to my father was a rich experience, and yet I wonder that if I could have risked falling out with him and coming back, I would have known I could risk more where there is love. I might also have known that it was for me to strike out on my own and follow my own path. I believe that life is woven and that for me the widest thread is religion. My image of the place of religion in my life is that there is a bridge to a spiritual life and that I was starting to cross this- religion may have formed part of that bridge —but then I hit a large windowless wall which barred my way. I could go no further until I had grown strong enough to get past that wall either by finding a way around it or sometimes by knocking through it with force. I had to get to beyond it and at times it has felt like a matter of life or death. Most of the time I now live beyond the wall.

Lindsay Smith

Religion and Me

I begin my story by introducing the various inner voices that have helped me write it. In this piece there are thoughts, from an adult perspective, and an 'inner voice' character called Sprite who asks questions from time to time. There are also recollections from the child's perspective pre-fixed by my childhood name Linnie.

Sprite is an authoritative part of me, untroubled by a need to please or anxiety. I have used her to ask straightforward questions. Connection with that part of me has helped me order my thoughts to write my story of a religious childhood.

Sprite: What do you remember about church and God?
Linnie: You went to church every Sunday and then you had dinner.

Underneath the pews in Christchurch in an itchy straw Easter hat… I was looking along those knees and legs under the pew. I liked the singing. The church was sunny and everyone looked happy.

Standing up in the dining room, family prayers, my dad said some words, I was quiet and put my hands together, I think my mum asked him to do it.

I got a tummy ache when I was asked to kneel down before bed and say my prayers, my knees hurt on the floor.

We went to the church at 'Gordon Square' because that's where it was. We sat in the gloom. An old man, the oldest man I'd ever seen, seemed to be the most important man in the church. I remember a lot of words, lots and lots of them, but the singing was nice.

We went in another room, which was dark too. A man talked to us about some stories about saints and other things. We were meant to learn something called a catechism. I don't think I learned it. I wasn't good at learning things off by heart.

One day my mum was gong to church on her own without me. We were in the drive, the gravel drive near the gate. I screamed and cried because I wanted to go with her, she still said no.

Sprite: Who is God?
Linnie: *(Draws a picture of an eye)*

A warning: God's eye. Watch for him coming.

The angel of death came up the gravel drive – we can't have been watching so he left a long slow death to the head of the household.

It wasn't our fault – we got punished.

My dad hurt

My mum hurt.

I hurt badly.

If you don't watch out bad things must come. If you are not waiting you will be hurt.

My daddy was the best daddy. They didn't make him a saint and they should of.

My dad's Christianity was gentle and normal. We went to church and he gave out the hymn books. He was a bit shy but he smiled at everybody. My mum was happy and proud. Then God came when we weren't ready and punished her.

I am so sad.

I tried and tried to believe in God's goodness but didn't succeed. As I got older my Mum wanted me to be saved so she went on and on about stuff that didn't make sense. I was scared of being bamboozled and scared of hurting her some more, and scared of being punished again. I didn't believe what she believed but I pretended I did. I pretended in church so the God might not notice, I was scared of that God who punished us by killing my Dad.

If God can kill your Daddy for being good, he can kill your Mummy too.

Sprite: How would you explain your religious heritage?

I was born in 1952 in Washington DC USA. My father was a British Army officer there for two or three years at the end of his career.

My parents met in India in the 1940's and both spent World War II travelling its length and breadth independently of one another. My parents married when the war ended, she was in her late thirties and my father in his forties. I was born when my mother was 45 years old. She was delighted to be able to have a family as by the time she was married she had given up the idea that she would. I am the youngest of three children. My brother was the oldest born five years before me. My sister is three years older than me.

My father was a quiet, conventional man. He was the treasurer of the church and a sidesman. He took a responsible role in helping out with the administration, and seemed to be an easy going average Church of England churchgoer. His parents seem to have had a similar involvement; I have little information about their thoughts on the subject.

My mother, by contrast, had a strong religious background. Her father, grandfather and great grandfather were all members of the Catholic Apostolic Church. Her mother had died when she was nine years old, and her father was a strong influence on her own faith and religious beliefs.

Sprite: What was the biggest religious influence in your family?

The Catholic Apostolic Church was the dominant influence in my maternal family for many generations. My mother's beliefs were powerful.

The Catholic Apostolic Church (CAC) was founded in 1835 by the members of a movement interested in spiritual events, healings, speaking in tongues and utterances of prophesies which were seen to be a sign that the world was approaching the time of judgement heralding the return of Christ. The founders were strong believers in the Old Testament.

The movement was preoccupied with eschatology – the part of theology concerned with death, judgement and destiny. The founders were expecting the Apocalypse imminently and twelve 'apostles' were appointed.

My great, great grandfather was a founder member of the Church in Edinburgh and from 1856 ordained an 'Angel'. (These appointments were made by the 'Apostles'.) My great grandfather was Archdeacon in the same church and became an 'Archangel' in 1895.

My grandfather was also a member of the CAC (third generation) followed in turn by my mother now a fourth generation member.

Once all the apostles died, there were to be no further apostles, as it was believed that they could only be appointed by Divine intervention, and in this way the church had a built in obsolescence. The last surviving priest died at the age of 95 in 1971 when I was nineteen years old. Members of the church and their post-clergy descendants describe time after this as the 'Time of Silence'.

'The members regard the 'Lord's Work' as having been withdrawn by divine act because of the rejection of the apostolic witness by the Christian Church as a whole.' (Flegg, 1992)

My mother would describe this to me, but I found it hard to grasp. I assumed that I was one of the ones who had 'rejected the witness' even though I had never been clear about the 'witness' in the first place.

There is in the CAC movement a resistance to any challenge to the doctrine. The history has evidence of dramatic excommunications and schisms. I have found this to be a feature of other doctrinaire organisations which have relevance in a later part of my story.

My mother is the key part in my story in relation to religion, as her beliefs came from this highly prescribed and doctrinaire background. In some ways I think as an infant my parents, particularly my mother, became the personification of my perception of God.

My grandmother died suddenly in 1918, when my mother was nine years old. After my grandmother's death my mother and uncle never had a home. My mother described a nomadic existence in relatives' homes, some welcoming and some not, a happy sojourn in a French boarding school, and in the holidays staying in hotels with their father. Here they invariably got into trouble for being noisy (being children). My mother did her best to grow into her mother's shoes, protecting her little brother and trying to help her father. Her father married again which my mum rather resented, but she later became resigned and learned to respect her stepmother.

My grandfather died when my mother was in her twenties. After her father died my mother moved to India to live with her brother who was by then an Assistant District Commissioner in the Indian Civil Service, working in a remote hill station. She was in India through most of the Second World War but spent one year in Iran (then Persia). She met my father and returned to the UK to be married in 'Gordon Square' when war in the East was over.

The Catholic Apostolic Church (CAC), as my mother explained it, wanted to unite people of Christian faith, she believed you should worship at your own parish church, and at the CAC church when you could and not as an alternative. Consequently we usually attended our C of E church but once a month or so, and on religious festivals we might also attend a CAC church. There was more than one of these in London where I was brought up but we were 'regulars' at the one in Gordon Square.

My mother was a charismatic, hospitable, generous and loving parent. She was also unpredictably strict, doctrinaire, uninhibited and creative. I remember the power of this especially when I was younger. She would love to sing to us, to play, and encouraged us to express ourselves in games of dressing up, doing little 'shows' (which we called 'circuses'), in the garden, swimming, cycling, and cooking. She was keen on family activities like picnics and sledging. She was especially attentive if any of us were ill, taking great pains to keep us comfortable and entertained. I think she nurtured us physically in a way she had not been nurtured.

She was a person who would speak her mind. There were many expressions of right and wrong but these did not involve physical punishment. However, she could be sharp and unforgiving. She had few secular expectations of her children and 'do your best' was a supportive philosophy. She carried a strong central vein of sadness and grief that I experienced when I turned nine or so, there was not a verbal expression of this but I remember her look of repose was of enormous sadness and worry. This she often projected onto me, noticing me as 'highly strung'. She could laugh loudly, and readily, and had a sophisticated sense of humour. As we got older my mother became increasingly controlling. She found the late 50's and 60's culture frightening, and fought hard to retain her vision of what a family should be, and how good Christians should behave.

My mother's interpretations of her religious beliefs were contradictory, confusing, illogical and not open to question. In common with the CAC teachings my mother maintained a level of secrecy 'we are not meant to talk about these things,' and yet wanted very much to teach me of the liturgy and theology of her church. The CAC had a preoccupation with control, order and hierarchy and I felt its influence as more and more suffocating the older I became.

My mother was an embodiment of her principles, and I admired this. Hers was a 'lived out' faith. She felt it her duty to care for others who may be disadvantaged, ill or alone. This was not only a Christian duty, it was, I believe, fuelled by her own experience of emotional neglect. She would 'adopt' people in trouble. She would cook for them, take them to appointments in her car, and try to sort out their financial difficulties. There would be no distinction made between people like Miss Batley (a lady from church with mental health problems) and Len, an isolated, depressed man living on a notorious estate in Mitcham that I think she met at a bus stop. This sense of duty was lived out even when she was in her late seventies. She was also committed to reading her scripture every day, gave her stipend reliably and was generous in her support of charitable organisations.

My mother exhibited little or no fear of strangers, or people different from herself. She would not be fazed by a drunk on the tube or a tramp sleeping in our caravan outside the front of our house. By contrast I always felt anxiety and fear in the face of difference. When she would encourage me to accompany her on one of her visits I would resist entering houses, I would be resentful at the time she spent on those people and guilty because when it came to it I was not as kind a person as she was able to be.

The themes that my mother spoke about were apocalyptic, she saw hope in the solution of the world's problems by the second coming. It gave her a feeling that she had some control over world events and also some responsibility for these. There was the promise of being saved from death. There was an emphasis on oratory skills which I translated to mean that I should be very interesting when I spoke and if there was a chance that I wouldn't be it was probably best to keep quiet. There was definitely an expectation that one should 'Speak Out' and stand up for what one believed. This I also experienced as a pressure, as it exacerbated my sense of responsibility for the 'wickedness' in the world. The stories she told would include miracles and messages from beyond that I mixed up with magic in my imagination.

Sprite: What's the connection between the Catholic Apostolic Church and your dad's illness and being sent away to school?

There is a history of childhood loss in my maternal family, and I believe the combination of that loss and the particular religious background provided a rather toxic heritage for me.

My father was an easy-going, quiet, balanced man with a strong sense of humour. He died when I was twelve years old, after an illness that my brother and I calculate began four years earlier. Initially my father became confused, getting up in the middle of the night to go to work, losing his way, anxious that he had neglected some task at a job he had retired from. This was followed by physical deterioration; he would wet himself, he would complain of pain, he had falls.

When my father first became ill he was mistakenly diagnosed with depression and was prescribed ECT. My mother and I (possibly my sister and brother too) went to visit him in hospital. I was eight years old.

My father's illness progressed and for at least two years my Dad was bedridden, with little movement, doubly incontinent and without speech. As an eight to twelve year old this was a disturbing experience and its effect on me was one of a gradual breakdown of trust in the world. The certainties I had enjoyed seemed fragile and my fears increased.

The first time I saw my father in bed in the hospital, I ran towards him with my arms outstretched. He recoiled in anticipation of pain if I were to touch him "They have stuck needles in me!" he shouted. I was rooted to the spot and I believe that in that moment my eight year old spontaneity was stunted and frozen. My spontaneity remained largely inaccessible for three decades, and if ever it surfaced I would shame myself deeply, particularly if it was met with any hint of disapproval.

I became acutely focussed on my mother, and her responses to me and particularly any of my misdemeanours became exaggerated. I broke a mixing bowl when she was out, and waited at the front window for hours to be sure to 'confess' on her return, desperate to be forgiven. She was reassuring but puzzled.

Like all children, I only knew my family – so it seemed normal to have an invalid in the front room. However, it was not easily explained to visiting friends, so I was keen to spend time at my best friend's home, sleeping over if possible, as here life was simpler and straightforward. Her mum gave me some special attention. This could lead to conflict as my mother would sometimes insist I come home to sleep (she wanted to see me, I imagine) when I just wanted to be at Sally's house.

My mother determined to nurse my dad at home and normalised this as much as she could. For the four years of his illness, we would kiss him goodnight each evening. I would try to 'nurse' my Dad. I would wrap him up in a scarf when he was sitting in a wheelchair in the garden. At other times I remember crossing the hall and hearing him shout out in pain, confusion or distress I wasn't sure which. He would look at you but there was no hint of him behind the eyes. There was no measure of his consciousness, but we knew to continue to respect that he might still be there.

I have traced back a history of four generations on my mother's side in which children of a similar age lost a parent. I think that the religious persuasion of my maternal family would not have helped them support, hold or comfort grieving children.

I don't know if it occurred before or after my father's illness, but I was a child that felt it her duty to look after others, and to sublimate my own needs.

Later in this period I failed my Eleven Plus as I had gone from being a bright, inquiring child to one who had lost a of understanding, and had become rather timid and confused. My mum decided (along with my uncle) that I might best benefit from going to boarding school. I also felt that perhaps looking after me was a bit of a strain for my mum and I could help out by agreeing.

Little did I realise that separation from my mother and sister (who had refused to go), would cause me so much emotional anxiety and pain. I managed boarding school well, finding friends quite easily and relating well to other girls. I was average academically and ticked over. However, the beginning of terms and the end of half terms were a terrible ordeal for me. I would get anxious many days before an impending separation; I would have panic attacks, bad dreams and devise as many strategies as I could to avoid the pain.

Religion at school was an every day occurrence, and at times I am sure I was quite pious. I think I was keen to think there was a safer container for my life than I had actually experienced. I don't think I could be brave enough to question what I was told. In some ways the fact that religion in school was so much more liberal and less significant that what was taught to me at home, gave me some freedom.

What was squashed in my need to conform and please, and not worry others, was my creativity and my spirit. I think I kept it going somehow, but it was hidden, and protected. Hiding this part of me became more important as I got older, because of my exaggerated feelings of hurt and rejection when I displeased people.

My father died in 1964 when I was twelve years old. I was in isolation in the sick bay at school when I heard the news.

This is the poem that I wrote in my fifties that describes the experience.

Bad News

I hadn' t practiced my piece.
I could avoid the freezing gutsick by pretending another illness.
Keep shame secret.
An excuse would douse the acid on my teacher's tongue.
So I caught the measles.
I was isolated in the gatehouse. I used the window to watch.
Entertainment

like TV and comics could broadcast germs like friends.
I watched the hockey players skidding on the flat field.
Wet girl's soles spreading puddles.
The shouts and whistles prisoners to the afternoon mist.
Watched the housemistress coming.
She looked like Jackie Kennedy at the funeral we stayed up for.
Widow composed.
In a short coat she trod her script to the tarmac path.
I waited, another widow's child.
With bad news she left sweets on the windowsill in an ornate jar.
Some white, some purple.
I thought I saw relief in their resilience.
I sucked one sweet each day ritual rationing the comfort.
Before and after.
One white, one purple.
I watched the school lights across the dark field and swallowed.
I hadn't practised my piece.

Sprite: So how did these experiences affect you in your teens and into adult life?

My mother's 'sermons' would be ignited as though you had switched her on. The trigger could be anything to do with bigger questions in life. Relationships, education, politics, anything could kick start it. Anything that was connected in any way to beliefs, values and behaviour was a touch paper. She would switch into sermonising and that would last for hours unless you could distract her out of it with an errand that needed to be run, a meal to be cooked, something practical.

I would respond to these sermons with a shutting down of senses, this would mean I would look as though I was listening, I would look intently, and make the right paraphrases, nod in the right places and make verbal prompts. Inside my stomach would hold an acid feeling of fear and guilt, guilt for pretending.

My adult life has been characterised by frequent feelings of guilt, which I feel are fading now after several productive years with a gifted therapist. I have lived with the sense that I should at all times be open to the pain and suffering of others – wherever they are, whoever they are and that I should act on relieving that suffering.

If I come across something that's 'not right' I should do something. Never pass by on the other side. I have developed a paradoxical defensiveness about requests for charitable work, resenting being asked to 'do good' like being phoned up by a charity to see if I will do a collection locally. This is mixed with the automatic physical response of guilt (the freezing gutsick I mention in the poem).

If I make a mistake and feel shame the first thing I want to do is to disappear – run away, get someone else to take it away. The need for forgiveness is almost compulsive; I become absolutely preoccupied with the anxiety of holding my guilt and planning the various ways in which to rid myself of it. Profuse, unnecessary extended apologising is one. Exaggerating and catastrophising is another. In recent years this feeling has been easier to contain, and lasts for less time. More recently I can contain the first flood of feeling and manage it better.

Guilt around sex and physical intimacy is an aspect of religious influence (or possibly under the guise of religious influence) which I believe was a damaging, constraining force in my late childhood, adolescence and into my adulthood. We were always encouraged to 'be modest' and 'cover up' from being quite small. My mother herself was ashamed of her own body and would demand that we 'not look' if ever we had to go in the bathroom when she was there. As I grew up and matured I found it difficult to accept any sexual feelings. This coupled with a highly exaggerated romanticised view of relationships led to some difficulties for me.

I could fall for someone and have romantic fantasies about that person but these would always be secret and undeclared. I would contrive to be close to them and engage in a somatic intimacy, an illusory consummation but any hint of physical contact I found shaming. So if a boy kissed me or touched me in any way I would find it frightening and I would experience feelings of dislocation from my body. I could become very scared and guilty very quickly, and this would be compounded by a sense of frustration at my hang-ups.

I associate some of the difficulties I had with expressing myself sexually as resulting from my letting my mother down by breaking a taboo, an unspoken rule. In even talking about sex I was exploding the family myth of sexual innocence as a presumed and desired state. Since my mother's perception was that sex outside marriage was a sin, she would have been frightened to admit to her own sexuality.

After going out with a boy for over a year I went on the pill. He did encourage me. He was called Paul. I didn't love Paul but we got on OK and he was a kind boy. Eventually he fell in love with me, but I didn't feel the same strength of feelings. I didn't tell him that because I didn't want to hurt him.

My mother must have discovered the pills, perhaps unconsciously my guilt made me let this happen. She asked me and I told the truth. I was flooded with shame. I was a nineteen year old woman, and I became an eight or nine year old girl. I was desperate for forgiveness. Desperate for her to forgive me this 'sin'. I promised all sorts. She went very cold on me. I got more desperate. I remember wanting so much to regain her love that I climbed into her bed with her, no forgiveness was forthcoming. I had a miserable few days and it was never spoken about again. Rejection was a big fear for me. Honesty about adult relationships and worries were kept away from my mother. I continued to struggle for my sexual independence from both mother and God, and although I have been able to recover, I am not sure the influence of those rules and regulations have been completely extinguished.

Sprite: What frightened you so much?

I was brought up with the Old Testament stories and the imagery to go with it. I imagine the crucifixion. The death of Christ, this quiet, wholly innocent man being murdered, the graphic torture and killing of Jesus, brings home to me the religious ideas and images that seeped into me in childhood.

While ever this murder was explained as a 'loving gesture' to the world, the justification seemed illogical. The use of the graphic representation of this killing as a symbol of Christianity carried a threatening and frightening message to me. The story of horror and terror was told in matter of fact ways, without fuss. This again seemed wholly confusing and when my father died it became more significant. My experience of the painful and slow death of my wholly innocent father gave this repeated image vivid connotations. I think it led me to a profound mistrust of the world. Perhaps this is a realistic mistrust, but introduced in my life before I had built sufficient resources to manage the threat and keep it in proportion.

Sprite: How has it affected you?

I find it very difficult to watch a film involving conflict, tension or violence; I suspend my disbelief easily and quickly. To watch a film featuring graphic images, particularly those of violence, is to experience it first hand, to be there as a witness and yet unable to act on the events in any way.

When I watched the film *Apocalypse Now* at the cinema it had a profound effect on me. I found myself in a state of distress, I think I experienced a kind of secondary trauma. I was incapable of conversation, tearful, and experienced flashbacks that led to sleep disturbance for several weeks afterwards. I appreciate that others may have been similarly affected, but I think the level of my reaction was out of proportion to that of others I have spoken to.

I think the graphic stories and imagery that was a backdrop to my childhood meant that in adulthood I subconsciously protect myself from anything that might surprise or disturb. This means I am rather closed to new experiences, and there are many films I have avoided which I believe could potentially have been thought provoking, expanding educational, even inspirational. This extends to music and graphic art also. I think the boundary between reality and imagery is thin for me, and I fear the intrusion of apocalyptic ideas that may overwhelm me or take me over in some way. I am inclined to be very wary of new art in all its forms.

Exposure to eschatological ideas (death, judgement, and destiny) and the imagery to match occurred when I was too young to hold representations of distressing events, those of pain, violence and injustice that were framed in a realistic way. The power of images are such that flashbacks from stories often come to me at times when I am living free – at a party after a couple of drinks, at times of family celebrations at intimate times of joy. The effect is one of killing positive feelings. In addition the fear of spontaneity leads to further reductions in spontaneity.

In adulthood I have difficulties in feeling I have the right to live in the fullest sense of the word, to experience carefree moments, without a sharp edge of darkness and despair. I am inhibited from a capacity to experience joy, to be spontaneous, to love, to laugh to speak out. I think I will tempt fate if I don't prepare for the worst, and therefore guard against any unbridled pleasure in anything. As I write these words I hear the generations of puritans in my family. I hear loudly the Scots Presbyterianism and gloom that emits from that brand of religion. I hear pessimism and negativity and recognise these in me.

I have managed the fear I hold in many ways. Being good and kind as a child and as an adult have been dominating scripts. I like institutions and hierarchies and rituals as these help me to know which tribe I belong to, and how to behave and keep safe. The script that led me to becoming an educator and a counsellor has an obvious source.

One time I did get angry, and it helped me survive, grow and change.

I was living at home with my mother in my early twenties, having spent much of my life living away. I had recently returned home to live after spending a year in a residential job, working at a children's home. I had started teacher training college but had to live at home for economic reasons.

The film *Blow Up* was on the TV and I wanted to watch it. My mother forbade it. I insisted I wanted to watch it. Eventually she turned off the TV and refused to allow it. I fled the house in a rage of tears. It was late in the evening and I walked and walked, it was a survival moment. I saw her drive by in her car looking for me obviously worried, but my anger was so great I didn't show myself. I stayed out very late and crept into my bedroom where I spent a sleepless night.

The next day early I left the house and went to Linda's house. Linda was a new friend I had made at college. We had only recently discussed getting a flat together. Her mother greeted me at the door and offered me whisky in tea as I clearly looked distraught.

Linda encouraged me to go to the doctor as I was suffering anxiety with depression, nausea and occasional panic attacks. These symptoms persisted for a few months. They felt lonely months despite moving from home into a flat with Linda as we'd planned. In a way I think my Mum understood. She helped me out financially so I could afford it.

I was assessed by a psychiatrist and placed in a therapy group.

Somewhere in my notes is the history that was taken by the psychiatrist at St. George's. He made no comment, but giving my history I realised I was troubled at that time in my life. It was the first dawning of awareness that my background had been a challenging one for me, and that I wasn't completely psychologically well.

Looking back I think I was brave to break away from my mother's need to control me. My request for help was a sensible bid for freedom. I was unlucky not to find quite the right kind of help at that time, but an acknowledgement that to stay at home and be swallowed up by my mother's beliefs, needs and culture would be to forfeit my health and freedom.

My mother's behaviour acknowledged this, perhaps she knew it too. She surprised me on occasions with her unconditional acceptance. Once around this time I had a disastrous attempt at a summer job in a hotel in Tenby, Wales. I returned within 24 hours deeply depressed. My mother tucked me up in bed, and allowed me time to 'be' and recover at home. She asked no questions. She encouraged me in my studies and I recovered with her care.

There was nothing much consistent about my mother.

Sprite: You have left out the story of losing your sister to a different religion

My sister left the UK when she was nineteen and I sixteen, it was 1970. She had become involved with Scientology through a boyfriend. She was keen to involve me in the excitement of her new-found doctrine. I was not attracted to another set of elaborate and illogical beliefs, and had already adopted the role of the daughter who needed to protect my mother's feelings.

The fight to stop my sister from being absorbed into the cult of Scientology took place between herself and my mother and uncle. I was young and a bit-player, but through my own responses to my mother's religion I recognised my sister's need to escape. She got married quickly to an American scientologist and within weeks she emigrated. The marriage did not last long, there was an amicable separation, but it emerged that her new husband was suffering with Hodgkinson's Lymphoma. He died nine months after they were married.

I was seventeen and at still at boarding school when I received the news of my brother-in law's death. It hit me very hard and I experienced numbness and shock which seemed to be excessive considering this was a man I had met briefly on two occasions, one of which was his wedding day. I think my response was a delayed reaction to both the death of my father, and the abrupt and unexpected separation from my only and beloved sister.

It is not surprising that a person brought up with absolutes in a doctrinaire church should find themselves drawn to an alternative and I feel that in this case Scientology robbed me of my sister. We have always maintained a contact but I have seen her only five times in the forty years she has lived in America. There have been restrictions on the contact between us and, up to 2008, would say that my sister had disappeared and an automaton had replaced her. However, that exagger-ated estrangement was ended in the summer of that year. I was able to meet with her on neutral ground. Here we were able to spend a couple of hours conversation in a Maryland coffee shop we were able to share something of our separate jour-neys. We were at last able to exchange truths about the past, share tears, regrets and misunderstandings.

In 1978 I married my husband. We had lived together as students and had a happy, largely uncomplicated relationship. I think that part of my attraction to my husband was the personality traits that I associate with my mother. Strong beliefs, that should be acted on, principles about making the world better, respect for the natural world, and support for those who suffer.

Shortly after we were married we bought our first house. My husband is a Marxist, and his beliefs are strong and uncompromising. I think he felt oppressed when we bought into the constraints of a mortgage. We were beginning to feel the effects of the newly-elected Thatcher era, and I too felt angry and betrayed that my sense of optimism in the future was being trashed, my values ignored.

My husband had been interested in the Worker's Revolutionary Party since college and became involved again. I was at first quite enthusiastic, although not to the extent of wishing to join myself. As the months progressed he became more involved and from my perspective I started to hear 'sermons' again. I did my best to keep open to the ideas, and to understand the principles which he was practising. Increasingly this became harder and harder, and I fell back on the light switch reaction.

After many months of misery I decided I had to leave to survive. This, coupled with a rift and schism that was emerging in the WRP, generated a new perspective for my husband. He decided to withdraw from the party and we began to repair our relationship.

I still have difficulty with strong belief systems, and feel resistant to any of those with a doctrine attached. I have strong ambivalence being both attracted and resistant to structure ways of behaving in organised hierarchies. I think I would be easily institutionalised and felt the safety of that in boarding school life. However, I have a fear of being 'taken over' and that extends to a deep suspicion of things that might influence me. My responses to new and provocative experiences are similar to my response to strongly argued ideas and perceptions. I am both drawn to them and actively cynical. This leads to a kind of atrophy at times, the drive to do something about injustices and inequalities with a fear of being duped by a doctrine or swallowed up by an organisation.

Sprite: What about other forms of spirituality?

I have had a very few experiences that I would want to characterise as 'spiritual'. As an earnest child and young adult I would certainly have been on the lookout for some sign or other to follow as I was insecure in the modern world and confused by all its mixed messages.

I can remember really trying to make my father appear after his death; a little concerned about ghosts, but still felt that he could reassure me from beyond the grave. It never happened, and I came to think of myself as just not that kind of person, not deep and not spiritual. I think my life experience has done little to alter that perception.

I have, however, had profound responses to people, situations and to some landscapes.

My mother had a curious interest in standing stones and early Bronze Age sites which I have inherited.

I remember being about fifteen when my mother visited school and took me to a Bronze Age burial mound which was hidden behind a farmhouse somewhere deep in Wiltshire. We had to borrow a torch and get directions from the farm house and stooped low as we entered the stone-lined barrow. I remember being very moved by the experience, imagining the burials of people so long ago, and in a curious way I found it very reassuring. I think in two ways. One because we were dealing with pre-Christian history so little chance for any sermonising – and indeed I remember none. The other that spirituality didn't have to mean rules and regulations, but seemed to be more about respecting and valuing the dead in relation to the landscape.

So I am not without a spiritual sense, although it is muted in me and not tied to any coherent group of ideas.

Sprite: Tell them about Karen

She and I were at teacher training college. I was a public school girl and she a working class girl from Middleton in Manchester. I was instantly drawn to her; she was funny and friendly, warm and kind.

We both had religious histories; she had a very strict catholic background. I think we were both scared of the liberal times in which we were living which clashed so fundamentally with our parents' expectations of us. We have kept in touch over many years and although we don't meet often I experience her as honest and reliable.

I have had experiences that involve Karen where I have experienced something beyond words, a healing effect that I cannot explain.

Unlike me Karen's path away from the organised and oppressive religiousness of her youth has taken her to alternative beliefs and she has trained in, and practises a number of therapies, none of them mainstream. Karen is a very unusual alternative practitioner in that her Mancunian wit and her inside experience of working class life and people make her someone who is grounded and earthed and for me, therefore, someone in whom I can trust.

One very hot summer when my children were very little and I was exhausted from a long academic year as a lecturer she offered me a treatment which involved no touch. I, desperate for some care and attention, happily volunteered. After it finished, I felt nauseous, dizzy and overwhelmed. Gradually this passed and I felt relaxed and enervated. I was surprised and suspicious that such an unscientific treatment could have an effect.

I witnessed this on another occasion when Karen visited us and gave a treatment to my daughter who was suffering from a virus with a temperature and sickness. Her fidgety distress left her and she slept for three or four hours, then woke without a temperature and ready to go.

Karen continues to be a close friend, and yet I struggle with her openness and commitment to new ideas and concepts (angels, past-lives, spiritualism). She is a trustworthy, honest and grounded individual and I cannot deny her truth. I think I might be more open to spiritual matters if I didn't feel the need to protect myself from being 'taken over'.

Another experience I find difficult to admit, given my fierce wish to be an absolute and confirmed atheist without doubts.

For several years at Christmastime I would be a bit disappointed with the celebration. The Christian elements of the festival held the connotations of myths to which I no longer wished to give credibility. That left a gap that was filled by my secular family with food, drink and presents. I found this lacked something for me so I took to attending communion at York Minster along with any number of other fairweather attendants. I most often went alone, but met up with my like-minded friend Sally. We were both ex boarding-schoolers who could enjoy a good carol and the atmosphere that such a beautiful religious building can provide.

One year I had been suffering with a bad cold, and felt really unwell as I walked down to the Minster. I had a headache, blocked nose and cough. I met Sally and we took our places at the back. I felt sweaty and shivery by turns and rather questioned why I had come out. I could no longer take communion with integrity so offered my bowed head for a blessing as invited. An unprepossessing bearded clergyman was in charge of the bread and passed his plate to his colleague placing his hands gently on my head. I felt a strong heat enter my head and pass down into my body. I was puzzled and oddly discomforted to have received this.

Sprite: So what's left? What do you believe now?

In preparation for writing this account I went on a visit to the Church of Christ the King my mother's church ('Gordon Square') London.

The church is closed to non-CAC members but was open for a service by a group called Forward in Faith. They turned out to be group against the ordination of women, not an organisation that I have any sympathy with!

At the beginning I was curious and intrigued; I enjoyed the familiar poetry of the hymns. As the service progressed I felt less and less, regarding any resonance of faith. All the words spoken seemed to be judgemental and contradictory.

For once I became aware of the threat and how it still has some power for me. If you don't believe in God, that is the worst sin, not sinning but not believing.

I began to experience the dilemma as anxiety. Here was I not believing and at the same time wanting to be understood and forgiven for not believing. I am up for judgement and I think I have avoided sinning too (watch out for pride there), but I don't believe in God so I am condemned to eternal punishment however well I behave. I still hold an irrational fear of judgement and want to be forgiven for my lack of faith.

Sprite: What kind of a caring, loving God does that?
Linnie: Well they say that you have to have faith, and if I don't believe then of course I'm not going to have the love of God… and I am condemned to eternal punishment

I got uncomfortable in the service, I felt alienated, bored, angry guilty and fearful. I certainly wasn't immune to the ideas being spread around here.

Sprite: So what were you left with?

The visit confirmed for me that I do not believe in the Bible's philosophy. I don't believe in the God described by religion, and I can survive being different from those that do believe. I can continue to behave well without the need for religion to tell me how to behave.

If God is love, then that's the only thing I can believe. When I see love expressed in all its forms especially in nature, I can find an interpretation for 'God'.

Sprite: Why would you want to do that?

Why, indeed!

If I only believe in things I can see, hear, feel, touch, smell and things that can be explained by logic, I cannot explain the small 'other' experiences I have had, and those that trustworthy people tell me about.

If I allow that there might be something 'other' I must also allow some truth to the myths of Christianity and allow in the confusion, anger and guilt it has brought me, and the pain and suffering it generates with its absolute practitioners, its fear of the other and its crazy interpretations.

If I don't believe, however honestly, I cannot shake the threat of punishment that was promised me in childhood.

I am still somewhat trapped by my past. I feel diminished by my conflicting feelings and lack of courage to pronounce my truth "I don't believe" without fear of retribution.

I feel constrained by anxieties that I could be taken over, like my mother was. These prevent me from exploring any 'other' spiritual dimensions in life for fear of being consumed, duped or deceived.

Sprite: Sounds a bit like a cul-de-sac.

Perhaps it is.
I will wander back to the road and see where it takes me.

Bibliography
Columba Graham Flegg, *Gathered under the Apostles: Study of the Catholic Apostolic Church* Clarendon Press Oxford 1992

4
Themes and Issues in the Narratives

With such a diverse range of stories and styles, the establishment of hard and fast conclusions about the influence of religion in childhood was always going to be difficult. In compiling this book we chose to encourage our contributors to tell their stories in their own words giving them only the briefest of remits. This has the merit of respecting that an individual's priorities lead them to emphasise certain aspects and perhaps not mention others. This chapter is designed to raise awareness of what we saw as the possible impact of early exposure to religion.

We have explored below some recurring themes in detail, but in doing so would first want to recognise the limitations of this study. The sample is small. The contributors come from an older demographic in terms of age (between 47 and 85 years) and religious tradition (all originally from Christian denominations). There are more women (seven) than men (three) in the sample. The contributors were self-selected in that they were recruited from an advertisement in a professional journal for counsellors and psychotherapists. Therefore they inevitably reflect the readership of that publication.

So what about the strengths of such an investigation? The 'lived experience' of personal narratives as a qualitative research method is now well established (see Chapter 2). The subtlety and subjective nature of such stories gives a substantial insight into how a child might absorb the religious influences around them. The additional advantage is that the adults in this case were able to reflect with insight and personal awareness on those experiences, and make some judgements about how they believed their religious childhoods affected them. The common denominator of a Christian tradition affords us the advantage of showing how varied and unpredictable the outcomes can be, even with a shared philosophical foundation. We also believe that some of the themes that we have identified could be recognised in other monotheistic religions.

Our aim was to uncover significant aspects from the narratives that had been identified by more than one contributor. We have looked for the strongest themes that emerged from the stories describing the landscape of religion in childhood. As mentioned in the Introduction, while these narratives come from those who experienced an early life in which religion was of major significance, we believe that these features or themes can be relevant to those who have experienced a perhaps less intense, but still meaningful brush with religion.

We illustrate each theme with references to, or quotations from, the contributors' narratives. Many other examples of the same theme may be found in the book, but we identify one or two examples of what we are describing. We have tried to stick to the explicit, but need to acknowledge that these themes can be present in a subtext, and we would hope that the full version of the narrative offers readers the opportunity to read between the lines.

For those involved in facilitative work these categories may suggest where therapeutic exploration would be most helpful. We have given this further thought in Chapter 5. The categorisation of the themes is not a clear one as many of them are inter-related, so this structure for understanding the key aspects of the narratives is, of necessity, a blunt instrument of analysis.

Common themes from areas explored in the narratives

Self Concept: how religion influences the way a child forms a view of him or herself and notions of being good and/or acceptable
Fear, Guilt, Shame & Anxiety: feelings commonly expressed in the stories
Responsibility: to and for others
Belonging: security, identification, fear of 'the other', acceptance and rejection
Creativity and Inspiration: art, music, dance, ritual and self-expression
Beyond the material world: the numinous or the spiritual
Perceptions of God
Questioning: doubts and doctrine
Moments of Change, Trauma, Loss, Separation: religion and difficult experiences
Family Origins and Cultural Legacy: ancestry, the wider contexts of childhood
Sex and Sexuality: desires, lust, love and religion
Gender: gender roles and church practice
Self Concept: How religion influences the way a child forms a view of him or her-

self; notions of being good and/or acceptable.

The term self concept here is employed in its most common usage 'as a person's view of him or herself.' (Merry, 2008: 33). Merry also offers a fuller definition harnessing present day thinking on the construct of the self, making it clear that the view that an individual holds of him or herself is a complex and fluid one. We acknowledge the many interpretations of the notion of self and for the purposes of this research, we apply the term in its commonest meaning.

Most contributors identified in their narratives the significance and importance of received religious templates of expectations, or prescribed patterns of what they should believe, and how they should think, feel and behave. They also recognised that such templates affected their view of themselves, and their sense of how acceptable they were both to themselves and others, including God. We refer in this section to those aspects relating to self-concept that seemed to draw on religious experience explicitly.

Parents and other significant care-givers were the strongest conduit of religion in the early lives of the contributors. Parents communicated religion according to their own views on the subject and brought up their children influenced by how they believed children in a religious household should be brought up. Contributors met the challenge of considering their parents' or care-givers' communication of religion with its message of how to be acceptable, by telling their stories as fully as they were able at the time of writing. When recollecting childhood experiences it is difficult to abstract with certainty the direct communication of religious teaching from the often filtered version that might have been incorporated in care giving, but individually the contributors have explored how much religion influenced their sense of self-acceptance and in what ways they valued themselves unconditionally.

Reading the full accounts you may want to consider whether the presence of religion in childhood intensifies or magnifies the impact of the usual process of socialisation. Socialisation, as Malik explains, is 'the process of the creation of self... of a child being inducted into society. It is the process whereby a natural creature is transformed into a social being, an object transformed into a subject, an animal into a person'. (Malik, 2001: 23)

Might the messages about self in childhood, the usual and ordinary influences in homes, carry added potency because of the implications of eternal life, eternal consequences and the presence of an all-seeing, all-knowing, all-powerful God? Some of the strength of that influence would depend on what kind of God was pictured by the child. This is an aspect that we explore later in this chapter.

Person–Centred Theory would apply the terminology, of explicit 'conditions of worth' in the templates for acceptable behaviour offered to these children. We could also use the same theoretical approach to reflect on the children's development of a 'locus of evaluation'. For those not familiar with this theoretical perspective more information can be found in the work of Rogers and other writers from this psychotherapeutic tradition. (Rogers, 1961, 1980, 1983; Mearns 1994; Merry, 2002; Cooper, 2000)

The way of being and behaving that was acceptable as described in these narratives included an external prescription from God or Church, on top of the usual expectations that form part of the process of parenting and socialisation. In these religious households, the encouragement to trust oneself and think for oneself and so grow towards an internal locus of evaluation was affected by the religious influence for which parents and care-givers provided a conduit. In many there was an emphasis on, and sometimes a requirement to look outside oneself for the right way.

In talking of their early life, we can hear what is true for many contributors articulated by Jane

'The first powerful message was that someone (or Someone) would be watching and noticing every detail of my behaviour, and even my thoughts, with an implication that He would see and take a dim view of any wrong move. I grew to have an instinctive sense that I had got it wrong'

Reliance on others' judgement (particularly that of adults) plays an intensely significant part in any child's ability to accept themselves. It is interesting that some of the contributors write of how they were impacted both as a child and in later life by their awareness of stated benchmarks set by religion and communicated in religious households. It seems relevant to understanding the influence of religion in childhood to consider how these templates or benchmarks were communicated.

In some households there was space for attention and respect of the individual child and sometimes an encouraging or at least a tolerant response to independent thoughts and actions. In others there was little or no room for the individual child, and a discouragement of questioning a rigid interpretation of doctrine, which was communicated severely. Sharon talks about how she 'cried out to be acknowledged'.

Examples of these differences are articulated by Jane and Anni who were both brought up in tightly knit religious communities which seem to have some traits in common. Yet they came away from these childhood experiences with a different view of the rules and structures with which they were brought up with.

'There was a curious mixture of theological teaching and pragmatic recognition by the adults that largely worked for us all.' (Jane)

'I mistrusted and disliked myself so much that I didn't need others to punish or judge me. I did this for myself.' (Anni)

Some contributors described the love and affection from parents and/or others within their religious settings that enabled them to feel valued and worthwhile, an experience that stayed with them into their adult lives, helping them in their darker days.

'At a time when I sometimes felt vulnerable and isolated, I was met by Christ through these Christian folk…those moments of my encounter with God through others has kept my faith alive.' (Peter)

'I was one of the lucky ones…the nuns laughed a lot, they worried about me, they cared for me… They gave me a deeply secure feeling of being loved.' (Wendy)

For others like Sharon, Lindsay and Anni the message of religious expectations seemed to be more dominant, and generated some confusion and uncertainty.

'Both my parents and God sent out waves in all directions to create the feeling of an earthquake of a highly unsettling and corrective nature.' (Sharon)

The struggle towards self-acceptance and trusting oneself has, for some, echoes of those messages from childhood which dictated a primary requirement of unconditional belief in God. Jane, Lindsay and Lucy all write about the difficulties of finding their own authority and autonomy, having been taught to defer to others to set the principles and practice of living.

'I've found it hard to think for myself, to speak up. I often feel guilty and as though I've got it wrong and will be censured'. (Jane)

'Authority also rested outside of me, and at times I still invest authority figures with disproportionate power, just as I can recognise an over- developed "authority" part of myself who needs to get things right.' (Lucy)

Whilst some still feel vulnerable to those childhood messages or templates, others tell us that they have found ways of moving towards an internal self-acceptance. Some, like Anni, have done this through turning away from the prescriptions of childhood religion, particularly from those childhood messages that she felt were damaging,

'Finally I had let go of the feeling of being "damaged goods" and of being punished for my wrong-doings…' (Anni)

Others, through their adult experiences and developed insights have been reconciled to the faith of their early years and value themselves in a way that is different to when they were young. John R's journey from being a Christian evangelist 'through therapy and into mysticism' involved embracing new and varied experiences and leaving behind others as he searched to contact his real self. He concludes:-

'More and more assumptions have been discarded at more and more levels, and each time it has felt like freedom and liberation.' (John R)

John Mc examines a fundamental difference he had with his training to be a Catholic priest which required him to be a man apart, when he felt strongly he wanted to be an equal member in the community:

'I wanted to be a man who belonged to the people-and that is what I've now found and I'm glad to be there.' (John Mc)

There is a sense that some contributors have found a way of seeing the influence of childhood religion as part of their tapestry of childhood, and, perhaps because it is inalterable, they accommodate it. Others who felt oppressed in childhood could see those experiences as grist to their developmental mill.

"As the child of my parents I have travelled far from their convictions but am grateful for their influence; the moral guidance they laid down and on the whole lived by…" (Catherine)

"It has taken me years (to) see that the conservative foundation stones that my parents placed under my feet did not destroy me. In a strange way they were a gift to make me determined to find a better way, a freer way. "Everything is useable, nothing is wasted …"(Sharon)

While it is clearly impossible to separate out the impact of religion from all other influences in the forming of self in childhood, the presence of structured religious expectations in the lives of the contributors does appear to have been of considerable significance in the development of their self-concept and most consider it in detail in their narratives.

Fear, Guilt, Shame and Anxiety

This group of feelings and responses figure prominently, frequently and powerfully in the landscapes of the narratives. These emotions, and reflections on them, follow on naturally from the reflections we have made on our section on the formation of self -concept.

At least eight narratives refer directly to specific experiences in childhood or early life when some or all of these feelings were associated with the contributor's relationship to God. Anxiety and fear appeared to arise out of a belief in judgement by God for wrong-doing. Often that wrongdoing would take the form of internal thoughts or feelings, or behaviour which did not involve anyone else. The anticipated punishment is often unclear. There are references to fear of immediate punishments in the form of banishment from the community, physical punishment by parents or loss of their affection, but there are also allusions to the fear of rejection by God and condemnation to eternal suffering. There are few references to the experience of receiving forgiveness. The fear of God can be equated to a terror which some of our narrators articulate as a constant feature in childhood.

'The ultimate punishment I felt was that I would end up in hell and not go to heaven.' (Anni)

For some contributors the echoes of fear can be heard in their lives now. Others have found that in adult life, and after much struggling, they have freed themselves from those early fears. Anni ultimately discovered a belief in her own strength and value which no longer involved the necessity of bargaining with God and appeasing him, and she rejected her early beliefs. Peter eventually found a way of reconciling his beliefs with his lived experience.

'This has been a long and sometimes tortuous journey of recognizing the reality of my body and my emotions, and wrestling with the guilt of experimentation whilst experiencing the pain and rich intimacy of both same-sex and heterosexual love. The way that I have reconciled my experiencing is that I have found God in all of these emotions and relationships, and can see the 'rightness', growthfulness and value of that intense love between two consenting adults - whether same-sex or heterosexual.' (Peter)

By contrast, Lucy, Lindsay and Jane describe how they found it difficult to shake off the fears of punishment generated in childhood and recognise how potentially guilt inducing and shaming it feels to make mistakes in adulthood.

'If I make a mistake and feel shame …the need for forgiveness is almost compulsive; I become absolutely preoccupied with the anxiety of holding my guilt and planning the various ways in which to rid myself of it. (Lindsay)

"I craved safety and had a desperation to get things right, as there seemed to be some unnamed punishment for getting things wrong, even when done innocently.' (Lucy)

Feelings of guilt and shame were often associated with falling short of the standard that particular individual expected of themselves, a standard reinforced for many by their religious background. Contributors evoke their fear of the consequences, and guilt and shame about the implications of doing or being different from the template offered in childhood. As Wendy describes:

On the one hand I felt empowered and happy, and on the other hand so ashamed, guilty and wicked. Where had that come from if not from centuries of condemnation of gay lifestyles from all the main religions? Why was I so terrified to tell anyone? Where had that come from? When all we felt for each other was a compassionate love.'(Wendy)

Anxiety features prominently in several of these accounts. (Lindsay, Lucy, Jane, Anni) It is present both in childhood and in adulthood, sometimes in relation to the apocalyptic threat of punishment by God for wrong-doing and sometimes present in daily life and the interpretation of it. Lucy, Lindsay and Anni describe a good deal of anxiety in both childhood and adult life which seemed to be based in an interpretation of how to avoid bad things happening. It seems as though they pictured a vigilant God who needed to be appeased in order for them to be free from anxiety.

'If God can kill your Daddy for being good, he can kill your Mummy too.' (Lindsay)

'I needed to try harder, that was clear. After all I knew what would happen if I didn't.' (Lucy)

'I was troubled by anxious thoughts and found it difficult to quieten my fears no matter how many rituals I made up and performed mentally or physically.' (Anni)

Some of those early fears seemed to persist resiliently into adulthood. These emotions seem to be tangled together and associated with the prescriptive nature of a religious childhood.

Responsibility
Most of the contributors referred several times to their strong sense of responsibility for and duty to others whilst they were growing up. John Mc refers to assuming a strong sense of responsibility for his widowed mother, 'I had to make my mum OK not upset or distress her'. Peter had the sense that it was his duty to evangelise, and this led to some bullying from others.

Faith in action seemed to be a theme for some contributors who, in adulthood, live out their religious beliefs in practical ways in their work or local communities like John McC, Catherine and Wendy. For some, the early religious beliefs that centred around responsibility and caring found a natural home in counselling training and practice as a counsellor.

'Here in the Person-centred way of being, I found the answer. I feel my eyes
pricking even as I write this: it has been such powerful stuff for me. And I am
not in the habit of admitting when I am deeply touched.' (Wendy)

'I continue to believe in healing, but unlike the Pentecostal Church that focussed solely on physical healing, I have experienced through diverse therapies,
especially Gestalt therapy, emotional and psychological healing.' (Sharon)

Lindsay's story refers to this sense of responsibility and duty as an overwhelming
sense of global responsibility still with her today.

'I have lived with the sense that I should at all times be open to the pain and
suffering of others – wherever they are, whoever they are, and I should act on
relieving that suffering.' (Lindsay)

There were some more general references to duty to family and commitment to marriage as exemplified in Catherine and Wendy's accounts.

For some, duty involved sacrifices, a price paid by some of the contributors or others close to them. Their fuller stories trace the present place of duty and sacrifice in
their lives.

'I don't know if it occurred before or after my father's illness, but I was a
child that felt it her duty to look after others and to sublimate my own needs'
(Lindsay)

'Throughout my childhood, I suffered bullying for my minority colour, my
father's fame and for my then naïve religious values that I tried to impose on
others- for I was taught that it was the duty of all Christians to spread the
"Good News", even if others did not want to hear it.' (Peter)

Perhaps it is not surprising that this theme emerged from contributors since their religious backgrounds stress the significance of commitment to community or group.

Belonging

The narratives reveal experiences of religion and religious communities that gave rise to a strong sense of belonging and of identification with a particular group.

> 'My early religious experiences... gave me a deeply secure feeling of being loved, a knowledge that "I'm OK, you're OK", that "I am known", and this causes me to behave and feel differently from someone who may have grown up with no such religious understanding' (Wendy)

Acceptance by the group could bring security and comfort in childhood - an atmosphere where a child could feel 'warm and safe.' (Jane) 'How favoured I must be', she muses from a childhood perspective. Belonging gave Peter some confidence too. Of early involvement in his Church he writes,' It gave (me) a sense of being part of a close-knit community, and enabled the overcoming of innate shyness...'.

The shadow side of belonging was for some the fear and suspicion of those outside the group and a need to stay inside. 'I became a clinger to survive.' writes Sharon. For her part Jane comments on 'how scary and dangerous all the people outside were.'(Jane)

These contributors also reflect on how difficult it was to mature within the tight grip of their religious communities

> 'I grew up hearing that we were the chosen ones and that we must never "be yoked together with non-believers". Having this constantly put into my thinking limited my relationships and screwed up my way of relating to men who were "outside the fold".' (Sharon)

> 'I rarely needed or wanted to look outside it [my religious community] but I grew up with a fear of people who are not part of the group... I also have a sense that in a strange way it is difficult to really grow up and properly mature in such communities. I'm not sure if this applies to both men and women but I think it has been difficult for me to become independent, self-determining and grown-up.' (Jane)

By contrast John R describes developing an experimental approach to understanding and relating to a group. His mother was High Church and his father 'Broad' Church.

He describes how, having become 'an evangelist' himself at the age of sixteen, he 'was going around the country delivering talks on 'What is a Christian and How does one become one?'' From this beginning he recounts how, during service in the Army, he began to explore new ideas and experiences, an exploration that eventually took him "through therapy and into mysticism".

> 'In 1969 I went to see a performance of *Paradise Now* by the Living Theatre, a play about the beautiful, non-violent anarchist revolution. I was very excited and moved and taken by it, particularly the freedom and the breaking of boundaries. Two friends (who had also seen the play) and I started a group called B Now, and we had a series of evenings where we would do nonverbal exercises for an hour, and then go into a group fantasy about the Best Society Humanly Possible, and then eat together, the rule being that you must not feed yourself but only someone else. At various points in these group meetings I had experiences which seemed to transcend the present scene and to take me into the space I labelled as eternity.' (John R)

Contributors spoke of times when they thought and felt differently from the rest of the religious group in which they were brought up. Peter reflects at length on this, expressing a need to belong to his childhood Church 'and community' while appreciating sometimes the benefits of being outside, which he says gives him 'freedom to be myself and to share my experiencing and thinking, and generate discussion.' John Mc reflects on his attachment to the church by saying 'I still need to belong to something that has been so much a part of my life'. Catherine talks about a 'hunger to belong'.

Some contributors describe the need to leave the group in order to find freedom of belief, thought and behaviour, like Jane, Lindsay, Anni and Lucy. Anni and Lucy experience this as a very painful process.

Creativity and Inspiration

The narratives reveal memories of both attraction and awe at the inspirational and the creative aspects attaching to the religions of childhood. The sights, sounds and smells associated with early religious experiences seemed to have stayed with the contributors and frequently are fondly remembered and connected with early feelings of excitement and novelty. John refers specifically to this element:

'…there were always incense and processions, bells and changes of costume, little palms on Palm Sunday and so forth, and plenty of stained glass.' (John R)

Wendy describes beautiful Harvest festivals and Easter flowers, Sharon the women in church dancing and twirling and Catherine the excitement of exploring the literature with her mother in the form of Bible stories 'that sent tingles down my spine'.

The rituals of the churches vary and whilst there is often childish excitement there is also a more complex response to them by some contributors. Sometimes this occurs at the time but more frequently later in life when the person has reflected on the implications and power of these rituals. This theme too may need to be considered in conjunction with others we have discussed particularly 'Belonging' and 'Beyond the material world', as ritual which gives access to a community that is special and invokes the divine, will be powerful in a child or young person's life.

Jane uses the word 'ritual' often in her account. She describes her baptism by full immersion at age 13 as 'a momentous step of commitment to God and the group.' Later in her life she reflects on her own experience of baptism and its implications when she goes to a similar occasion and recognises how difficult leaving such a group would be for that person once they were seen as 'safely in the fold'. Jane's uncertainty in later life about the benefit of some unquestioned rituals in her early life is illustrated by how the Church's insistence on hat wearing could be both a source of excitement and pleasure for her (her father's delight in her) and a symbol of repression of her emerging self concept.

For Lucy, the church building and her memories of playing and doing little jobs in the church as a child, mean that she is warmed by the sight of a church, but at other times the religious symbols can be threatening and disturbing. She is uneasy about attending a service. Whilst she could see that her father found meaning in the rituals of a service, she could not share that experience then or now.

It is clear from the accounts that some considerable pleasure and stimulation was experienced in relation to the creative aspects of religion and worship. Most of the contributors will have been growing up in wartime or in the immediate post-war years. These colourful aspects of life might have been welcome in a rather grey and austere time. It is also the case that the elements of drama as a creative force expressed in stories such as Sharon's and John R seem viscerally exciting and contribute to the development of the child's creativity.

Beyond the material world - the numinous or the spiritual

It would seem that it was religion in childhood that introduced our contributors to the numinous - that part of their nature that was eager to engage in areas of belief beyond what can be scientifically measured or materially evidenced. We have used the term 'numinous' to describe those elements of the narratives which exhibit 'a religious or spiritual quality.' (Oxford Dictionary Thesaurus 2001)

Hay & Nye refer to this spiritual quality as 'awareness that there is something other, something greater than the course of everyday events' (Hay & Nye,2006; 60) Lucy knows and believes that, for her, life has this quality.

'Having been introduced so young to another 'dimension', a non material world where thoughts were known and judged by a being who lived in the sky with his son and special dead people, I guess that I have gone on trying to make some sense of what that was really about. Without something to lay over it I could not leave it alone and it would not leave me alone, so my spiritual quest has not felt like an option..........That life has a numinous quality, an otherness, I know and I believe that it is my early life that has given me such certainty.' (Lucy)

John R's narrative contains many references to his journeys of 'psychospiritual development' from his family origins in religion. He describes the influences that gave him insight and 'mystical experiences' and those which led him to become a writer and practitioner of Transpersonal Psychotherapy.

Peter places religion at the core of his being, but the words seem to indicate a spiritual quality.

'Religion has been, and still is, a consistent influence in my life. It is impossible to say who I would be without my relationship with God and the Church. It informs all of who I am and my potentiality to become that which is divine within me – that which I am capable of.' (Peter)

Catherine and Lucy describe vividly experiences of the numinous as do others both in childhood and in adult life: Lucy when she is banished from 'the garden of Eden' and Catherine's experience while her husband is dying in hospital.

Anni's path took her away from the religion of her childhood, and her personal quest found a home in women's spirituality:

'I had loosened the grip of my Baptist upbringing. I had rejected a religion that I perceived as being made up by men for men, one in which women seemed to have a 'walk-on' part and in which men had the 'upper hand'…my travels took the form of an inward quest.

Together with some friends we formed a Matriarchy Group with the purpose of exploring women's spirituality.'

Lindsay describes how a religious childhood served to make her wary of any kind of spirituality, made her frightened to explore and suspicious of the numinous.

'I feel constrained by anxieties that I could be taken over, like my mother was. These prevent me from exploring any "other" spiritual dimensions in life for fear of being consumed, duped or deceived.'

So in this context the contributors had strong responses to the numinous and spiritual elements of their religious childhoods. In adult life these responses could remain and draw them towards the beliefs of their childhoods, or encourage them to look elsewhere for these qualities or else generate a strong resistance to the idea of anything beyond that which can be explained and understood.

Perceptions of 'God': Then and Now

It seems important to raise the question of who or what God is, or was, to each of our contributors in their childhoods and whether the development of these concepts changed as they grew into adults, whether or not they continued to believe in a God.

What difference might it make to the impact of religion on them as adults if they now no longer believe in God, or if their God still reflected the one known in childhood, or if the nature of the God of their adult years had changed?

Contributors were not asked directly to write about this, but it does seem that for some of those who still retain a faith in God, that the God to whom they refer later in their stories is different from the one that they met as children. Two contributors talk of no longer believing in the existence of God. Seven contributors have stayed

? w Christ

173

within church settings, although their comfort in being there varies as do their reflections on the God of their current beliefs. Sharon doesn't recognise the 'sacred/secular split' but describes seeing God in all things. For John R there is an early movement that indicates a leaving behind of the familiar and a search for the transcendental.

John R. refers in his story to a movement from seeing God in terms of his early evangelical teaching to being attracted to Spinoza's work where 'God and Nature were one and the same'. He talks of still being impressed by Spinoza's quote that 'The effort to understand is the first and only basis of virtue'. From his army days onwards, John's story traces his journey deeper into the transpersonal with no reference to his experiences of the God of his early years.

For Wendy, Peter, Catherine, Sharon, and John Mc there appears to be something of a change in the nature of the God that they experienced as a child and the one in whom they grew to believe in adulthood.

Sharon summarises her movement to her own understanding of God's nature at the end of her story, having gone back to visit her family in America, as follows:

'During those two years I saw more clearly the narrow-mindedness of my family. I was appalled by the right-wing fundamentalism that kept showing pictures in black and white. My biggest discovery was that I was not to blame'.

Wendy charts her journey from her early days of church-going in the village church through to a loving experience at her Roman Catholic convent boarding school. This was followed by her best friend's conversion by Billy Graham from whom she learnt of 'a very different God who was into punishment. I learnt to feel guilty, a failure in God's eyes because I couldn't believe everything they said.' Wendy continues 'This new Church view disturbed and confused me. And I think put back my emotional development for many years.' Thereafter, she set out on a path of exploration of her own. 'I always wanted to know the reason "why?" This proved a hard path as she came to terms with her sexuality, but, with help, she eventually found her understanding of God, not through following rules but by trusting 'my own "actualising tendency" - for which I read "God".'

Peter was born into the Moravian church. His father was an ordained Minister and at the time of writing his story Peter had applied to the Church for training as an ordained Minister. God has been fundamental to his life: 'It is impossible to say who I would be without my relationship with God and the Church'. He refers to 'a long and sometimes tortuous journey' of self-acceptance. So how did Peter come to believe that he was loved and accepted by God? He refers in his story to many people from his childhood onwards who showed him such love, often at times of great personal difficulty, and how at these times he felt that he had found God. Faith and the true nature of it for Peter are captured by him as follows: 'But amongst all the damage that has been inflicted on me and my family, those moments of my encounter with God through others has kept my faith alive, and enabled me to distinguish between what is a distortion of faith and what is true faith.'

Catherine starts her story with a profound experience in her adult life whilst her husband is very ill. It leaves her with an assurance that 'What did matter was that we should love one another, that the nurses should work from love, that everything we do should come from love.' At the age of twelve, terribly lonely at boarding school she 'turned to religion.' Whilst finding comfort, she also found that 'We were expected to accept the teachings of the Church and the school, and the emphasis was on sin and salvation. We were never quite good enough, always sinners. Criticism, not praise, was the norm. When I came to leave… I had been quite thoroughly brainwashed.' This was to change. Reflecting on what God means to her now - 'whether he is a concept or a creator' - she agrees with Keats that 'We would be better off if we were capable of 'Being in uncertainties, mysteries, doubts, without any reaching after fact and reason".' Catherine has found herself able to reach an 'attitude to spirituality and to the Church to which I belong that is as adult and thought out as I can manage.'

For John Mc, his decision to leave the priesthood of the Roman Catholic Church meant a dilemma. The training in his early life had told him that his life was to be one of duty. In falling in love and wanting to get married, his individual wishes had somehow to be reconciled with this teaching. Eventually he decided to leave the priesthood, although not the Church, and subsequently became a counsellor. From that place he reflects that 'Spirituality, Religion and Churches do not necessarily all fit together-they may do but not necessarily so'. His emphasis is on the importance of the individual and what faith means to them. Sometimes he wonders where religion exists in his work as a counsellor. He has moved from the priesthood and found himself thankful that he made that move.

Jane's movement in the paragraph headed 'A propensity to guilt' is summarised as follows: 'I became immersed in it [Christianity] and embraced it at a personal level and have never felt much interest in seriously investigating another version-I suspect they all have similar pros and cons. That statement represents a huge journey for me, since I come from a tradition which would see it as seriously heretical, since it holds that IT is the only right way and all others are wrong and to be feared.' Jane's early experience was of a loving warm (and very closed) community with perhaps a rather more enlightened attitude to sex than many contributors recalled. However, there seem to be 'pros and cons' in her story about her gain from this early life and some struggle still with its legacy.

For Lucy there are references to times when belief and the struggle with it seemed 'like a matter of life and death'. She acknowledges that the God who dominated her life until recent years had not grown or changed, but retained the form from child-hood. She says that 'I was more than a little uneasy to discover that the picture of God that I still held was the child's one of a bearded old man in the sky - he (very male) carried a stone tablet, the 10 commandments, scowled and had the narrow judgement of a vindictive village gossip.' Her story follows her wish and attempts to change that 'picture', and how that may take her away from her Christian roots. At times she still feels influenced by the God of her childhood.

Punishment, fear and guilt appear large in Anni's early life: 'Punishment for wrong-doing in the eyes of the Lord was a big feature of my early childhood, and that the Lord was watching my every doing and knew my every thought.' Despite the em-phasis on 'born evil' and 'born to suffer', Anni had 'a strong sense of innate goodness' within her. This feeling separated her from her family and she 'felt different from them.' And later 'nothing was actually going to destroy my spirit which throughout my life, for as long as I can remember, has felt like a strong thread running through me.' However, Anni recognised that she was still 'Godfearing' and she talks of her struggles to appease God by doing the right thing, and of her fear of punishment if she doesn't. This feeling continued to follow her into adult life until at 20 a traumatic incident convinced her that she can not accept the interpretation of God from her childhood religious experience and she says '…I had to find my own truth.' Her truth eventually takes her to a rejection of her early beliefs which she states as a joint view shared with her husband, 'We do not believe in God nor in any "afterlife"; this is our one precious life to live - and it gives me courage and a huge sense of relief.'

The God of Lindsay's childhood is perhaps captured in her child's voice at the start of her story, the piece ending with 'If God can kill your Daddy for being good, he can kill your Mummy too.' The messages that she heard from her mother confused and frightened her, and the loss of her father when she was 12 compounded this. Lindsay believes that 'In some ways I think as an infant my parents, particularly my mother, became the personification of God.' However, she also knew that she couldn't believe what her mother told her and that she was pretending to. Whilst a more liberal interpretation of religious teaching at school offered 'a safer container for my life', the God of childhood became evident again at the end of her story when she talks of her feelings during a recent visit to the Church she used to attend as a child: 'For once I became aware of the threat and how it still has some power for me. If you don't believe in God that is the worst sin, not sinning but not believing.' The answer to the question she asks herself 'So what were you left with?' ends with the words '….If God is love, then that's the only thing I can believe. When I see love expressed in all its forms especially in nature, I can find an interpretation for "God".'

Questioning: Doubts and Doctrines

It is clear from the stories that all the contributors have, at some time in their lives, wanted to question the doctrines given to them as children. For some the opportunity of writing about their experiences seems to have helped them.

For some contributors questions were not voiced until later in life, as it was apparent that the religious contexts in which they were brought up discouraged questions and argument. For Anni a dilemma emerged vividly as she grew up and began to grapple with the ideas she had been given, and as she began to ask more and more questions.

'The more I grew up the less certain I became. I was frightened. It was as if every step I took towards Jesus took me away from him. The answers that I received to my questions did not satisfy my curiosity…what was asked of me was to "trust in the Lord Jesus". This, for me, proved to be a step too far…' Some questions simply could not be answered, and yet what would become of me if I rejected totally the Lord Jesus Christ? Would I be thrown out of family and home? Would I be struck down?'

In some cases the questioning of authority took a more personal direction but became generalised to religion as well.

'It was not until years later that I realised that my animosity towards my father, and repudiation of all that he believed in was due at least in part to my anger that he lived while my mother had died. All authority was now anathema to me… At this time I gave up God.' (Catherine)

Her final section offers some definition of the paradoxical responses to the influence of the church and its teachings.

How many suffered significant loss – childhood/adolescence

'My emotional need for belonging and comfort was to some extent assuaged by religious practice, and my reason engaged by the impossibility of simple belief.' (Catherine)

We have looked to see in these stories whether there were non-religious models for a child to observe, perhaps in the wider family, or perhaps through available literature. We found few direct references to secular influences. This is not surprising given the brief of the task. We are in no position to say that there weren't any, but it seemed that the narratives would indicate that the dominating culture was pervasive for our contributors.

What place was afforded these contributors to question religion as a means of self-discovery? We have found evidence in many stories that, for these children, doubts and questions were not just unwelcome but actively discouraged. For many, questioning and striking out on an individual path was not something that came naturally.

'I have been an ex-priest now longer than I was an actual priest. I have mixed-up feelings about the Church ...For all its faults it seems right for me to continue to be a Catholic. I feel angry at the Catholic Church but sad about it at the same time – if truth be told, more sad than angry, and maybe some shade of guilt about leaving the priesthood when I know that there is a shortage of priests.' (John McC)

For others, the act of questioning or adopting an autonomous stance was seen as a risky thing to do and in certain cases it was what made them psychologically and even physically unsafe.

'I had to make up stories and lies so that I could join something that my parents believed was wrong, dangerous and immoral [dancing]... I continually argued with my mother and father..."How can I respect you when you don't respect me?"He pushed me down on the bed, removed his belt and spanked me. My dread was that my friends would be able to hear me crying. I was fifteen years old.' (Sharon)

We could say that conformity was prized in the households where our contributors were raised, on the evidence of what they have written.

For many the act of writing their narratives generated painful reflections. Lucy describes a pivotal moment when she discovered a capacity to actually find her first fundamental question about her religious beliefs. This happened when she was in her fifties.

By contrast John R seems to have been a person to have begun his adult life questioning and exploring, and he does not refer specifically to any fears or anxieties associated with questioning.

In the act of writing these narratives contributors have inevitably questioned themselves and others about their memories and experiences with religion. The writers were all volunteers for a project designed for those who wished to question and reflect, so whether or not a capacity for reflection is affected by a religious childhood is not one we can necessarily answer. However, we would suggest that encouragement to openly question fundamentals was on the whole very limited in the childhoods described.

Personal growth as an adult and staying within the group was possible for a few, but for many the questioning was a part of growth that took them away from their origins, and for some very far away. Why did some stay in a traditional religious setting, either the one from childhood or another, albeit after much questioning and examination? Why did others leave as soon as they could and never return? We don't think we have any definitive answers for these questions but can only speculate. Perhaps it is sufficient that those who stay can do so because they can go on asking questions that they did not ask before or hold what might be seen as conflicting thoughts and feelings without too much tension. They can be true to their adult selves, no longer silenced by their childhood fears. Others find the doctrines of childhood no longer carry truth for them, and they have forged a new and different path where they feel they can be authentic and liberated.

Moments of Change: Trauma, Loss, Separation,

Religion as a backdrop to significant life events gave those events particular meaning for each individual. A religious reference point or interpretation seemed integral to the understanding that the child or adult had of such events. Trust in the world and in oneself can be shaken by trauma; the explanations provided by religious references seemed to result in a range of responses to difficult experiences.

The contributors write about some of the experiences of life that affected them deeply. John Mc, Catherine and Lindsay all suffered the death of a parent in childhood. Wendy was separated from her father and maternal family. Catherine, Anni, Lindsay, John McC and Peter were all sent away to school. Peter also experienced the significant move from one culture to another. Sharon experienced constant spontaneous change of home and community. In adulthood Anni describes a deeply traumatic assault and many sad losses, and Lucy describes the effect of her father's death on her. Catherine describes the difficulties with a husband with mental health difficulties.

For some, the responses to difficult experiences resulted in a move away from the religion of childhood, either soon afterwards or later in life. For others, there appears to be a deepening of commitment. The age at which these events occurred obviously have additional relevance for the way in which a contributor would make sense of them.

There are examples in the narratives of a trauma in childhood or early in life which were perceived as a punishment for being bad or breaking a promise to God. It seems that traumas had the power to confirm the contributors in the anxiety or fear that was already a significant part of their lives.

Lindsay is able to access her response to the loss of her father at the age of 12 through an internal child's voice who expresses how she interpreted her father's illness and death:

'I was scared of that God who punished us by killing my Dad.'

Lucy felt a profound abandonment when she broke a promise she had made to her God:

'I felt condemned. I felt abandoned. God had never been more real or more angry. I had stepped into a different world.'

Both Lucy and Jane struggled to manage that fear through re-establishing a trust in themselves and their ability to manage their lives. It seems that if a pervasive experience of a negative self-concept exists, subsequently overlain with a trauma or negative experience, this can lead to a belief that the experience is a punishment from God, with its concomitant consequences.

'I emerged from the experience even more determined to save myself. I feared that I would be judged as 'having asked for it' and worse that I deserved it for having 'turned my back on the Lord'. The experience had been my punishment for all my wrongdoings. Deep inside me I knew this could not be true, that it was a lie, and that I had to find my own truth.' (Anni at 20)

God was also experienced as present when there were moments of change in a different way. Sharon was brought up to believe that her father's healing from tuberculosis was instant and God-given and this belief of her father's dictated her early life, a life of rigid conviction and constant moving on as they were all now pilgrims. Their religious beliefs took them to numerous places and these moves seemed often to be precipitous and unplanned.

'I quickly discovered that moving away from home didn't mean leaving the trappings behind. Since we had moved so many times in my childhood, uprooting didn't seem unusual…I can count up to nine different towns we lived in before I left home, and this included three different Western States in the US…After all, we were pilgrims and before I became disillusioned, I could sing with the loudest of the Pentecostal worshippers…

1.   'So many words from the old songs are embedded in my memory, but I sang them without knowing that they were reinforcing my parents' understanding of God, Church and religion and seeping down into my psyche. I wasn't on my way home, but in desperate need to get away from the restrictive scene and get a dose of what the Pentecostals called "sin."'

In Catherine's early life she had turned to religion for comfort and found it.

'At the age of twelve, a few months after my father re-married I was sent to boarding school. I was 'too friendly', apparently, so no one would speak to me for about two terms. I have never experienced such isolation and, as prisoners in solitary confinement do, I turned to religion.'

In adulthood Catherine experienced another moment of change which gave her a firm belief in the power of love 'in which religion and politics seemed small things'. It seems that when faced with distressing events the religious experiences of childhood are activated quite vividly. They may provide comfort and strength or the reverse.

Family Origins and Cultural Legacy

The narratives reveal that in many cases the writers felt part of a bigger history, either culturally or as a result of their family origins. This, like many other of the elements common to the contributors, was experienced differently by each individual. The power of one's family history in this regard is self-evident.

> 'To be training to be a priest in the light of this tradition carried with it a sense of walking in the footsteps of giants. It was a privileged profession one was entering and it carried an awesome sense of duty. Becoming a priest was no light matter!' (John Mc)

> 'Throughout my life I have had a strong desire to be part of the ordained ministry. There has never been a time in my life when this has not been in my awareness at some level. I have pictures of me as a small boy, aged about four, in my underpants and wearing my father's dog collar, supposedly 'preaching' to a group of assembled teddy bears. At that level, there is something about unconsciously imitating my father and grandfather, for whom I had deep love and respect.' (Peter)

Whether or not religion as part of a family history is any more or less influential than a particular political affiliation or professional association, or even supporter of a particular football club, is a matter for debate. As this issue was raised in several narratives it seems important to include it here.

Sex and Sexuality

Peter starts to explore sex and sexuality in his narrative under the heading 'The Church as "sexless"'. Almost all of our contributors related how little their backgrounds had to offer by way of helpful guidance when it came to issues of sex. It seemed that what was available to them seemed to condemn sexual activity of any kind, although heterosexual sex within marriage seemed to have a sort of dispensation. To be sexual, even to feel sexual feelings, for many, was to be a bad person.

The resulting grief and pain for those youngsters coming into sexual awareness needs to be read in individual accounts (for example in Lucy's, Lindsay's, Jane's, Wendy's and Anni's stories) to be fully appreciated. Although many have found ways as adults of reconciling their sexual feelings and/ or sexuality with their faith, others still carry deep seated damage to their sense of self-worth as sexual beings.

All our contributors were growing up between the 1930s and the 1960s, and the narratives reflect the culture of these times. This period included wartime promiscuity, and the popularising of the 1960s 'sexual revolution' at a time when many of the writers were young adults. Those times must have been threatening for the parents and families of these young people. Some responded by ignoring it, and others by carefully controlling it.

'What I do know is that boys started to become really important. Not that I said anything – what was there to say? Sex was not a word that anyone mentioned – I think that I mean anyone. Not much on TV and acute embarrassment all round at home when it was….Any mention or portrayal of sex on television at home and the air would chill as some attempt was made to find a diversion.' (Lucy)

'Then there would be hot chocolate and several hours when the adults would try to get the teenagers to fall asleep and much chasing of miscreants around the camp site. This was all the greatest fun while people fell in love with God and each other, adults and youngsters all involved together, mostly good-naturedly. My first kisses were experienced just outside the light of the Camp bonfire, largely sanctioned, even encouraged by the adults, as long as things didn't go too far.' (Jane)

Those who offer accounts of their experience of Church and sexuality characterise it as something that was not relevant to be talked about, or seen in polarised terms. It seemed to generate feelings of guilt and shame sometimes becoming a taboo.

'The way of life in the seminary at that time seemed geared up to promote and develop this view – an all-male establishment, away from home and family, disciplined monastic-like routines. And sex and intimate relationships? Well sex was tied in with marriage and since priests did not marry then sex was not going to be an issue. And close friendships with either men or women should be avoided as these could be fraught with danger. And what of sexual thoughts and feelings? They were temptations to be resisted and denied.' (John Mc)

'I wanted desperately to talk to my parents about what was happening ...I was not married. I had obviously had sex, and I was pregnant.
In my vulnerability and frightened state of mind and body I feared that this indeed was God's wrath for my wrongdoings; for everything that I had ever thought, felt and done that would, in the eyes of the Lord, be considered sinful. Although close friends and my partner were supportive I felt on my own, lost and frightened. I was in unknown territory' (Anni)

'Guilt around sex and physical intimacy is an aspect of religious influence (or possibly under the guise of religious influence) which I believe was a damaging, constraining force in my late childhood, adolescence and into my adulthood. We were always encouraged to 'be modest' and 'cover up' from being quite small... As I grew up and matured I found it difficult to accept any sexual feelings. This coupled with a highly exaggerated romanticised view of relationships led to some difficulties for me.' (Lindsay)

'For me, religion as I received it stunted the first attempts at releasing inner desires and brought a lack of trust in my own instincts and wants. I craved safety and had a desperation to get things right, as there seemed to be some unnamed punishment for getting things wrong, even when done innocently. I became ashamed of, and distanced from, my body and my needs, trying to avoid an awareness of them.' (Lucy)

Others explore their experience of discovering themselves outside the mainstream in terms of sexual orientation. We can only reflect on the impact that religious teaching had on those who found themselves well outside the expectations of their original religious teachings.
Wendy found herself in love with a woman...

'Why was I so terrified to tell anyone? Where had that come from? When all we felt for each other was a compassionate love. But I couldn't not know that every Christian church would condemn us as "wicked." Particularly the Roman Catholic Church. I met several RC lesbians who were vitriolic about their former Church, would never go back: had given it up forever. And although there was a group called "Quest" for Roman Catholic lesbian women it was not well supported at that time and most RC women I met were very damaged by their experiences, and wanted nothing to do with an organisation that had so demonised them.' '(Wendy)

Peter, as a bisexual person, recounts his sexual awakening and how he reconciles these with his religion:

'It was then that I had a regular experience of same-sex nudity and I found it pleasurable. At that same time, the culture in the school was extremely homophobic (not necessarily overtly, but implicitly among the pupils through humour and teasing), and so I had to keep these feelings to myself. I was also increasingly aware of some biblical teaching that stated that homosexuality was 'wrong', and of some Christian teaching that masturbation was sinful. I was also fascinated with girls, but that was 'wrong' too (or so I thought then). It has taken me years to reconcile my bisexuality, and my pleasure in masturbation, and to see them both as a gift from God - as an embodiment of the divine within me, rather than as something to be ashamed about. This has been a long and sometimes tortuous journey of recognizing the reality of my body and my emotions, and wrestling with the guilt of experimentation whilst experiencing the pain and rich intimacy of both same-sex and heterosexual love.'

We can conclude that sexual development is not an area where many of our contributors found much openness, support, advice or understanding from their religious roots.

Gender

The majority of our contributors were women in middle and late middle age. Many were young adults at the time of the development of the women's liberation movement. This seemed to be reflected in their awareness of the dominance of men in the religious groups in which they were brought up or were members. Anni, Catherine and Jane all refer to this in their stories. Lucy identifies the maleness of her perception of 'God'.

Other contributors identify times when they had difficulty with the opposite sex these issues may or may not be a direct consequence of religion introduced in childhood.

'In such an atmosphere I grew up being told that we were the chosen ones and that we must never 'be unequally yoked together' with non-believers. Having this constantly put into my thinking limited my relationships and screwed up my way of relating to men who were 'outside the fold' (Sharon)

'It occurred (a spontaneous therapy session) as part of a whole series of experiences to do with my own therapy which brought to an end my hatred of women, and from that point on I was much more aware of the feminine, and of the Great Goddess' (John R)

John McC describes the constraints placed upon him as a Catholic priest who is not allowed to marry, as distinct from his Church of England counterparts who can join the Catholic Church and remain married. Issues around gender, sexual relations and marriage remain contemporary in the various Christian Churches and these have clearly marked our contributors.

References

Boyd Webb, N (1993) Helping Bereaved Children: a handbook for practitioners. New York: Guilford Press

Brom, D, Horenczyk, RP, Ford JD (2009) Treating traumatised children; risk, resilience, and recovery. London; New York:Routledge

Cooper,M, O'Hara, M, Schmid, PF, & Wyatt, G (2007) The Handbook of Person-Centred Psychotherapy and Counselling. Basingstoke: Palgrave Macmillan

Mearns, D (1994) Developing Person-Centred Counselling London: Sage.

Merry, T (2002) Learning and Being in Person-Centred Counselling 2nd Edition PCCS

Hay, D & Nye, R (2006) The Spirit of the Child. London: Jessica Kingsley.

Rogers, C.R (1961) On Becoming a Person Boston Houghton Mifflin (Currently published by Constable)

Rogers, C.R (1980) A Way of Being Boston Houghton Mifflin

Rogers, C.R (1983) Freedom to Learn for the Eighties. Columbus, OH: Charles Merrill

5
Professional Applications

This chapter aims to address two questions. Firstly, how much are therapists aware of their assumptions and blind spots in relation to their own experience of religion and how might this affect their work with clients? Secondly, we explore how the themes we have identified in the previous chapter might present in therapy, and how they might be explored if they do.

We have used the term 'therapist' to include counsellors, psychotherapists, psychologists and pastoral workers and, where relevant, supervisors of those practising in these professions. We have used the convention of applying the pronoun 'she' when we refer to therapists and 'he' when we refer to clients, although the intention is not to be gender specific.

We considered whether there might be an inherent reluctance on the part of a therapist to engage with work that draws on a religious past and how a therapist without experience of early religious teaching might relate to a client who brings such issues. How would a therapist with a religious history herself hold in mind the impact that her personal experience might have on her therapeutic relationship and interventions? Is it enough to say that professionals are trained to work with difference and diversity, and that dealing with matters of religion needs no special awareness?

As humanistic therapists we aim to respect the autonomy of our clients as a core condition of the therapeutic alliance. As Rogers (1992:38) puts it, we want to form a relationship characterized 'by a warm acceptance of and prizing of the other person as a separate individual'. We strive to accept clients with unconditional positive regard. 'an unconditional acceptance, a positive regard or caring, a non-possessive love.' (Thorne, 1991:38)

We would recommend that therapists do not mistake that for an excuse to treat their client's religious beliefs as taboo or off limits. To explore the place of this area of a client's inner world might very well involve raising and addressing fundamental questions posed both by therapist and client. While questioning beliefs adopted in childhood is not always straightforward for a client or therapist brought up in a religious household and can shake a person's foundations, we suggest that not doing so can leave clients alone and abandoned in their existential 'trauma of self-consciousness' (Spong, 2007:65) without the support of the facilitative companion that a therapist can be.

This therapeutic work is as much about therapists themselves and their experience of religion as it is about their clients' worlds. Much has been written about the need for therapists to explore their own psychology before, and while, they work with their clients. (Wosket, 1999; Merry, 2002) This includes attention to the therapist's religious beliefs. A therapist with strong religious views can be challenged in training to articulate these and integrate these in such a way that her clients are provided with a clear opportunity to go where they need to go in terms of exploring religion and beliefs should they want to do this. It is more likely, however, that there will be therapists in training who have strong religious conviction and who have not explored that aspect of their culture and would prefer to avoid that area of enquiry, perhaps because of fear that their own doubts and uncertainties might be unearthed in such a process. They might offer up an unsophisticated blanket defence for this in the form of 'respecting difference', indicating that this is a 'no-go' area. This is a position that should invite challenge, both from trainers and fellow trainees.

> 'A widespread assumption, which nearly everybody in our society accepts - the non-religious included - is that religious faith is especially vulnerable to offence and should be protected by an abnormally thick wall of respect, in a different class from the respect that any human being should pay to any other.' (Dawkins, 2006: 42)

A few therapists have such deafening religious noise of their own that they run the real risk of influencing, or even exploiting, a vulnerable client whose religious background may have dictated that they should defer authority to others. The threat of damnation and the seduction of forgiveness are extremely powerful concepts. A therapist brought up with these values will need to have actively engaged with their own philosophical and emotional development to ensure that a hidden agenda of evangelism is not operating in the guise of facilitation in the therapy room.

We are advocating that therapists coming for training both need to be prepared to unpack their religious bags, and to inspect and explore the content thoroughly with the supportive challenge of others, some of whom need to be of a different and therefore independent background. Training programmes where trainers and all the trainees share a religious perspective risk a closed and collusive approach to this area of development, and there is a distinct possibility that this necessary training work is not undertaken.

West (2004) supports the view that spirituality and religion are important issues for counsellors to address with clients and advocates that training should challenge the trainee to be aware of where she stands.

'What I would call for is that all therapists during training are exposed to basic information about the major faiths within their society; various ways of mapping people's spiritual development; issues around spiritual emergence and awakening; a deep sense of their own relationship with religion and spirituality'. (West, 2004:86).

Ross (2006) recognises the challenges posed by religion in therapeutic work and the need to engage with these challenges. He describes religion as 'a difficult subject to deal with as it provokes so many different, often polarised reactions. These responses need exploring to help understand what happens in a counselling relationship when issues of religion or spirituality emerge.' (Ross, 2006: 172)

This is echoed in the British Association for Counselling & Psychotherapy's information sheet G13 entitled 'Working with issues of spirituality, faith or religion.' In this sheet, Harborne alerts therapists to the likelihood of having clients with a 'wide variety of faiths, spirituality and religious backgrounds and experiences'. She encourages therapists to 'maintain an attitude of non-judgmental enquiry', in order to clarify these and 'ascertain whether therapy is the most appropriate intervention?' (Harborne, 2008:2). Clients may be reluctant to bring these issues up, but a therapist can provide the openness, the patience and the empathy that provides them with the opportunity to do so.

Similarly, therapists with their own history of religion may collude with a client in avoiding exploration of religion, not only because of a shared blind spot, but also because it may engender fears of punishment for the therapist. Our section on 'Questioning' in Chapter 4 may be of particular relevance here

It is understood (at least in the Person Centred tradition) that for a therapist to form an effective therapeutic relationship, not only will she be unconditionally accepting of her clients, but she will also, amongst other things, be real or genuine. This realness is anchored in the therapist having a well developed self-awareness, which remains available to her whilst she listens to her clients.

> 'In, essence, this realness depends on therapists' capacities for being properly in touch with the complexity of feelings, thoughts and attitudes which will be flowing through them as they seek to track their clients' thoughts and feelings'. (Thorne, 1991: 39)

It does not necessarily follow that clients need to be exposed to all the therapists' own processes, but the therapist does need to be sufficiently transparent to be experienced as real. Communicating transparency is a skill and challenging in these circumstances. The therapist's simple 'I am a Christian' or 'I am Muslim' says little. We can see that in our narratives such a statement carries with it a lot that might be assumed but be inaccurately understood. A similar statement from a client would reveal almost nothing of what that means. A shared dialogue about beliefs is preferable. The most important thing is that the door is opened and the therapist and the client can look beyond the door as and when the client chooses. The therapist carries the responsibility to indicate that there is a door marked 'religion' that may be significant, and that this is done in such a way that the client feels that there would be active support should they choose to explore what lies beyond.

The assumption that unexplored religious beliefs, however precious and valuable to the individual, are a beneficent force in a client's developing psychology, is challenged by our contributors in the way they describe their experiences. So when and how the subject of religion is raised in the therapy room is a matter for consideration. West advocates that the client's religious and spiritual frame should be part of the assessment process, however informal that process might be. He draws on the work of Richards and Bergin to explore why he believes this to be beneficial and draws attention to specific questions that could be asked at this stage in therapy. (West, 1997:78) This would automatically raise the awareness of the client that the therapist is open to that area of work, and that religion may have a significant part to play in the therapy. Introducing the subject early and alongside other possibilities would also remind the atheist or agnostic therapist of the significance of religion as a possible element in the therapy that is planned.

The atheist or agnostic therapist would then need to be alert to any responses that a religious client might engender in them. Therapists without a religious background might find it hard to empathise with a client whose beliefs are alien to them, and they may struggle to appreciate the impact of what they consider to be irrational beliefs. This may be the case even though those therapists have absorbed an awareness of the existence of such beliefs from a shared culture, and fully support the importance of acceptance of difference and diversity in clients.

> 'Some therapists may have difficulty in offering unconditional positive regard to clients who hold strong or inflexible religious views…which may be perceived by the therapist as an avoidance of acknowledging their own responsibility for the consequences of their actions… For therapy to be successful, the client must be in psychological contact with the therapist. In some cases …the client's ability to stay in psychological contact with the therapist is limited, and, in some cases may demonstrate a significant resistance to change. As a result the therapist my be left feeling powerless or may struggle with congruence or experience a sense of collusion. Such issues for the therapist could subsequently become the focus of supervision and/or therapy' (Harborne, 2008:2)

Religion can arouse strong feelings in the non-religious practitioner, or the practitioner who has rejected religion, as well as in the religiously devout one. By contrast, some practitioners might not recognise the relevance of religion, even when it is a significant part of a client's background. They might find themselves unconsciously screening out those references, for reasons of their own or for those alluded to above. An empathic, respectful and mature therapist may set out to accept the significance of a client's experience of religion, but perhaps this is not enough. 'Acceptance does not mean much until it involves understanding.' (Rogers, 1961: 34) The client may not perceive a sufficient degree of acceptance from a therapist who has not appreciated the complexity of the influence of religion in childhood, and the depth at which it may have been experienced. The communication by the therapist of acceptance with real understanding can be further complicated when the client may have been encouraged by their religious experience to think of themselves as not good enough, not acceptable. A therapist's usual skill in communicating empathy and acceptance with understanding may need particular attention in these circumstances in order to ensure that a client is fully understood. Only when this is successful, and the client and therapist are in psychological contact, will a client feel the confidence to choose to explore the significance of their religious experiences.

In the second part of this chapter we want to reflect on how the themes in our previous chapter might surface in therapy and how further exploration of them might be facilitated. Clients may bring 'explicit and implicit spiritual issues' (Harborne, 2008:2) to a therapeutic setting. We would expand this statement to include religious issues. Some clients may voice their desire to explore their early experience of religion, while others may not. As with any other cultural aspect the impact of the religious childhood of the therapist and/or the client has an influence on both parties and on the therapeutic relationship they form. The extent of that influence will vary and may be of no great significance.

We found some evidence to suggest that the intensity or scope of the religious experience does not alone dictate the extent or degree of the effect. While all of the contributors came from backgrounds where religion was a consistent presence, there was no correlation between the denomination or style of their religious experience and the degree of influence on the individual's self-development. An immersion in a community culture will affect individuals in disparate ways. Lucy and Jane had very different introductions to religion and yet it is possible detect similarities in their responses. Therapists should be alert to the possibility of unpredictable effects on individuals with religion as any part of their childhoods, however brief or occasional that might have been. As with any other cultural awareness, a therapist would need to understand the internal interpretation that a client had made of their unique experience.

Here perhaps lies another discovery and one that may inhibit a client in their self- exploration. The degree of impact of early religious teaching may be so core, that to explore it in therapy raises profound ambivalence for a client. Since many religions have a tenet of faith ('believing' being a primary requirement), if a client explores and asks questions they risk punishment (and that punishment may be 'eternal') for their sin of lacking faith. Moreover, should they express doubts or questions openly they may risk potential abandonment by church, community and even family. Here may lie one reason for a client's reluctance to enter this area. As with any other potential change that a client chooses to make in their lives, the impact can be profound. What we are suggesting is that there is a risk that a therapist may not understand that even a seemingly conventional and ordinary experience of established religion can carry that profundity.

A second restraint on exploration may arise from the existential answers that religion provides to individuals both in how they live their lives and how they manage a fear of death.

'The manifestation of an almost universal yearning... finds expression in most religious systems. It arises, I believe, out of the existential awareness of the trauma of self–consciousness. The idea that human beings might be alone in the universe, buffeted by natural forces over which they have no control, gives rise to more fear than can be absorbed. That fear is banked by the idea, which becomes a growing human conviction, that there is a power far greater than that which human beings possess - a power that watches over us and intervenes to help us.' (Spong, 2007:65)

Rowe talks of how our attitude to death dominates how we live our lives and how the popularity of religion comes from its 'promise to overcome death'. For her these beliefs about the nature of death are 'guesses or fantasies', but they are nevertheless of fundamental importance in our lives.

'...if we have constructed these beliefs with a view to which beliefs would benefit us or which beliefs we can live with most comfortably, we can be very reluctant to change them, for to do so would mean changing the way we live our life.' (Rowe, 2009: xiii)

There are other useful sources for therapists who wish to address existential aspects of therapy including Yalom (1980), Frankl (1985) and Spinelli (2001). For a client who has accepted without question the protection from existential doubts and difficulties that their religion has provided, to begin to explore this area may feel exposing and dangerous. This might be especially true for those where 'God' has remained an unquestioned figure formed in childhood. Our section on 'Perceptions of God' in Chapter 4 summarises our findings with regard to this and we return to look at what issues might be helpful to explore with clients later in this chapter.

However, there may be a third and even deeper psychological restraint to clients and their therapists exploring religion. This takes the form of the threat to identity that such an endeavour may generate. If a person is given a prescribed view of how to be and yet their felt experience is that they do not conform to this template, a dilemma arises. There is a gap between their felt experience of self and the self that religion has taught them that they are or should be. Religious clients may experience this position as a highly threatening double bind. It may be a choice between abandoning their felt selves or their religious identity. It may be less traumatic to abandon the former than the latter. The potential for severe emotional consequences such as anxiety and depression are revealed in the narratives of this book in Chapter 3. In addition, as mentioned above, the family ties can be stretched or broken if a client's path leads them to question their religious identity, and this can feel like 'an earthquake' (Sharon).

'When clients of any faith lose the trust which they have previously held in that faith, they may also lose trust in themselves and experience anxiety and stress or even a profound sense of self-loathing, failure and shame.' (Harborne, 2008:2)

Rowe reminds us that reluctance to discuss beliefs can be based in the shame and fear of not being understood:

'We hide our beliefs from others to prevent them from laughing at our childish faiths, or belittling our deepest fears, or chiding our foolish optimism. Or simply not understanding what was being told'. (Rowe, 2009:84)

The stakes can be high where religion is concerned.

In the face of these challenges it would be surprising if there were not reluctance on the part of clients to explore their religious pasts, and sometimes on the part of therapists to accompany clients on this path.

However, if a client is able to bring religion to therapy and wants to share that aspect of their life, we offer below some areas of exploration that may be fruitful.

These are based on the themes that the narratives uncovered.

The narratives provide ample evidence of the sustaining element of religion.

The contributors emphasise the comfort that religion and religious experiences can bring. Many of the stories explore safety and comfort, belonging, being seen and valued. Peter describes people in his life who have offered this sense of being valued. Wendy talks about the loving nuns in her convent. The power of community is strong and many of our contributors still belong to a religious group of one kind or another. Some narratives hint that these communities offer safety and comfort for them. This is a constructive area of potential support that counsellors might want to explore with their clients who have experienced religion in childhood. As a therapist you are often part of a wide system of care and support. It would seem helpful to talk through with any client the advantages and drawbacks of involving their community system, depending on what issues arise for the client in therapy.

Our narratives show that many of our contributors have developed a sense of guilt and shame as part of their core self-perception. This in itself is not an unusual issue to come across in the therapy room. However, our narrators also provide evidence that hiding those aspects of self is very likely among those brought up to fear a judgemental God.

Striving to be good, and a fear of not being good, seem to be very strong features in these accounts. Many of our narrators describe themselves as pious and conforming children. They describe the positive feelings which derived from having achieved a standard of 'goodness'. Others mention being praised for their humility. Sometimes this had the corollary of feeling 'chosen', 'special', and 'different'.

Lucy's story describes the depths to which her shame needed to remain hidden, in order for her to continue to function. Indeed, at times she was overwhelmed and unable to function. The power of this shame has the potential to be overlooked by a therapist who doesn't quite understand the resilience of religious influences in childhood. Therapists need to be alert to the client's potential depths of guilt and shame. The place of guilt and shame in the client's self-concept may mean that to probe this area could threaten to dismantle core beliefs about their 'good-ness' including exacerbating or reviving deep fears of eternal punishment for not being good enough. Therapists need to provide the support for the client to build resources in the face of such strong emotions, understanding the fear that may have to be faced in exploring this aspect of their experience.

Specific psychotherapeutic approaches to the phenomenon of shame may be of use to the therapist here. Practitioners such as Bradshaw (1988), Jacoby (1991) and Kaufman (1993) write specifically about strategies for working with client issues of guilt and shame.

It is perhaps to be expected that some religious communities applaud the notion of self -sacrifice and can be discomforted by those of self-care and self-interest. It is noticeable from the contributors' accounts that giving to others seems to have involved subjugating their own needs.

Therapists, in their efforts to restore an appropriate level of self-care, autonomy and personal power in their clients, can stress the 'I' factor and challenge clients to take responsibility for their lives, including responsibility for those choices that may have led them into difficulties. When working with a client who has had a re-ligious influence that stresses conformity and subservience to the group, therapists may find it challenging to enable a client to locate sufficient confidence in their capacity for self-determination.

Anger and frustration are rarely mentioned explicitly in the narratives, but these emotions are detectable between the lines. All the religious contexts described in the narratives seem to have been characterised by rules, some direct and specific relating to behaviour (wearing of hats, or not going to the cinema) and others more general and open to interpretation (being good, doing good). The impact of authoritarian organisations on individuals was considered by Bowlby to be 'inimi-cal to the promotion of good personal relations, of goodness.' (Bowlby, 1947 in Holmes, 1993:201) While this may be an extreme view, the impact of rule-bound childhoods can produce extremes of rebellion as well as extremes of conformity. Clients coming from these backgrounds and having the latter reaction can be pre-occupied with being good clients. These clients may be less likely to complain, disagree or correct a therapist's misunderstanding. Building a relationship where clients can trust enough to question their therapist or be angry with their therapist is often difficult. This will be more so when a client has been brought up with religious imperatives of humility and conformity. These clients may also be those who can quickly move into a shamed state if their attention is drawn to a bound-ary issue. Therapists can be alert to this and help to feed back to clients when they think this short circuit may have been triggered, acknowledging the source of such sensitivity.

The contributors to this study make it clear that anger and frustration were not emotions that were well received or sat comfortably with 'being good'. Anger seems to have surfaced in some parents, however, who meted out punishment often described as 'in the best interests of the child' to learn what was not acceptable.

The energy of anger can be a healthy factor in restoring personal authority. Anger, as with creativity and spontaneity, are natural components of human expression. Expressing it can bring relief and a stronger sense of self, which can be translated into more zest for life and enjoyment. Therapists can encourage and welcome anger and help clients unused to this as a positive emotion to find its therapeutic potential and manage their possibly intense fear of punishment that may arise when they express it. Gestalt psychotherapy has much to offer in its non-judgmental attitude to strong emotions such as anger. Anger is seen as part of a healthy functioning psychology.

'in Gestalt aggressiveness as defined in the original sense of 'reaching out' is indispensable to life, love and productive activity... It becomes negative when you never let yourself express your hurt or your rage.' (Clarkson, 1989: 54)

Curiosity and spontaneity appear to be the casualties of some religious childhoods. Sharon, Anni and Lindsay all refer to a negative response to their curiosity and spontaneity. Experimentation and spiritual exploration may be variants of this. Sharon, John R and Anni describe their energy to go out and actively search for and engage with spiritual experiences. Wendy and Lindsay, by contrast, describe a fear of spiritual experiences bringing back 'big ideas'. As Jane puts it, there is an anxiety of being 'swept back into a vulnerable state'. So for some the big ideas of religion and spirituality have been a stimulus, whereas for others this has translated into a fear of the numinous. Having the supportive companionship of a therapist in explorations of belief can be very valuable in this respect.

For clients wishing to explore what can seem like unusual thoughts and experiences 'may be anxious that faith issues will be considered pathological if brought to therapy' (Harborne, 2005: 4)

'Therapists may need an understanding of what is considered 'delusional' within different cultures. A willingness to be open to understand the client's experiencing within the context of their culture and community and to explore these ideas where relevant, both with clients and with other professionals within therapeutic, mental health and faith perspectives as well as in supervision is therefore necessary.' (Harborne, 2008:2)

As a therapist it might help to make explicit when working with people who refer to 'God' who or what they mean by this reference. Their reply would assist anyone involved with them therapeutically to appreciate whether this concept had remained unchanged from childhood. As explored further in the section entitled 'Perceptions of God' in Chapter 4, the fear of the God of childhood may hold clients in a place dominated by childhood anxieties. It may be worth helping a client to articulate how they formed their understanding of God as a child and how that may or may not have changed.

Rizzuto's paper *Object Relations and the formation of the image of God* provides a clear review of psychoanalytical theory on how the concept of God is formed. She hypothesises that 'the elements unconsciously used to form the image of God originate in early object representations and interactions; and that these images – more or less integrated with the God provided by the environment – become an internalization with a life of its own.' She also proposes that this created image can change and refers to the influences that can effect that change, but concludes,' the early object relations of an individual are the most lasting and more important elements in his internalized image of God.' (Rizzuto, 1974: 88)

There is some evidence from the narratives that those who have found a measure of peace with themselves and the God of their adult years have done so after much struggle in which professional help has played a substantial part. In addition to the work of establishing the client's current perceptions of their God, it is worth pointing out that, as with other potential transferences in a therapeutic relationship, the therapist has the potential to represent God to the client. Some understanding of attachment and psychodynamic perspectives may be of help in these circumstances (Jacobs, 1988, Holmes, 1993)

The aims of this chapter, and indeed of the whole book, have been to raise awareness amongst professionals of how open and willing they themselves are to recognise and embrace this subject when their clients need them to, and to emphasise how important and in what way this area can be to clients' well being and self development. The inclusion of this subject in training programmes would ensure that practitioners could become aware of the possible influence of religion on themselves, how they relate to religion and how their clients may be affected by their own religious experiences, especially those in their childhood.

References

Bradshaw, J (1988) *Healing the Shame that Binds You*. Deerfield Beach, Health Communications Inc.

Clarkson, P (1989) *Gestalt Counselling in Action*. London, Sage

Dawkins, R (2006) *The God Delusion*. London, Black Swan

Frankl, V (1985) *Man's Search for Meaning*. Washington, Square Press

Harborne, L *Working with Issues of Spirituality, Faith or Religion* Information Sheet G13, British Association for Counselling & Psychotherapy

Holmes, J (1993) *John Bowlby and Attachment Theory*. London, Routledge

Jacoby, M (1991) *Shame and the Origins of Self-Esteem: A Jungian Approach*. Brunner, Routledge

Jacobs, M (1988) *Psychodynamic Counselling in Action* London, Sage

Kaufman, G (1993) The Psychology of Shame: *Theory and Treatment of Shame-based Syndromes*. London, Routledge

Merry, (2002) *Learning & Being in Person-Centred Counselling*. Ross-on-Wye, PCCS

Rizzuto, AM, (1974) *Object Relations and the Formation of the Image of God*. British Journal Medical Psychology, 47, 83.

Rogers, C (1961) *On Becoming a Person*. Boston: Constable Houghton

Rowe, D (2009) *What Should I Believe?* Routledge

Spinelli, E (2001) *The Mirror and the Hammer. Challenging Orthodoxies in Psychotherapeutic Thought*. Continuum.

Spong, J S (2007) *Jesus for the Non-Religious*. USA: Harper Collins

Thorne, B (1991) *Person-centred Counselling: Therapeutic and Spiritual Dimensions*. London, Whurr

West, W (2004) *Psychotherapy and Spirituality*. London, Sage

Wheeler,S (2006) *Difference and Diversity in Counselling: Contemporary Psychodynamic Perspectives*. Basingstoke, Palgrave Macmillan

Wosket, V (1999) *The Therapeutic Use of Self*. London, Routledge

Yalom, ID (1980) *Existential Psychotherapy*. New York, Basic Books

6
Personal Conclusions

From Lindsay

Contributors and editors have shared their intimate childhood experiences for readers of this book in the hope that something can be learned and better understood in the process. I trust that readers will respond to this privilege and tread softly on our endeavours. The narratives explore the light, shades and textures of personal experience and It is from these stories that the reader will draw the most significant lessons. As a co-editor I have tried to stick to an open exploratory approach as a starting point. I think this book begins to explore what might be the consequences of introducing religion early in a child's life.

The research and writing of this book have represented a profound and unending exploration of meaning for me. Writing about my own experience of religion and studying the experience of others has freed me to engage with the numinous qualities of my life without the lens of religion and god. I feel more liberated to look at aspects of life and the world that are not readily explicable, without the old fear of being taken over by a religious group or person, and without the need to protect others from my agnosticism. Since completing the book I have found myself an atheist. God and religion do not seem to feature much in my inner thoughts. I can approach people with faith without an anxious response that used to mean I wanted to fight them or keep clear of them.

My attitude to the institutions of religion remains intolerant. I am not sure that my position has changed since compiling the book. I believe that the negative effects of religious beliefs and concepts in the world are greater than the undoubted positive and precious contributions that individual religious people make to the lives of others.

One particularly dark influence that concerns me is the way children's freedom to dream, to explore and to understand can be stamped on by the heavy feet of religion. It is this conclusion that stays with me since completing the book.

I find it very difficult to see how the benefits of a religious childhood, especially one introduced before the age of seven, can outweigh the risk of a significant reduction in the freedom of an individual to develop psychologically and cognitively to their potential . For me it restricts and restrains rather than facilitates. I am well aware that the contributors and my co-editor will have a different view from me.

My interpretation of the material in this book has led me to believe that it is inadvisable to involve children in religious activities before the age of seven. I believe that the psychological health of children is not promoted by the early introduction of those powerful religious concepts such as an all-seeing, all-knowing God, original sin, evil, devils and even angels. I think these ideas have the power to frighten and coerce, and that certain children are particularly sensitive to them. Children are inclined to take these absolutes literally (and perhaps this is intended), internalizing them into a poor self-concept where shame punishes and restricts and fear can dominate spontaneity and inquiry.

I appreciate that there are numerous other powerful ideas that children are exposed to, and I do believe that children grow through their experiences. Children can not, and should not, be shielded from all that is potentially confusing or troubling. However I think that, wherever possible, the child is better off if encouraged to discover rather than have ideas imposed. I also believe that children could be introduced to religion, just as they might be to other difficult aspects of life in the world such as death, sex and war, in a way that is age-appropriate and in a way that gives them the best opportunity possible to make up their own minds. Children need a safe base to explore, where they are reassured and protected enough to make forays into the complexity of adult life without the fear of being judged, hurt or punished for doing so. Religion, as described in these narratives, does not seem to offer this freedom to children.

Having different views from my co-editor Lucy has been a great advantage for this book. She has been an incomparable writing companion. We have accompanied each other in many and different ways. We have been like the old weather-vane couple, when she has been motivated I could be found skulking inside the weather-house, when she has found herself preoccupied with other responsibilities I have found my enthusiasm. I have been in a hurry to complete and she content to let it take its course. Her attention to detail and commitment to subtlety and accuracy has been a foil to my tendency to generalise and over-state. Somehow we have found a collaborative writing style that has been productive and tenacious. One has not dominated the other and the differences have been positive spurs to find common ground and acknowledge and state our disagreements. We remain very close friends.

Lindsay Smith
December 2011

From Lucy

In deciding to write this book I had a fundamental dilemma. I had come to recognise that religion, as I had experienced it, had been core to my personal development. However, during many years as a counsellor and supervisor I had rarely met clients who wanted to explore the impact of religion on them, or indeed who voiced any interest in, or concern with, religion. I was also aware that, until the last few years, I had rarely referred to a struggle with religion in my own therapy sessions, and that when I had, such references seemed to have no life in them and were allowed to fade as material, perhaps more familiar to therapy, took over in the sessions.

Over time, as I became more confident that religion had indeed played a very significant part in my personal development, and as I got to know Lindsay and we shared our stories, we recognised how early religious teaching/input had influenced us in ways that had similarities. We wondered whether there were others who, like us, had been fairly immersed in religion as children and had emerged with issues that troubled and confused them. So we set out to find out, and this book is the result.

That the impact can be profound is, I believe, evident from this research. That how it impacts is unpredictable is also clear. Religion can offer comfort and encourage spiritual insight and it can also damage. So I am left questioning how safe it is for children to be taught what to believe. Encouraging children to explore their responses to religion that is taught in an open and mature way, and being respectful of such responses, may remain the best safeguard. How religion is taught to children is beyond the scope of this book, but it does, I believe, pose the question.

To return to my dilemma. Having written this book I am clearer that early religious influence (and I include here not only immersion in religion but also what we have called in the book having a 'meaningful brush' with religion as a child) can have a profound and unpredictable affect, but how widespread the impact is remains unclear. Perhaps there are reasons why this subject does not surface often in therapy, and we have voiced some of those in Chapter 5. Or perhaps it is just a few individuals who can identify with the struggles that many of our contributors spoke of. If this is the case then this book will, I hope, be of help to them and those professionals who work with them.

Lucy Birtwistle
December 2011